# Joyce's *Ulysses*
## and the
## Assault upon Character

# Joyce's *Ulysses*
## and the
## Assault upon Character

James H. Maddox, Jr.

THE HARVESTER PRESS

Publication of this book was partially
supported by The George Washington University.

First published in Great Britain by
The Harvester Press Limited, 1978
*Publisher: John Spiers*
2 Stanford Terrace
Hassocks, Sussex, England

ISBN 0 85527 612 6

First published in the USA by
Rutgers University Press, 1978
Copyright © 1978 by Rutgers,
The State University of New Jersey
Printed and made in the United States
of America

*To Lucy*

# Contents

# Preface

My primary indebtedness in this study is to previous writers on Joyce. Joyce's works and *Ulysses* in particular have been lucky in drawing to them a remarkable number of scholars and critics of great good sense. Among the scholars I am most indebted to are Walton Litz, Father William Noon, Robert M. Adams, and Weldon Thornton, who have brought to light different parts of the incredibly complex background—Joyce's mind—which produced *Ulysses*.

Among the critical books, there are two whose importance to this study I wish to acknowledge. I was first overwhelmed by S. L. Goldberg's *The Classical Temper* when I was an undergraduate, and I still find it probably the best work on *Ulysses*. In particular, Goldberg's treatment of the aesthetic theories contained within *Ulysses* and the *Portrait* seems to me definitive, and I have not attempted to go beyond his elegant argument. A second book, Marilyn French's *The Book as World*, appeared after my work was already in manuscript. I hope I will not be suspected of oblique self-praise when I say that I have found her work excellent—the best since Goldberg's—and at several points complementary to my own. I have revised a good handful of passages in my study in order to acknowledge Professor French's precedence. On two general points of similarity, however, I have left my text intact: the first is the proposition that Joyce's characterization is predicated upon the coexistence (not the resolution) of opposites; the second is the proposition that Joyce's stylistic variations are the corollary of Stephen's axiom in "Proteus" that the world can be known only through its refracted signatures.

On these two points I gladly acknowledge that Professor French got there first.

I am grateful to The George Washington University Committee on Sponsored Research for two generous grants in support of this book; to Random House, Inc. and The Bodley Head, Ltd. for permission to quote extensively from *Ulysses* (copyright 1914, 1918 by Margaret Caroline Anderson and renewed 1942, 1946 by Nora Joseph Joyce); and to the University of Texas Press for permission to include in Chapter 6 of this book a revised version of an article on "Eumaeus" which first appeared in *Texas Studies in Literature and Language*, Vol. XVI (1974). And I am very grateful indeed to Robert Kellog and Bernard Benstock who read the manuscript for the Rutgers University Press. Professor Benstock in particular called my attention to several hair-raising errors which I have corrected. Whatever hair-raisers remain are my own.

Finally, there are the people to whom one can never give sufficient thanks, who have fathered and mothered this book through their friendship and encouragement. I thank Sherman Hawkins, Laurence Holland, Cecil and Violette Lang, Bill Wilson, Lisa Kiser, and the late George McCandlish. Walton Litz, besides being a member of the foregoing category, kindly read the manuscript and gave me wise advice.

# Abbreviations of Works Cited

*FW*: *Finnegans Wake* (New York: Viking Press, 1958), eighth printing with the author's corrections incorporated in the text.

*PA*: *A Portrait of the Artist as a Young Man,* ed. Chester G. Anderson (New York: Viking Press, 1968), Viking Critical Edition.

*U*: *Ulysses* (New York: Random House, 1961), new edition, corrected and reset.

# Introduction

Perhaps nothing could be more fortunate for a writer in the twentieth century than to have been born Irish. The typically Irish combination of cosmopolitan cultural yearnings and a deep love-hate for the homeland created out of an incredibly small population the greatest English-speaking poet, novelist, and playwright of the century. Far more than Beckett, even more than Yeats, Joyce was held rapt by the blessing and the curse of being Irish. One's Irishness afforded one the condition of embattled and oppressed integrity; it also, as Joyce maintained throughout his life, afforded one the opportunity to betray one's ideals, one's leaders, and one's national artists. By choosing to live on the Continent, away from his homeland, Joyce raised his own Irishness to a new exponential power; he could be most Irish, most heroic and embattled, only once he had transformed Ireland herself into his persecutor, the Poor Old Woman into the old sow that eats her farrow.

The dilemma of Irishness was present to Joyce not simply as a political metaphor, but as a part of the very language he spoke and wrote. As a young man, he was scornful of the Gaelic League's effort to revive the ancient Irish language, but at the same time he was sensitive to the logic which was a part of the League's appeal: English was the language of the oppressor, at variance with the Irish sensibility and with Irish patriotism. In *A Portrait of the Artist as a Young Man,* there is an interesting moment when Stephen runs headlong into the alien nature of English. In Chapter v, Stephen and the English dean of studies have trouble naming a humble object which Stephen calls a tundish and the dean calls a funnel. Stephen smarts under the dean's polite interest in "tundish," evidently an Irishism, and reflects:

1

The language in which we are speaking is his before it is mine. How different are the words *home, Christ, ale, master,* on his lips and on mine! I cannot speak or write these words without unrest of spirit. His language, so familiar and so foreign, will always be for me an acquired speech. I have not made or accepted its words. My voice holds them at bay. My soul frets in the shadow of his language. (*PA,* 189)

The joke, as Stephen later discovers, is that "tundish" is "English and good old blunt English too" (*PA,* 251). There is something paradigmatic about this encounter between Stephen and the dean. Stephen is more self-conscious and curious—and ultimately right— about the language than the dean is precisely because Stephen is a foreigner, an exile from the language he himself speaks.

If, in his self-imposed exile, Joyce was able to be most truly Irish, in his self-conceived exile from his own language he was able to become the world's greatest master of words.[1] There is at once familiarity and diffidence in Joyce's treatment of language; like Nabokov, a more obviously "foreign" writer, Joyce sometimes engages in that pedantic, even prissy search for the *mot juste* which is often a sign of the alien writer's intense self-consciousness. And there is in both writers a relentless awareness of language as a somehow foreign medium which at any moment may break free— sometimes creatively, sometimes rather frighteningly—from any denotative function:

His own consciousness of language was ebbing from his brain and trickling into the very words themselves which set to band and disband themselves in wayward rhythms:

> *The ivy whines upon the wall*
> *And whines and twines upon the wall*
> *The ivy whines upon the wall*
> *The yellow ivy on the wall*
> *Ivy, ivy up the wall.*

Did any one ever hear such drivel? Lord Almighty! Who ever heard of ivy whining on a wall? Yellow ivy: that was all right. Yellow ivory also. And what about ivory ivy? (*PA,* 179)

1. Richard Ellmann quotes A. Francini Bruni's report of Joyce's remark in Trieste: "The Irish, condemned to express themselves in a language not their own, have stamped on it the mark of their own genius and compete for glory with the civilised nations . . ." (*James Joyce* [New York: Oxford University Press, 1959], p. 226).

For Stephen Dedalus, language often threatens to drift free of its referential function and become a plastic, contentless material. We must return presently to the crucial question of why, given his own diffidence toward language, Joyce himself does not fall into the dilemma of some of Beckett's characters who find that the world of words has become completely unglued from and irrelevant to the world of objects.

Joyce's proud rejection of Gaelic was in large part a symbolic act: Gaelic, after all, was never a true alternative for a writer whose artistic ideals and goals were Continental. More real and more intense was Joyce's rejection of the Irish writers who were his contemporaries and immediate predecessors. His broadside "The Holy Office" (1904), a combination of Swiftian invective and rather embarrassing adolescent posturing ("And though they spurn me from their door/My soul shall spurn them evermore"), is an attempt to set himself apart from the entire Irish literary scene, all the way from Yeats down to Oliver St. John Gogarty, the original of Buck Mulligan. The poem is in the same vein as the comically pretentious and perhaps apocryphal remark Joyce is supposed to have made to Yeats: "I have met you too late. You are too old."[2] The attempt of the young Joyce—like the attempt of the Stephen of the *Portrait*—was to remove all the external definitions of himself so that he could stand free, self-defined like the Nietzschean *Ubermensch*. His dilemma came to be that of the Stephen of *Ulysses,* who has cut away at all of his own supports and now laments, "If I had land under my feet" (*U,* 46).

In his life, according to Richard Ellmann's convincing reading, Joyce got back to land when he first walked out with Nora Barnacle on June 16, 1904—and this is of great importance if we read *Ulysses* mainly in terms of Joyce's biography. It is more relevant here, however, to understand the literary means Joyce used to fill the vacuum created by his rejection of the Irish language and the Irish literary establishment.

Again, a passage from the *Portrait* is apropos:

The rainladen trees of the avenue evoked in him, as always, memories of the girls and women in the plays of Gerhart Hauptmann. . . . His

2. Ellmann reports the anecdote and discusses its validity. *Ibid.,* pp. 105–106n.

morning walk across the city had begun, and he foreknew that as he
passed the sloblands of Fairview he would think of the cloistral silver-
veined prose of Newman, that as he walked along the North Strand
Road, glancing idly at the windows of the provision shops, he would
recall the dark humour of Guido Cavalcanti and smile, that as he went
by Baird's stonecutting works in Talbot Place the spirit of Ibsen would
blow through him like a keen wind, a spirit of wayward boyish beauty,
and that passing a grimy marinedealer's shop beyond the Liffey he would
repeat the song by Ben Jonson. . . . (*PA,* 176)

This passage is sometimes quoted as one of Joyce's more stinging
rebukes of Stephen. There is something mechanical in Stephen's
foreknowledge of the places which will remind him of his favorite
authors; indeed, that foreknowledge is dominated by the same sort
of deadening routine that Dublin itself represents to him. But the
irony of the *Portrait* is very seldom single edged. In that collocation of writers—Hauptmann, Newman, Cavalcanti, Ibsen, Jonson—
there is an attempt to form, if not a new conscience, then at least a
new sensibility, based upon something more substantial and more
positive than the simple rejection of things Irish. Joyce-Stephen's
search for the slightly obscure or unappreciated author in Guido
Cavalcanti is characteristic; so is the love of the rebellious Ibsen;
and so, finally, is the love of Newman—for Joyce-Stephen always
delighted to find possible material for his art in the bosom of the
Church he had rejected.

Setting out consciously to form one's own artistic sensibility is a
risky business, attended by the dangers of self-conscious posing and
overrefined aestheticism which the young Stephen and the young
Joyce both fell victim to. In this hazardous process of soul-making
there is, in fact, a virtual equation between Stephen and the young
Joyce. Much of the thinness in Stephen's character in the last
chapter of the *Portrait* lies in the merely literary nature of his
self-created identity. But by the time of *Ulysses* he has already
come to recognize and loathe the attenuated quality of his predominantly literary imagination: "Reading two pages apiece of
seven books every night, eh? I was young" (*U,* 40). Stephen is so
devastating a portrait of the hyper-literary mind—and, by the time
of *Ulysses,* so aware that his self-portrait is devastating—that he
comes to represent his author's awareness of the hazards of his own

methods. And yet Stephen's weakness is not that he is bookish but that he is so *exclusively* bookish. His mind contains the intellectual categories of experience but not the experience itself, the kind of experience that Villiers de l'Isle Adam (quoted approvingly by AE in *Ulysses*) was too willing to consign to his servants. And even if Stephen's mind is only an intricate skeletal structure in search of content and substance, the structure itself is sound, not simply built of phrases taken from Jonson and Hauptmann, but founded upon the bedrock of Aristotle and Aquinas.

———•—•———

It will be more useful than it may at first appear to tread over again the old ground of Aristotle, Aquinas, epiphanies, and acts of perception—ground that has already been masterfully surveyed. Joyce's basically simple use of Aristotelian and Thomistic philosophy—and in particular their epistemology—is at the very heart of his work. Not only does his Thomism provide a gloss on Stephen's theoretical musings; it also provides the generative philosophical assumptions from which Joyce derives his own aesthetics and ultimately his method of characterization and his manipulation of style.

The first point to make is that the Aristotelian-Thomistic philosophy is the ancilla of Joyce's art and not the reverse. Hugh Kenner assumes that Joyce is so thoroughgoing a Thomist that we must register an ironic mark scored against Stephen each time his aesthetic theorizing wanders from the strict sense of St. Thomas.[3] Joyce and Stephen, however, are *applying* Aquinas, and there is even some question as to what Joyce took Thomism to be. Father Noon in his valuable study *Joyce and Aquinas* tells us something of great import about the intellectual atmosphere in which Joyce studied Aquinas:

> the mid-twentieth-century reading of Aquinas differs in not a few important respects from the reading which was given even in Scholastic circles fifty years ago. Cartesianism in one or another of its derivative idealistic forms had long been in the ascendancy, and one tended, in spite

———

3. For Kenner's argument, see *Dublin's Joyce*, Beacon Paperbacks (Boston: Beacon Press, 1962), Chapter 9.

of oneself perhaps, to read Aquinas, much as one read everyone else, through Descartes' spectacles.[4]

This observation either complicates or drastically simplifies the question which has engaged most of the critics who have discussed the bases of Joyce's aesthetics: is the central perceptual event in Joyce's art, the epiphany, entirely an objective happening (this is Kenner's claim), or is it appreciably colored by the subjectivity of the particular observer? If we are pure Thomists, we are likely to place emphasis on the objective nature of perception, and if post-Cartesians, on the subjective. The question is actually quite germane to our reading of *Ulysses,* since if we favor the objective event, our reading is likely to be pretty severe in its irony (why can't the character see what *I* see?) ; if we favor the subjective bias, we are likely to withhold judgment on a character's epiphany at least until we have seen it as an event within the context of the character's psychology. Father Noon's description of the intellectual climate in which Joyce read Aquinas suggests that the attempt to find in Joyce a "pure," pre-Cartesian Thomism is unnecessarily Procrustean.

S. L. Goldberg, whose treatment of Joyce's aesthetics should be read by every serious student of Joyce, resolves the question brilliantly. Here is a very general summary of Goldberg's elegant treatment of Joyce's aesthetics by the time of *Ulysses:* Aristotle, Aquinas, Stephen, and Joyce all commence with the premise that we can know the world only through our senses; through a reading of the "signatures of all things," the intellect appropriates the form of the thing. The artist, who has faithfully observed the world, consults his own soul in order to apprehend and understand the forms imprinted there. His expression of "the word" is a faithful reduplication of the world, but the world seen within the particular configuration it has assumed in the artist's own experience. The supreme artistic act is thus simultaneously an act of "realistic" observation and an act of self-knowledge, since in exploring his own soul the artist comes to know both the world and himself. Goldberg's version of Joyce's aesthetics manages to

4. William T. Noon, S. J., *Joyce and Aquinas* (New Haven: Yale University Press, 1957), p. 10. See also p. 38, where Father Noon discusses Stephen's tendency to wander away from Aquinas toward Kant.

keep both the baby and the bathwater. Joyce in his art remains faithful to the "realistic," the "objective," but he structures the objective world as it is actualized in the necessarily subjective mind of a perceiver.[5]

An epiphany, a privileged moment of perception, is a phenomenon of two different sorts. It is a moment of special luminousness experienced by a character in a book or story, and it is a moment of revelation which is recreated in literary form by the artist and in which the reader may participate. Like the manifestation to the Magi of God in the flesh—the event from which the epiphany takes its name—the epiphany is a miracle, but a miracle occurring in a secular, here-and-now world. For a character in one of Joyce's works, an epiphany is a moment when the subjective consciousness of a perceiver meshes exactly with the details of the scene before him, so that the scene becomes symbolic of an intellectual and/or emotional complex which is actually grounded in the scene, but which only this particular character can perceive. In their most intense form, epiphanies bring a character's whole life to a sharp point and the character himself to a moment of self-discovery which may be terrible ("A Painful Case") or joyous (*Portrait,* Chapter IV).

In recreating epiphanies through his art, Joyce must, of course, do more than rely upon the chance advent of that rare reader whose subjective experience might by coincidence happen to tally with Joyce's own. His method of creating and arriving at epiphanies is especially clear in *Dubliners* (and grows more and more complex in his later works). In the typical *Dubliners* story there is usually a feeling of something being amiss, something not quite right in the life of the central character—something, moreover, of which the reader is only vaguely aware until he rereads the story with a new awareness. There is usually a feeling of the character's unease or insecurity which we can sense but not quite put our finger on until a particular, meticulously described collocation of events brings that vagueness into a sharp focus which gives the story a retrospective order and shape we had not quite suspected.

There is a wide spectrum along which *our* experience of an

5. S. L. Goldberg, *The Classical Temper* (New York: Barnes and Noble, 1961), Chapter III.

epiphany in the *Dubliners* stories coincides or does not coincide with the characters'. Some of the characters are so controlled by the immediacy of emotions they do not understand (Eveline), so controlled by frustration and anger (Farrington in "Counterparts"), or so dimwitted (Maria in "Clay") that, as it were, they have no awareness of the stories of which they are a part. Other characters—the child (children?) of the first three stories, Little Chandler in "A Little Cloud"—have a mediate level of intelligence (the child simply because he is a child; he is potentially the most intelligent character in *Dubliners*): they have just enough consciousness of their lives to have become aware of their own prison bars. Mr. James Duffy of "A Painful Case" and Gabriel Conroy of "The Dead" are the two most intelligent and sophisticated characters. They fulfill the potential of the boy in "Araby," as they come to a full and shattering consciousness of their own natures. (The cases of Mr. Duffy and Gabriel Conroy, moreover, remind us that the epiphany is not only the central aesthetic and perceptual unit in Joyce's work; it is also the central *moral* unit. The vocabulary of "subject" and "object" takes on a new meaning at those moments when a character can transcend his own ego to understand what is beyond himself.)

And yet, even in the cases of Mr. James Duffy and Gabriel Conroy, there is a subtle but distinct difference between the character's epiphany and our own. For all the character's accession of self-awareness, he moves toward his revelation within the limitations of his own personality—Mr. Duffy passing through scorn to rigorous self-judgment, Gabriel Conroy passing through self-pity to great tenderness—as, of course, any character or human being must. The reader's epiphany is set within a slightly larger framework which includes the character's epiphany as well as its context. Joyce was well aware of that necessity, which Henry James stressed in his prefaces, to have an intelligent character who can come to an awareness of his world and yet who must be, if only minimally, more befuddled than the observing audience of author and reader.

———————————•—•———————————

The epiphany, a fusion of objective fact and subjective consciousness, is based upon two subsidiary assumptions which are of surpassing simplicity, but which protect Joyce's art from its own centrifugal tendencies. The first of these is the evident reality of the physical world. When Stephen Dedalus at the beginning of the "Proteus" chapter assures himself that the world is "There all the time without you: and ever shall be, world without end," the moment is slightly ludicrous but nonetheless significant. He is forcing himself to accept a world which is there, other, ineluctable. He is working toward a realization such as that central to Wallace Stevens's poetry: we can imaginatively transform the world only after we have accepted its alien, inhuman reality. In his art, Joyce can allow himself such a long tether and can wander into the most Byzantine of stylistic distortions because the narrative has its very roots in objects and facts.

There is nothing very surprising about Joyce's fidelity to the real: one is reminded of Carlyle's reaction to Margaret Fuller's announcement that she accepted the universe: "Gad, she'd better!" But the second assumption underlying the epiphany is somewhat more surprising, in a century when the very reality of character and identity has been so thoroughly called into question. If Joyce accepts the universe, he also accepts the reality of individual identity. "Soul" is one of the most crucial words in Joyce's vocabulary and represents perhaps the most important of his beliefs which remained unchanged after his departure from the Church. The "soul" is Joyce's word for the irreducible identity a human being possesses and which he is free either to develop and actualize or to barter away in an act of "simony." In this light, it is not often enough realized what Joyce has done by giving Stephen Dedalus a symbolic name. Sir Politick Would-Be and Lady Wishfort have names which accurately predict their behavior, but of course they are not aware of their own symbolism. Stephen Dedalus has a symbolic name *of which he himself is aware* because he contains within himself from birth the soul of a potential artificer. From a point early on in his life he is vaguely conscious of a mission which corresponds to his name and which he can accomplish only through the efflorescence of the powers he already contains within himself *in potentia*. The major criterion of judgment in the *Portrait* is Stephen's fidelity to the promptings of his own soul.

How, though, does an artist go about portraying a "soul"? The

answer to that is in large part the story of Joyce's style, for like
the world itself, the inapprehensible soul of a character can be
known only by way of its "signatures"—typifying phases of mind,
repetitive or obsessive mental gestures which point toward his
innermost being. Here another crucial Joycean word has to be
examined: the closest we can come to knowledge of a character is
knowledge of the character's "rhythm."[6] What Joyce meant by this
sometimes opaque word is relatively clear in the opening paragraph
of his 1904 essay, "A Portrait of the Artist":

> The features of infancy are not commonly reproduced in the adolescent
> portrait for, so capricious are we, that we cannot or will not conceive the
> past in any other than its iron, memorial aspect. Yet the past assuredly
> implies a fluid succession of presents, the development of an entity of
> which our actual present is a phase only. Our world, again, recognizes
> emotion.[7]
> its acquaintance chiefly by the characters of beard and inches and is, for
> the most part, estranged from those of its members who seek through
> some art, by some process of the mind as yet untabulated, to liberate
> from the personalised lumps of matter that which is their individuating
> rhythm, the first or formal relation of their parts. But for such as these
> a portrait is not an identificative paper but rather the curve of an

In this extraordinarily seminal passage, Joyce is defending two
points of view at once. First, he is insisting that character can be
properly known only within the medium of time. Second, he is
anticipating objections by other novelists such as Virginia Woolf
and D. H. Lawrence against the unsatisfactory means of characterization in the conventional realistic novel. The only true characterization, says Joyce, is one which reproduces the patterns of a
character's response to the world, the slow, groping movements of
a soul, "the curve of an emotion." (Yeats, in recalling the "You are
too old" conversation, remembered Joyce saying something very

6. Jackson I. Cope has discussed "rhythm" in Joyce's aesthetics and has brought
together most of the passages which I discuss in this context. See his "The Rhythmic
Gesture: Image and Aesthetic in Joyce's *Ulysses*," *ELH*, xxix (1962), 67–89.

7. "A Portrait of the Artist," most readily available in the Viking critical edition of
*A Portrait of the Artist as a Young Man,* ed. Chester G. Anderson (New York: Viking
Press, 1968), p. 257.

similar to this: "He had thrown over metrical form, he said, that he might get a form so fluent that it would respond to the motions of the spirit.")[8] Style itself must become the vesture of the literary character's soul. The soul is mysterious, unknowable; it is the task of the artist to mold his words around that mysterious central identity, to give as clearly as possible its contours and movements.

Such a process of soul-mapping was Joyce's enterprise in *A Portrait of the Artist as a Young Man*. Through two important means, he conveys the rhythm and traces out the curve of Stephen's soul. First, through the *style indirect libre* which he learned from Flaubert, Joyce infuses his third-person descriptions of Stephen with what we might call the first-person immediacy of the emotion which Stephen feels. The prose, which changes as Stephen changes, is itself a register of the growth of his soul. Second, Joyce gives to Stephen a cluster of significant attitudes and associations (an aversion to water, the desire to express his own version of reality, the concern with symbolic women, etc.) which are at once constant and changing—constant in that Stephen never loses touch with these forms of experience, changing in that the concerns become deeper and more complex from chapter to chapter. The literary device of the motif becomes in the *Portrait* the index of the rhythm of the soul.

Joyce's mapping out of his characters' souls reaches its most perfect form in the stream-of-consciousness narrative of *Ulysses*. Here Joyce all but literally gives us the "rhythm" of his characters, as he not only transcribes their specific thoughts but also structures those thoughts to follow an emotional curve which is the shape of the character's being—hence, for example, the sine curve of Bloom's euphoria and depression, his urge toward fantasy and his hyper-realism. And yet even here we do not arrive at the character's essence—nor do we ever arrive there. We know Bloom, for example, in great part through what his thoughts do *not* tell us, through those subjects which we see him avoiding. Even in "Circe," Joyce does not give us the final secret, the final keys to personality. It is a paradox of *Ulysses* that although no character has ever been subjected to such intense scrutiny as Mr. Bloom, neither has any character ever so triumphantly escaped final definition.

8. Ellmann, *James Joyce*, p. 106.

We can now turn for a moment to a question I raised earlier:
given his interest in portraying the encounter between mind and
world, why does Joyce not fall into the plight of Beckett's Car-
tesian characters who find the mental and physical orders hopelessly separate? The simple answer is that the objective world and
the soul of a character are for Joyce at once knowable from a
thousand perspectives and eternally mysterious, noumenous. We
can never know the essence of things—we do not have the angelic
intuitive apparatus for that—but we can take sightings upon that
essence (the form of a thing, the soul of a character) through repeated, many-angled perspectives upon the superficies of the world
or of a character's consciousness. And if Joyce always retains a
fidelity to the physical order—even though it is ultimately unknowable—so do his characters. There are solipsistic and narcissistic
tendencies aplenty in Joyce's characters, but one of Joyce's most
definite judgmental criteria is the character's ability to return to
and accept the physical world.

———————•·•·———————

Joyce's art is the art of the unspoken, an art of surround and
periphery, implying and evoking but never naming the center. The
epiphany is a circle of details all pointing toward the central,
undenoted subject. Consciousness is a collection of mental attitudes
given shape and unity by an underlying unknowable identity. It is
symptomatic of the art of *Ulysses* that Stephen's crucial demand at
the climax of his day—"Tell me the word, mother, if you know
now. The word known to all men" (*U,* 581)—goes unanswered.
Joyce gives us words as our only means of access to "the word."
The result is an art remarkable both for its underlying simplicity
and unity and for its bristling, crowded surface. And *Ulysses* provides us with many metaphors to describe this relation of surface
to substratum: parallax (the process of learning the truth through
observation from different perspectives), metempsychosis (the
transmigration of a single soul through various surface forms), and
Proteus (the incarnation of the one in the many).

Joyce's use of allusion is an integral part of this effort at evoking
the unspoken. Take as an example the Moses parallel in the
"Aeolus" chapter. By this point in the book we have seen Stephen

for three chapters and Bloom for three. Now Joyce brings them together within the context of the Moses story, and the "true" subject of the chapter becomes that of the integrity of the exile, Bloom-Stephen-Moses. Moses is not simply a yardstick by which Joyce measures his heroes; the Moses story is an ordering matrix which forces us to see Stephen and Bloom in a new configuration. Ideally (if not actually), all the parallels within *Ulysses* operate this way: the juxtaposition of the events of Bloomsday to Biblical, literary, or historical events generates a *tertium quid,* some fundamental pattern of behavior common to both levels—exile, for example, or homecoming, or spiritual renewal.

The most striking implication of Joyce's allusive method is its projection of essential, archetypal patterns of experience. When Joyce uses the motif of "met him pike hoses" in *Ulysses* or, more extensively, the Viconian historical schema in *Finnegans Wake,* it is implicit within his method that certain behavioral patterns are incarnated again and again throughout human history. This belief (whether poetic or literal) becomes increasingly prominent throughout Joyce's career. Stephen Dedalus in the *Portrait* is heroic to the extent that he defines himself as an individual *against* the context of religion, family, and culture. Bloom is a transitional hero—or, more properly, a hero who synthesizes Joyce's opposed definitions of heroism. For the most part, Bloom is still the kind of hero whose heroism arises from his uniqueness within his society: we like him mainly because he is different from his fellow citizens. But Bloom is already developing into a hero of a different sort: a plucky, comic, faintly ridiculous representative of humanity. This representative quality of Bloom's leads finally to Earwicker who is a hero only because, howlingly funny man, he represents the plight of all mankind. Joyce's allusive methods are the chief expression of this archetypal vision of humanity. The Homeric parallel is not simply a structural device; it is the statement of a psychological and historical assumption. The same patterns repeat themselves throughout history, and the allusions to Ulysses—or to Moses or Shakespeare—are illustrative of those patterns.

Such, most readers would agree, is the theoretical rationale of the Homeric parallel, but there is considerable disagreement as to the parallel's actual success. As he set about acquainting the public with his novel—through Valery Larbaud, Stuart Gilbert, and others—Joyce himself stressed the importance of Homer to his book. Essentially opposed to Joyce's own estimation was Ezra Pound's early comment with which many subsequent critics have agreed: "These correspondences are part of Joyce's mediaevalism and are chiefly his own affair, a scaffold, a means of construction, justified by the result, and justifiable by it only."[9] Although the last two phrases of Pound's judgment balance the initial negative phrasing, the idea of the Homeric parallel as Joyce's "own affair, a scaffold," has (not without some reason) become a commonplace of Joyce criticism.

The difficulty involved in making any absolute judgment on the Homeric parallel is that it functions so variously within the book. Paradoxically, the parallel can be least useful when it corresponds most closely to the surface level of the plot. We gain little, I think, from knowing that Stephen's interview with Mr. Deasy is like Telemachus's with Nestor: it is already clear that an older man is offering somewhat sententious advice to a younger man, and the parallel reinforces the action without adding any new dimension to it. The parallel is usually most rewarding when Joyce takes over some detail from Homer and transforms it into a radical metaphor. In "Proteus," Joyce unhesitatingly violates consistency by transforming Stephen from Telemachus to Menelaus in order to dramatize the struggle to perceive unity beneath multiplicity, a struggle which becomes one of the most important conceptual metaphors in the book.[10] The parallels can be extraordinarily successful when they create this kind of metaphor capable of including Bloom or Stephen or (most happily) both within a framework which brings into sharp focus some aspect of the human dilemma. The parallels are not rigidly and sternly judgmental. (Does anyone seriously believe that Joyce spent eight years demonstrating that a psychologically traumatized and cuckolded Jew in a land of anti-Semites is less of a conventional hero than a great warrior who

---

9. *Literary Essays of Ezra Pound*, ed. T. S. Eliot (New York: New Directions, n.d.), p. 406.

10. See Kenner, *Dublin's Joyce*, p. 181: "That the fundamental correspondence [between Homer and *Ulysses*] is not between incident and incident, but between situation and situation, has never gotten into the critical tradition."

consorted with gods and goddesses? Yes, some readers believe
this.) Instead, they are comic and serious at once: they call forth
our amusement at the idea of Homeric or Biblical heroism in
Bloom's Dublin, and they demand that we see a certain justness in
the comparison. The reader who cannot entertain the notion that
ennobling acts can also be funny will fail to enjoy the spirit of
*Ulysses.*

In spite of the misgivings one may feel about Joyce's methods
in their most extreme form, his technique of allusion is an immensely important and functioning part of his novel. If we prefer
not to see Ulysses, Shakespeare, Moses, or Elijah stalking through
the background of the book, we still have the incomparable figure
of Bloom himself, but we miss many of the overtones of that
melancholy comedy which informs Joyce's last two works and
which is in fact consistent with Bloom's philosophical outlook: the
past repeatedly surges up into the present, both to offer us some
sense of rebirth and to remind us of the futility of achievement.
This was to become the central, bittersweet lesson of *Finnegans
Wake:*

> Since the bouts of Hebear and Hairyman the cornflowers have been stay-
> ing at Ballymun, the duskrose has choosed out Goatstown's hedges,
> twolips have pressed togatherthem by sweet Rush, townland of twined-
> lights, the whitehorn and the redthorn have fairygeyed the mayvalleys of
> Knockmaroon, and, though for rings round them, during a chiliad of
> perihelygangs, the Formoreans have brittled the tooath of the Danes and
> the Oxman has been pestered by the Firebugs and the Joynts have
> thrown up jerrybuilding to the Kevanses and Little on the Green is
> childsfather to the City (Year! Year! And laughtears!), these pax-
> sealing buttonholes have quadrilled across the centuries and whiff now
> whafft to us, fresh and made-of-all-smiles as, on the eve of Killallwho.
> (*FW*, 14–15)

Whether we are speaking of the epiphany, of characterization,
of the manipulation of style, or of the use of correspondences, the
primary configuration within *Ulysses* is the same: a collocation of
details which point toward an unnamable center. Joyce's art is thus
Catholic and sacramental in the extreme. He can list all, *all* the

characteristics of accident, but he can only evoke or point toward substance. Moreover, what is accident early in the book becomes substance later on. In the opening chapters Joyce gives us a close account of the thoughts, dialogue, and action as indices of what Bloom and Stephen are "really" like; later in the book, by an exact analogy, Joyce offers more obscure hints as indices of what Bloom and Stephen are "really" thinking, saying, or doing.

There is another way in which what is accident in the first part of the book later becomes substance. Early in the book we—and Joyce—are interested in defining and understanding the individual characters of Bloom and Stephen. It is the tendency of the later chapters to regard Bloom and Stephen themselves as accidents, as examples of some yet deeper substratum of humanity. As early as "Aeolus," the first chapter in which both characters have speaking parts, we must see the two of them as examples of an underlying experience of which Moses too is an instance. And we should not be surprised when we occasionally see other Dublin wanderers who remind us of Bloom, for certainly it is one meaning of *Ulysses* that Bloom's doings are a signature of the general human lot.

Amid the book's general movement from the clear to the opaque and from the specific to the general, character is the closest thing to a constant; the only thing tying together chapters as diverse as "Sirens," "Cyclops," and "Nausicaa" is the common denominator of Bloom's character. The progression of *Ulysses* may be described as a series of trials of character, whether the trials be existential and contained within the action (Bloom is forced to flee from his wife's lover whom he sees in the streets) or stylistic, obviously imposed by the author (an eighteenth-century voice calls Bloom's masturbation an act of treason against the state). The perspectives by which character is seen are so various that I have adopted what may at first appear a haphazard arrangement of the chapters of *Ulysses*. I have singled out different movements which take place in the book and arranged this reading accordingly. My categories are these: the Stephen-chapters; the Bloom-chapters; those chapters in which the copresence of Stephen and Bloom gives rise to a new conceptual framework including the two; chapters of an even larger conceptual dimension in which Bloom and Stephen tend to merge into the background of humanity or the universe; and two

chapters in which the author's style most insistently intrudes between us and the characters ("Oxen of the Sun" and "Ithaca").
Finally, inevitably, "Penelope." These groupings demonstrate in
an economical way the variety of perspectives *Ulysses* demands
that we take in order to understand, in the end, the mystery of
being.

Style and narrative perspective gradually diminish the individual
importance of character in *Ulysses,* but there is an underground
current—the reader's own interest—running counter to this dimin-
ishment. Few readers, I suspect, ever experience total indifference
concerning the fates of Bloom, Stephen, and Molly, even when they
are viewed, in "Ithaca," from the cold of interstellar space. After
an earlier generation of critics had attempted to demonstrate,
sometimes bumblingly, that Molly and Bloom will soon resume
their sexual life together, more recent criticism, beginning with S. L.
Goldberg and continuing through Richard Ellmann and Marilyn
French, has insisted that this whole question is irrelevant.[11] To be
sure, the question of the characters' future fates is unanswerable,
but it is not irrelevant. If we insist too strongly upon the brilliant,
cosmic impersonality of "Ithaca" and upon Bloom's attainment of
equanimity, we are too partial in our responses to the novel. We
may admire Bloom's pacific acceptance of his wife's sexuality, but
we should not forget that here as elsewhere Bloom's strengths and
weaknesses are imbued with each other. His final acceptance of
Molly's adultery is also an instance of his evasion of action—and
a cause of pain to Molly herself. Molly's lambent, lyrical cry is an
objection to the movement of "Ithaca" and to the entire male
enterprise of which "Ithaca" is the culmination. She objects to
cosmic insignificance and insists that tomorrow's breakfast is as
important as any star in the delta of Cassiopeia.

---

11. See Goldberg's *The Classical Temper,* Ellmann's *Ulysses on the Liffey* (New York:
Oxford University Press, 1972), and French's *The Book as World: James Joyce's "Ulysses"*
(Cambridge, Mass.: Harvard University Press, 1976). A major argument of French's is
that the impersonal, Olympian styles of *Ulysses* force the reader into sympathy with the
human, all-too-human characters. She agrees with Goldberg, however, that the final
question of whether the characters have changed by the end of the book is irrelevant. See
in particular *The Book as World,* p. 87.

# Chapter I
# The *Telemachia*

Like Mallarmé's Hamlet, whom Mr. Best refers to in "Scylla and Charybdis," Stephen Dedalus *se promène, lisant au livre de lui-même* (187). Stephen is like Hamlet, the one difference being that he *knows* that he is like Hamlet, and this self-consciousness strongly affects his behavior. (Similarly, Joyce gives Stephen a blatantly symbolic name and then makes Stephen aware of that symbolism.) Stephen's reflexive consciousness of his own actions follows so directly upon the actions themselves that he is frequently unable to distinguish between his impulse and the parody of the impulse which his mind offers to him as immediate feedback. The *Telemachia*, the first three chapters of *Ulysses*, traces Stephen's attempt to distinguish between his sense of a true self and the poses which he knows to be inauthentic.

What we mainly see of Stephen as the book opens is this self-parodic manner—the manner, as Buck Mulligan says, of "an impossible person." Stephen moves about with a proud weariness. With an exquisite languor he "suffers" Mulligan to "pull out and hold up on show by its corner a dirty crumpled handkerchief" (4). There is much the same adolescent, bathetic quality about Stephen's thoughts which have been filtered through Joyce's precisely satirical *style indirect libre:* "Pain, that was not yet the pain of love, fretted his heart" (5); "Stephen, shielding the gaping wounds which the words had left in his heart, said very coldly . . ." (8). The prettified self-consciousness of these phrases falsifies the emotion they

19

attempt to express. There is the same effect in Stephen's spoken words. Many of his speeches have a formal, prepared air, as if he were indeed reading from a book: "You behold in me, Stephen said with grim displeasure, a horrible example of free thought" (20); "I fear those big words, Stephen said, which make us so unhappy" (31). It is reasonable to suspect that some of these phrases have been stored up, to be trotted out at a suitable time— just as Stephen mentally files away his definition of a pier as a dis- appointed bridge: "For Haines's chap-book. No-one here to hear. Tonight deftly amid wild drink and talk, to pierce the polished mail of his mind" (25).

This is the stiff, pompous, self-conscious Stephen whom many readers and critics cannot abide; yet it is necessary to see that Stephen himself has a growing awareness of his own failings. Having flown by the nets of family, nationality, and religion, he seeks his only center of value in himself, but he has gradually found that self grievously inadequate. Hence he is in a far more desperate state than Bloom. Like Bloom later on, Stephen sometimes reaches a dead end in his self-explorations, some painful point beyond which he cannot progress. But unlike Bloom, Stephen has divorced himself from the physical world and does not have any alternative solace beyond the self to fall back on. He has reached a crucial impasse, the point at which romantic self-assertion has ended in terrifying solitude. He feels the self-loathing and the claustrophobia of the creature contained within the walls of its own self, and in his very worst moments he displays a desperation closer to the manic than most critics have realized.

Joyce once remarked to Frank Budgen—apparently with grim satisfaction—that he had treated Stephen quite harshly in *Ulysses*. Joyce's mixed feelings of admiration and distaste for his former self are well known; what is important for *Ulysses* is that this process of self-revaluation has already begun in Stephen himself. For example:

> Cousin Stephen, you will never be a saint. Isle of saints. You were awfully holy, weren't you? You prayed to the Blessed Virgin that you might not have a red nose. You prayed to the devil in Serpentine avenue that the fubsy widow in front might lift her clothes still more from the wet street. (40)

Such a passage precisely defines Stephen's attitude toward himself during the day: his struggle for self-knowledge is still baffled by a strong self-revulsion. Yet the struggle for self-knowledge is itself Stephen's chief hope. Like all of Joyce's intellectual characters, from Mr. James Duffy to Shem (all of whom are to some extent Joyce's self-portraits), Stephen has reached a crisis in which he must either realize his place in the cycles of experience which subsume him or be forever doomed to the prison of his own egoism. The realization, to be sure, cannot occur fully within the limited scope of one day, but that day does provide several hints of things to come.

One such hint lies in the shape and direction of the *Telemachia.* The most obvious progression here is from surface to depth, from outside to inside, from the sunny parapet of the Martello Tower to the intricate maze of Stephen's thoughts as he walks on the beach. The progression at first seems to be in the direction of egoism, as Stephen descends further and further into his mental labyrinth, but this is not really true. Rather, the progression is from the subjective personal anguish of Stephen's dream to a moment of distanced self-understanding. The death of Mrs. Dedalus continues, perforce, to trouble Stephen throughout the day; but in the course of these three chapters he comes to accept, in a proto-Bloom-like way, the process by which that death is subsumed.

## "Telemachus"

The first chapter of *Ulysses* is dominated, not by Stephen, but by the wit and physical exuberance of Buck Mulligan. Mulligan is the false hero of this first chapter, just as the lightheartedly blasphemous Mass he celebrates is a false version of the book's celebration of life. Mulligan does more than usurp the Martello Tower; in the first scene of the drama he completely upstages the young hero.

Mulligan is a usurper, in ways that go beyond the Homeric parallel. Above all, he is a usurper of roles, capable of stepping into any disguise which will serve his purpose. His and Stephen's actions with the cracked mirror are significant in this respect. Whereas

Stephen characteristically gazes into the mirror with an uneasy self-consciousness, Mulligan flashes the mirror from the parapet, offering to the world its own image. His own name for himself is apt: mercurial Malachi. There is a dazzling, scintillating play of masks as he performs in turn before Stephen, Haines, and the milkwoman and in the intervals indulges in various forms of mimicry. He even outdoes Stephen at playing the high priest of the new religion of art: it is Mulligan who wishes to Hellenise Ireland (as Joyce was to do in *Ulysses*), and it is Mulligan who speaks glibly of Swinburne, Nietzsche, and Wilde.

Stephen's dislike of Mulligan is perhaps natural, but it grows out of sources deeper than personal resentment or envy. Their deepest disagreements are implicit in the argument over Stephen's refusal to kneel at his mother's deathbed. Here at the book's outset, Stephen *seems* to be placed in the worst possible light and Mulligan in the best, but that is not quite the case. Stephen is touchy and quick to take offense because he is arguing from a set of principles which he has carried to inhuman conclusions. But Mulligan's argument is more false, because it has no principles whatsoever:

—And what is death, he asked, your mother's or yours or my own? You saw only your mother die. I see them pop off every day in the Mater and Richmond and cut up into tripes in the dissecting room. It's a beastly thing and nothing else. It simply doesn't matter. You wouldn't kneel down to pray for your mother on her deathbed when she asked you. Why? Because you have the cursed jesuit strain in you, only it's injected the wrong way. To me it's all a mockery and beastly. Her cerebral lobes are not functioning. She calls the doctor Sir Peter Teazle and picks buttercups off the quilt. Humour her till it's over. You crossed her last wish in death and yet you sulk with me because I don't whinge like some hired mute from Lalouette's. Absurd! I suppose I did say it. I didn't mean to offend the memory of your mother. (8)

For perhaps the only time in the book, Mulligan is thrown off balance. He is unsure whether to speak in the language of reduction ("It's a beastly thing and nothing else. It simply doesn't matter") or of solemn high-mindedness ("I didn't mean to offend the memory of your mother"). Take the sentence, "You crossed her last wish in death and yet you sulk with me because I don't whinge like some hired mute from Lalouette's." First Mulligan appeals to Stephen's sense of guilt, then he sidesteps his own involvement by trivializing it. There is an excluded middle in this sentence, as there is in the entire speech. The key to the speech— and a key to Mulligan—is the phrase, "Humour her till it's over." His most essential criticism of Stephen is that he did not "humour" his mother—that he did not act the part he was called upon to perform.

Mulligan's momentary confusion is one of the most revealing touches in the chapter. Although Stephen has tired many readers by his melodramatic posturings in "Telemachus" (Mulligan himself calls Stephen a "mummer"), it is Mulligan who is the most egregious actor in the novel. Stephen's two most pointed epithets for Mulligan are "mocker" and "pretender," and the two taken together suggest why Stephen's reactions to Mulligan are always so charged with emotion. Mulligan's mockery destroys everything, leaving no ground for itself: and, analogously, his pretending is a continuous creation of selves which denies the existence of any enduring, subsistent self.

"Contradiction. Do I contradict myself? Very well then, I contradict myself. Mercurial Malachi" (17). Here is Mulligan's great charm and, in Stephen's eyes, his great weakness: he is mercurial, protean, all surface. It is no accident that Mulligan, the primrosevested dandy, is fond of Wilde, for he is an embodiment of self-canceling paradox, an exemplar of the self as a series of successive personae. He has the same thinness as Conrad's Decoud or Malraux's Clappique, in that he must constantly perform in order to continue to exist. He is thus a particularly frightening figure to Stephen; for Stephen, who has proclaimed the supremacy of the ego, now watches an ego continually dissipating itself, dissolving into so many phenomena.

If Mulligan is the purely phenomenal self, it is not surprising that Stephen is acutely aware of his own surface appearance. As he looks into Mulligan's mirror, for example, he thinks, "As he and others see me" (6). Later, he walks between Mulligan and Haines: "In the bright silent instant Stephen saw his own image in cheap dusty mourning between their gay attires" (18). These are the first instances of a particular form of self-consciousness which afflicts Stephen throughout the day—an obsessive sense of being watched, even when, as in "Proteus," there is no one present to do the watching. Hence Stephen's vestigial need of a God, not so much to insure his future immortality as to *see* him in the present and thereby guarantee his existence. He is acutely self-conscious because he is unsure of his own identity and is therefore forced to regard himself as object and to endow himself with an identity which he does not feel.

Stephen has thrown in his lot with Mulligan and now finds that he is unable to lead Mulligan's life. He sees in Mulligan all of his heroic ideals embodied in grotesque form. In the *Portrait* Stephen grandly declared his allegiance to "the angel of mortal youth and beauty"; Mulligan offhandedly declares that mortality ends as tripes on a dissecting table. Stephen has undergone the trauma of rejecting the Church; Mulligan is a carefree blasphemer. Stephen has declared the supremacy of the self over those forces that have shaped it; the example of Mulligan calls into question the very conception of a self.

## "Nestor"

The figure of Buck Mulligan establishes a theme central to both Stephen and Bloom: the question of the continuity of the self in time. The "Nestor" chapter enlarges upon that theme and prepares for its full orchestration in "Proteus." "Nestor" begins in the middle of Stephen's history lesson:

> YOU, COCHRANE, WHAT CITY SENT FOR HIM?
> —Tarentum, sir.
> —Very good. Well?
> —There was a battle, sir.
> —Very good. Where?
> The boy's blank face asked the blank window. (24)

These fitful jerks and starts of historical detail provide the context for Stephen's thoughts: "I hear the ruin of all space, shattered glass and toppling masonry, and time one livid final flame" (24). This vision of history as meaningless, a nightmare—"Time shocked rebounds, shock by shock" (32)—is an expansion of Mulliganism: like the personality, history may have no continuity or ultimate sense, but instead may exist simply as a series of phenomena with no underlying order.

Stephen's way of running a class only emphasizes this air of discontinuity. The history lesson centers upon a scene of destruction—"From a hill above a corpsestrewn plain a general speaking to his officers, leaned upon his spear" (24)—and then is followed by a jerkily recited *Lycidas* which stops short of the resurrection. Moreover, Stephen in his offhand remarks to the class speaks with a nervous energy which puzzles the students by apparently discontinuous leaps of association. Kingstown pier, he says, is a disappointed bridge. To an inconclusive riddle he supplies an inconclusive answer: "The fox burying his grandmother under a hollybush." Finally, even the day's schedule adds to the feeling of incompleteness. It is Thursday, only a half-day, so that the lessons are never completed.

In the mental background of this scene, Stephen thinks of historical figures who, like Kingstown pier, were disappointed, destined to be stopped short of completion: "Had Pyrrhus not fallen by a beldam's hand in Argos or Julius Caesar not been knifed to death?" (25). And, in an especially rich passage, he thinks of teachers whose work went unregarded:

> Gone too from the world, Averroes and Moses Maimonides, dark men in mien and movement, flashing in their mocking mirrors the obscure soul of the world, a darkness shining in brightness which brightness could not comprehend. (28)

This is one of those complex crosscurrents of allusion to which the reader of *Ulysses* soon becomes accustomed. There is first of all an implicit comparison between Stephen himself and the two philosophers—all of them disregarded teachers. In the phrase "mocking mirrors" Stephen consciously recalls Mulligan, whose flashing mirror shines at the beginning of "Telemachus" and whose mocking manner resembles the flashing, dazzling intellects of the two dark men. Stephen has mentally elevated Mulliganism into an historical principle of transience. But, outside Stephen's consciousness, the

two Semitic philosophers also anticipate Bloom, himself a mirror
reflecting the obscure soul of the world. The passage at once sums
up Stephen's thoughts on mutability and anticipates the appearance
of Bloom, who is capable of maintaining an integral self in a muta-
ble world.

The covert reference to Bloom seems especially appropriate in
a chapter which has to do with teachers, pupils, and the trans-
mitting of wisdom. Bloom is present *only* by reference, however,
and the relations between teacher and pupil in the course of the
chapter are—like Stephen's view of history—fragmented and incomplete. In the course of the chapter, Stephen plays the part of
both teacher and pupil. In the first half of the chapter he tries—
unsuccessfully, it would seem—to impart the knowledge of the past
to his unruly students; in the second he is a more decorous but no
more willing listener to the platitudes of Mr. Deasy. Both of these
situations convey one of the major burdens of the "Nestor" chapter:
continuity has failed; there is no fruitful linkage between event and
event or between past and present.

Yet there is a countercurrent to the feeling of chaotic discontinuity in "Nestor." Earlier in the day, Stephen held Mulligan's
shaving bowl and remembered: "So I carried the boat of incense
then at Clongowes. I am another now and yet the same" (11). In
a similar way, before going in to see Mr. Deasy, Stephen reflects
on his hapless pupil Cyril Sargent: "Like him was I, these sloping
shoulders, this gracelessness. My childhood bends beside me" (28).
It is a moment of gentleness and pity, squeezed in between the
public performances before the class and before Mr. Deasy; and
it amounts to an answer to Mulliganism. Opposed to Stephen's
perception of disconnected serial selves in Mulligan is his own
actual *experience* of a perduring self which links his present with
the past of his childhood.

Nestor himself, though, is the strongest opponent of Stephen's
idea that history is sheer meaningless process. Mr. Deasy's very
essence is his unchanging allegiance to old saws. When Stephen
enters Mr. Deasy's office, he is aware of entering a timeless zone:

> As on the first day he bargained with me here. As it was in the begin-
> ning, is now. On the sideboard the tray of Stuart coins, base treasure of a

bog: and ever shall be. And snug in their spooncase of purple plush, faded, the twelve apostles having preached to all the gentiles: world without end. (29)

The phrases from the Gloria Patri emphasize Mr. Deasy's stability—even if it is the stability of outworn worldly wisdom. The reference to the Apostles preaching to the Gentiles is another anticipation of Bloom—and appropriately so, for Mr. Deasy is the first of Stephen's surrogate fathers we encounter in the book.

Mr. Deasy is not, of course, a serious contender for spiritual fatherhood in *Ulysses;* he plays Polonius to Stephen's Hamlet. But like Polonius, Mr. Deasy sometimes speaks the truth, even though he may drown it in a deluge of cliché. He is not unlike the prudent and frugal Bloom when he approves of the motto, "I paid my way." And he comes very close to the lesson which Stephen is trying to learn when he says blandly, "To learn one must be humble. But life is the great teacher" (35). Later, in one of his moments of willed humility, Stephen will speak to himself in similar terms: "Dublin. I have much, much to learn" (144). Stephen is amused by Mr. Deasy's avuncular rhetoric ("If youth but knew. . . . You think me an old fogey and an old tory . . . I like to break a lance with you, old as I am"), and he resists the paranoia of Mr. Deasy's misogyny and anti-Semitism, but he has a grudging respect for the older man's stability and earnestness: "The lions couchant on the pillars as he passed out through the gate; toothless terrors. Still I will help him in his fight" (35–36).

Mr. Deasy also tells Stephen: "All history moves towards one great goal, the manifestation of God" (34). Stephen has no literal belief in the teleological Christian pattern which Mr. Deasy describes (he replies, in fact, with one of his more churlish retorts: "That is God. . . . A shout in the street"), but Mr. Deasy is once again surprisingly close to Stephen's essential concerns. Earlier in the chapter, Stephen thought of an Aristotelian conception of teleology which would give sense to the self and to history: "It must be a movement then, an actuality of the possible as possible" (25). Stephen's thought here is fragmentary; it will not receive full articulation until the library scene in "Scylla and Charybdis." But his conception of potentiality constantly moving toward actuality al-

lows him to give at least intellectual faith to the idea that the distinct
phases of the self lead toward and will finally issue in an awareness
of the enduring self.

For all his unknowing wisdom, however, Mr. Deasy is inadequate as a figure for Stephen's emulation. His timeworn phrases
represent stability, but it is the stability of paralysis and stagna-
tion. Stephen thinks:

> The same room and hour, the same wisdom: and I the same. Three
> times now. Three nooses round me here. Well. I can break them in this
> instant if I will. (30)

As was the case in the *Portrait,* Stephen has an almost obsessive
fear of being tied down: the imagery of nets and nooses holds for
him a particular horror. What is new in the Stephen of *Ulysses* is
his willingness to negotiate with the forces which he once so un-
equivocally rejected.

## "Proteus"

The first two chapters of *Ulysses* establish, through the opposition of representative characters, the deepest thematic conflict of
the book: the mercurial present of Mulligan and the frozen past
of Mr. Deasy. It is important to see that Stephen is defined in the
opening chapters primarily through his reactions to these two characters. The romantic egoist of the *Portrait* is now ironically forced
to look to others in order to achieve any degree of self-definition.
In this light, the subject of Stephen's history lesson is symbolic:
his denial of the forces of family, nationality, and religion has been
at best a pyrrhic victory. He has attained to the position of the
*Ubermensch,* but he finds the hyperborean air there too thin for
survival.[1]

---

1. It is interesting to notice that Joyce's two characters who consider themselves
disciples of Nietzsche receive very harsh treatment: Mr. James Duffy (of "A Painful
Case"), who reads *Thus Spake Zarathustra* and *The Gay Science,* and Buck Mulligan,
who is fond of quoting Nietzsche. In rejecting Mulligan, Stephen is also rejecting
Nietzsche's philosophy of total self-sufficiency. (Ellmann records Joyce's own attraction
to Nietzsche around 1904 [*James Joyce* (New York: Oxford University Press, 1959)
p. 147].)

The placement of a single character—Stephen—between two extremes—Mulligan and Deasy—is itself characteristic of *Ulysses*. Such triadic relationships are so integrally a part of Joyce's work that we must call them not simply devices of structure but components of Joyce's very vision of the world. In the first two chapters alone, there is the large contrast between Mulligan and Deasy; and the second chapter itself falls into two halves, Stephen-as-teacher and Stephen-as-pupil—the two halves being joined by the symbolic scene of Stephen gazing upon his own childhood in the person of Cyril Sargent. (The list might be extended. The book has two heroes who are set in relief by the third character, Molly. Stephen is located between Scylla and Charybdis, Bloom between the reductive and inflated styles of "Cyclops." Or the hero himself can be one of the two poles: Bloom is the countertheme in "Sirens," played against the theme of the Ormond Bar, and he is the voice of detumescence balanced against Gerty MacDowell's tumescent fantasizing in "Nausicaa.")[2]

These triadic patterns are so important to Joyce's art because his imagination is at once ironic and synthetic. Joyce seldom makes a statement without acknowledging the truth of the counterstatement, and the effect is not that of canceling out but that of holding together. It is fair to say, in fact, that Joyce tries the mettle of his characters by testing their ability to hold together opposed ideas without losing their sense of an essential identity. (Mulligan is so intriguing because he is *nothing but* opposite poses.) All of Joyce's major female characters embody this *discordia concors*—sometimes, perhaps, too easily. So does Bloom, in more complex ways. And, supremely, so does Earwicker, who is superior to his two sons because he combines their two natures, Shaun's pompous self-image and Shem's knowledge of sexual guilt. Looked at in this way, "Proteus" is Stephen's *rite de passage,* for it tests his ability to combine mutually repugnant ideas.

True to its title, "Proteus" is on its surface the most fluid and unstable chapter of the book, but in its underlying structure it is

2. Richard Ellmann has suggested a very systematic use of triadic patterns in *Ulysses* (*Ulysses on the Liffey* [New York: Oxford University Press, 1972] pp. 1–2). See my subsequent discussion of Ellmann's idea, at the beginning of my section on Bloom.

perhaps the most beautifully balanced and coherent of any of the chapters.[3] It is an epitome of its own theme, as it combines a teeming surface multiplicity and an ironbound underlying unity. It begins, as many of Joyce's works begin, with an overture which makes a preliminary statement of theme and anticipates the movement of the whole.[4] The fundamental opposition Stephen establishes in this overture (37) is that between substance and accident, between the thing in itself and its signatures, the signs which may be read by the senses. The premise from which he begins—from which he patiently forces himself to begin—is the ineluctable modality of the visible and the audible: the inescapable sensory modalities through which we perceive the world. He cannot know the world through direct intuition of its essence; he can know it only by means of its superficial signs. And he shudders at the idea that the signs are the total reality—whether a deceitful shimmer created by God or a projection of his own consciousness. The thing in itself and its protean manifestation: this is also to be his dual vision of himself during the chapter. Is there an ungraspable but nevertheless identifiable entity Stephen Dedalus, or is there simply a flickering series of different selves—"Disguises, clutched at, gone, not here" (43)?[5]

An important turn in Stephen's thought occurs in this opening section when he thinks, "Rhythm begins, you see. I hear" (37). As the collocation of seeing and hearing suggests, rhythm combines two modes, the *nacheinander* and the *nebeneinander*: in its recurrent patterns, rhythm incorporates permanence within change, stasis within kinesis. Much later in the day, in "Circe," Stephen will return to this notion of rhythm:

3. See Goldberg's excellent summary of the process of the chapter in *The Classical Temper*, (New York: Barnes and Noble, 1961) p. 158.

4. These thematic "overtures" characterize Joyce's work from *Dubliners* through *Finnegans Wake*. The three words which fascinate the child on the opening page of "The Sisters"—"paralysis," "simony," and "gnomon"—are a preliminary statement of the thematic centers of *Dubliners*. There is a similar effect in the opening section of the *Portrait*, in the musical prelude to the "Sirens" chapter, and in the opening paragraphs of *Finnegans Wake*.

5. The questions which Stephen proposes to himself at the beginning of "Proteus" are central to the epistemology of *Ulysses*. "Proteus" was written early in the composition of *Ulysses* and received only minor revision. It is something like the intellectual keystone of the book, and there are few large ideas in *Ulysses* which cannot be traced back to it.

So that gesture, not music, not odours, would be a universal language, the gift of tongues rendering visible not the lay sense but the first entelechy, the structural rhythm. (432)

Stephen conceives of the ideal art as the one which would convey most perfectly an incorporeal form through a perfectly adapted medium (in this case, gesture). This point is made clearer in his reference to "the gift of tongues," the Pentecostal descent of the Holy Spirit. Rhythm is thus for Stephen an incarnation of the ineffable, a capturing of substance within the perfectly accommodated form.

After his mention of rhythm, Stephen opens his eyes and half-seriously assures himself of the continuing, independent existence of the physical world: "There all the time without you: and ever shall be, world without end" (37). The closing phrase from the Gloria Patri hearkens back to the identical phrase which came to Stephen's mind in Mr. Deasy's office (29). If we look back now at these opening paragraphs of "Proteus," we find, in fact, that Stephen has moved from Mulligan to Deasy, from the phenomenalism of ineluctable modality to world without end. This movement, from chaos to an at least tentative certainty, is to be the movement of the chapter; and, as in this brief overture, the turning point of the chapter will be the rhythm of a poem.

The terms *nacheinander* and *nebeneinander* help to describe the structure of the chapter. "Proteus" is clearly divided into two halves, the first temporal, the second spatial. For the first half of the chapter, Stephen's thoughts follow the temporal progression of his selves from birth up to the present moment. The sight of the two women (whom Stephen mentally transforms into midwives) sets his mind at work upon his own birth (38) and family life (38–39). Then, proceeding through a brief memory of Clongowes (39), he passes on to a recollection of his religious phase and the period of his first artistic efforts. Here he reaches a crucial stage, the departure at the end of the *Portrait,* and his external action matches the crisis in his thoughts: "The grainy sand had gone from under his feet" (40). Moreover, he sees "at the land a maze of dark cunning nets." The phrase conflates several of the most important details of the *Portrait:* the Dedalian labyrinth, the nets past which Stephen said he would fly, and the phrase "silence, exile and cunning"—but now it is the nets rather than Stephen which have the dark cunning power. The phrase presents a compressed reevaluation of his earlier exuberant departure from Ireland. Stephen now turns northeast, and his thoughts shift to the more recent experience of his stay in Paris (41–44). Again he walks too close to the land's edge, and again his action is the corollary of his thoughts: "Turning, he scanned the shore south, his feet sinking again slowly in new sockets. The cold domed room of the tower waits" (44). And with this feeling that he is already beginning to stagnate in his new surroundings the first half of the chapter is rounded out. The second half of the chapter seems less coherent than the first because it is organized, not around a temporal progression, but around discrete objects in space: Sir Lout's toys, the live and dead dogs, the man and the woman. The bipartite structure of the chapter is thus an eloquent statement of Stephen's problem. Unable to experience fully the continuity between his present and past selves, he must seek some coherence in the present protean world of discrete phenomena.

There is another polarity in the chapter, less obvious, but as important as the polarity of time and space: that of male and female. It arises in part from Stephen's unresolved attitudes toward both parents, for he is haunted by the idea of his father as well as by the more harrowing specter of his mother. He is trying to relocate himself with respect to them as surely as he is trying to locate himself with respect to space and time—and in the end the two efforts are the same.

Like Bloom—and, for that matter, like Joyce—Stephen thinks of the world of process as essentially feminine. Occasionally a woman is for Stephen a sexual object ("What else were they invented for?" [40]), but more often a woman is for him an avatar of Woman, identified with the moon, the tides, and the eternal, unprogressive forces of Nature. Like Mulligan, Stephen thinks of the ocean as "our mighty mother" (37); he makes of the woman he sees on the beach an incarnation of process; and, in one of the loveliest passages in *Ulysses,* he sees the ocean as a weary woman (anticipatory of the weary Anna Livia in the closing pages of *Finnegans Wake*):

Under the upswelling tide he saw the writhing weeds lift languidly and sway reluctant arms, hising up their petticoats, in whispering water swaying and upturning coy silver fronds. Day by day: night by night: lifted, flooded and let fall. Lord, they are weary: and, whispered to, they sigh. Saint Ambrose heard it, sigh of leaves and waves, waiting, awaiting the fullness of their times, *diebus ac noctibus iniurias patiens ingemiscit.* To no end gathered: vainly then released, forth flowing, wending back: loom of the moon. Weary too in sight of lovers, lascivious men, a naked woman shining in her courts, she draws a toil of waters. (49–50)

Women in Stephen's mind do not exist to any appreciable extent as personalities. Although he has a very concrete sense of his father (see, for example, his imitation of his father's speech, p. 38), his mother is to him less a personality than a mood and a faint odor of wetted ashes. He imagines men, on the other hand, with varying degrees of concreteness. Women represent unmitigated process, men represent the *principium individuationis.* (Again, Stephen's sexual mythology goes beyond *Ulysses.* All of Joyce's major male characters are anxious to assure themselves of their own identities; his major female characters are never preoccupied by problems of self-definition.) The men whom Stephen thinks of in "Proteus" are on the whole an unavailing lot. There is Simon Dedalus, witty but self-pitying and even at times mean-spirited. There is Richie Goulding, whom Stephen imagines as a bedridden father domineering his son. And, most extensively, there are Kevin and Patrice Egan. Patrice is another son overawed by his father: *"Je ne crois pas en l'existence de Dieu. Faut pas le dire à mon père"* (41). But Stephen's major sense of identification is with Kevin Egan himself, the heroic but pathetic exile. Among the host of older men in Stephen's mind, Kevin Egan seems in many ways a likely spiritual father to Stephen, but he has in fact offered Stephen the most searing of insights into the loneliness and desuetude of exile: "They have forgotten Kevin Egan, not he them. Remembering thee, O Sion" (44).

Men are far more sharply defined in Stephen's mind than are women, but the men are personalities gone rigid, frozen in typical attitudes: Simon's tawdry wit, Richie Goulding's tired hospitality, Kevin Egan's burned-out patriotism. The strong sexual division in Stephen's mind is further reinforced by the almost total separation

of the men's world from the women's. Simon is a widower who tries
to avoid his daughters; Richie and Walter live at "Aunt Sara's,"
but we never see her; Kevin Egan is "Loveless, landless, wifeless"
(43). Earlier in the day, Mr. Deasy offered another example of
this sharp division in his misogynic lecture to Stephen:

> A woman brought sin into the world. For a woman who was no better
> than she should be, Helen, the runaway wife of Menelaus, ten years the
> Greeks made war on Troy. A faithless wife first brought the strangers
> to our shore here, MacMurrough's wife and her leman O'Rourke,
> prince of Breffni. A woman too brought Parnell low. (34–35)

The reality the women represent is frightening to Stephen because
it is always changing; but the men, in their distance from the feared
woman's world, represent the true Dublin disease: paralysis.

The forms of polarity I have been discussing make clear the
kind of synthesis that Stephen is seeking (although "seeking" is
not quite the right word, since Stephen is not yet aware of certain
kinds of experience). Both philosophically and existentially, he
seeks some reunion between his sense of himself as a series of so
many flickering serial manifestations and his sense of himself as an
enduring entity. In the terms of the sexual mythology which the
book proposes, he longs for immersion in the world of feminine
process, but he fears the loss of discrete identity which might come
from immersion in that world. Later in the day, he will meet a
man capable of reconciling these opposites, but it is important to
see, in the context of "Proteus," the ways in which Stephen briefly
manages to reconcile them himself.

Stephen's moment of reconciliation begins when he sees the
woman on the beach and formulates a poem in his mind:

> Across the sands of all the world, followed by the sun's flaming sword,
> to the west, trekking to evening lands. She trudges, schlepps, trains,
> drags, trascines her load. A tide westering, moondrawn, in her wake.
> Tides, myriadislanded, within her, blood not mine, *oinopa ponton,* a
> winedark sea. Behold the handmaid of the moon. In sleep the wet sign
> calls her hour, bids her rise. Bridebed, childbed, bed of death, ghost-
> candled. *Omnis caro ad te veniet.* He comes, pale vampire, through
> storm his eyes, his bat sails bloodying the sea, mouth to her mouth's kiss.

Here. Put a pin in that chap, will you? My tablets. Mouth to her
kiss. No. Must be two of 'em. Glue 'em well. Mouth to her mouth's
kiss. (47–48)

When he first saw this woman on the beach, Stephen thought, "I
see her skirties. Pinned up, I bet" (46). The detail of the lifted
skirts recalls the other girl Stephen saw on the beach, at the end of
Chapter IV in the *Portrait*. Stephen makes symbols of both women,
transforming them into representatives of the life experiences which
he has yet to encounter. But the moment of vision in "Proteus" is
the more complex—and the more valid—because it takes into full
account the costs as well as the benefits of experience. Thus Stephen
stylizes the image of the woman in "Proteus," but only in order to
emphasize the ambiguity of her physicality and mortality. She is the
beginning and the end of Biblical womanhood—both Eve being
driven from Eden ("followed by the sun's flaming sword") and
Mary at the Annunciation ("Behold the handmaid of the moon").
Like Molly and Anna Livia, Stephen's woman is both the cause of
the Fall and the source of the Antonement.

The woman is also May Dedalus: she goes forward to meet the
sinister "pale vampire," and Stephen describes her with the phrase
"bed of death, ghostcandled," which recalls his earlier recollection
of his mother's deathbed: "The ghostcandle to light her agony"
(10). Stephen's series of images is a restatement—and momentary
acceptance—of the fact of his mother's death. Mental image and
objective fact have become reconciled, and so Stephen thinks: "Put
a pin in that chap, will you?" He is telling himself to stabilize the
image and make it into a poem, but his language also creates two
further meanings: he drives a stake through the heart of the vampire and, unknown to himself, he fulfills the Homeric parallel by
pinning Proteus. Stephen has for the moment made process ac-
ceptable because understandable: it exists in the terms which he
himself creates and proposes.

We do not see the poem itself until four chapters later, in
"Aeolus," when Stephen remembers it:

> *On swift sail flaming*
> *From storm and south*
> *He comes, pale vampire,*
> *Mouth to my mouth.* (132)

It is startling to find that the poem has been written from the point of view of the woman. Stephen does not simply describe the woman: he speaks in her voice. The poem is thus both an act of Stephen's distanced, conceptualizing imagination which stands outside process and—through his identification with the woman—a statement of submission to process. Even Stephen's actions while composing the poem dramatize this double awareness:

> His shadow lay over the rocks as he bent, ending. Why not endless till the farthest star? Darkly they are there behind this light, darkness shining in the brightness, delta of Cassiopeia, worlds. Me sits there with his augur's rod of ash, in borrowed sandals, by day beside a livid sea, unbeheld, in violet night walking beneath a reign of uncouth stars. I throw this ended shadow from me, manshape ineluctable, call it back. Endless, would it be mine, form of my form? . . .
>
> He lay back at full stretch over the sharp rocks, cramming the scribbled note and pencil into a pocket, his hat tilted down on his eyes. That is Kevin Egan's movement I made nodding for his nap, sabbath sleep. *Et vidit Deus. Et erant valde bona.* Alo! *Bonjour,* welcome as the flowers in May. Under its leaf he watched through peacocktwittering lashes the southing sun. I am caught in this burning scene. Pan's hour, the faunal noon. Among gumheavy serpentplants, milkoozing fruits, where on the tawny waters leaves lie wide. Pain is far. (48–49)

Stephen first exults in a feeling of proud imaginative sovereignty over his world and then accedes to his perception of his place in that world: "I am caught in this burning scene." The moment of composition is both dominant and passive, as Stephen experiences first his superiority and then his submission to process.

Stephen's pinning of Proteus, the stabilizing of process which is necessary to him before he can submit to it, shows the relation in Stephen between intellect and experience. He is a character who must be assured of his own existence metaphysically before he can feel confident to live existentially. There are two passages, one before the poem and one after, which demonstrate the degree to which the very act of imagining the poem gives Stephen a new self-assurance. First, this moment of panic:

> Would you do what he did? A boat would be near, a lifebuoy. *Natürlich,* put there for you. Would you or would you not? The man

that was drowned nine days ago off Maiden's rock. They are waiting
for him now. The truth, spit it out. I would want to. I would try. I
am not a strong swimmer. Water cold soft. When I put my face into it
in the basin at Clongowes. Can't see! Who's behind me? Out quickly,
quickly! Do you see the tide flowing quickly in on all sides, sheeting
the lows of sands quickly, shellcocoacoloured? If I had land under my
feet. I want his life still to be his, mine to be mine. A drowning man.
His human eyes scream to me out of horror of his death. I . . . With
him together down . . . I could not save her. Waters: bitter death:
lost. (45–46)

Everything that Stephen fears comes together here: Mulligan, the
water which is both thing and symbol, the drowned man who is at
once Stephen himself and another human being crying out for
Stephen's help, his mother—all this accompanied by that paranoid
feeling Stephen has all day of some enemy lurking just outside his
field of vision: "Who's behind me?" In the very intensity of its
claustrophobia, the passage is an instance of the resources of stream-
of-consciousness narration. The most crucial phrase, perhaps, is "If
I had land under my feet." It exactly sums up Stephen's dilemma
in the novel: the problem of reaching any self-definition when he
has no ground upon which to stand and build.

A second passage, this one near the end of the chapter, again
centers upon the drowned man, but the shift in tone is extraordinary:

Five fathoms out there. Full fathom five thy father lies. At one he
said. Found drowned. High water at Dublin bar. Driving before it a
loose drift of rubble, fanshoals of fishes, silly shells. A corpse rising
saltwhite from the undertow, bobbing landward, a pace a pace a porpoise.
There he is. Hook it quick. Sunk though he be beneath the watery floor.
We have him. Easy now.

Bag of corpsegas sopping in foul brine. A quiver of minnows, fat of
a spongy titbit, flash through the slits of his buttoned trouserfly. God
becomes man becomes fish becomes barnacle goose becomes featherbed
mountain. Dead breaths I living breathe, tread dead dust, devour a
urinous offal from all dead. Hauled stark over the gunwale he breathes
upward the stench of his green grave, his leprous nosehole snoring to
the sun.

A seachange this, brown eyes saltblue. Seadeath, mildest of all deaths
known to man. Old Father Ocean. *Prix de Paris:* beware of imitations.
Just you give it a fair trial. We enjoyed ourselves immensely. (50)

There is disgust in this passage, but it is contemplative—even, toward the end, humorous. (One of Joyce's nicest forecasts of the appearance of Bloom is the ad for drowning which Stephen devises here.) If this is the distaste of Hamlet, whom Stephen resembles in so many ways, it is the Hamlet of Act v: the peace which settles over both Stephen and Hamlet comes from a half-anticipated, half-achieved faith in the benevolence of process. Hope and fear are almost precisely balanced. The references to *The Tempest* and *Lycidas* augur a resurrection which actually takes place—the drowned man "breathes upward . . . his leprous nosehole snoring to the sun"—but it takes place in a physical world of "urinous offal." (Again, Joyce points toward Bloom, whose grilled mutton kidneys "gave to his palate a fine tang of faintly scented urine" [55].) It is a resurrection, not into the stasis of eternity but into the kinesis of the phenomenal world. And notice what else has happened in this "seachange": the sea itself has changed, from "our mighty mother" at the beginning of the chapter to "Old Father Ocean" here at the end. If "Proteus" contains the paradox that Stephen can reach calm and equanimity only through submission to kinetic process, it also contains the proposition that he can reach his own male maturity only through his acceptance of what he fears as feminine. By the end of the chapter, Stephen identifies with the drowned man; and the sea, originally the emblem of the feminine, becomes the emblem of fatherhood.

In the course of the "Proteus" chapter, Stephen seeks to know the "hypostasis" of things, the substance underlying surface appearances. As his inquiry applies to himself, he seeks to know the essential Stephen Dedalus, the enduring self which underlies his various successive personalities. This search is painful for Stephen because although his natural tendency is to leap toward direct knowledge of essences, he is forcing himself to realize that the signatures of things are the only avenue he has to knowledge of the things themselves. Philosophically, he is a Platonist reluctantly forcing himself to become an Aristotelian. The thing itself continues to exist for Stephen—hence his conclusion when he opens his eyes, "There all the time without you: and ever shall be, world without end"— but he can know the thing only through apprehending its superficies. "Proteus" thus momentarily reconciles the conflict of the two preceding chapters, the conflict of Mulligan and Deasy, of mercurial change and frozen stasis. Stephen forces himself to accept the world of change because he realizes that only through the physicality of that world can he arrive at the world of idea. He at least urges himself toward commitment to the world of process, because he has come to realize the paradox that he can achieve personal stability only by accepting change.

Like most of his hopeful thoughts during the course of the day, the conclusions Stephen reaches in "Proteus" are only tentative, still unrealized. He has mapped out a course of action, but he has yet to bring it to fruition. Nevertheless, we should not minimize the kind of projected resolution Stephen is capable of reaching, even apart from his meeting with Bloom. The peace at the end of "Proteus" comes from Stephen's resignation to Bloom's world:

> He turned his face over a shoulder, rere regardant. Moving through the air high spars of a threemaster, her sails brailed up on the crosstrees, homing, upstream, silently moving, a silent ship. (51)

The ship Stephen sees suggests the Church with its three "crosstrees." (Joyce insisted on keeping "crosstrees" even when Budgen told him the word was incorrect.) The ship, indeed, suggests *all* the institutional forces which seek to dominate Stephen's soul. In "Telemachus" Stephen said to Haines, "I am the servant of two masters. . . . And a third" (20). By means of a muted pun, the ship is all three masters. The symbolism of the ship is heightened, moreover, when we remember that Stephen is "rere regardant" not only here but at the end of the two preceding chapters, as he looks back at his two oppressors, Mulligan and Deasy. And yet the tone of the passage is anything but threatening. The sense of calm which Stephen has achieved in the closing pages is transferred to the silent, homing ship. For the moment, Stephen can gaze with equanimity upon the very forces which at other times bring him to the verge of panic. As he prepares to leave Sandymount Strand and gazes backward at his receding past, we are reminded of those other ships, the ships of Menelaus, at last freed to continue on their journey after the conquering of Proteus.

## Chapter II

# The Essential Mr. Bloom

The first three chapters of *Ulysses* force us to see Stephen as a character defined between opposing extremes. Bloom's first three chapters force us to see him as a character defined by the extremes he contains within himself. Thus in order to summarize Bloom it would be necessary to account for the contradictions of rosy optimism and reductive pessimism, of fantasy and severe empiricism which make up his character. Bloom has an inclusive consciousness, that ability to encompass conflicting attitudes which is the paramount quality of Joyce's mature heroes.

Bloom's combinations of opposites are reminiscent of Buck Mulligan ("Contradiction. Do I contradict myself? Very well then, I contradict myself"). For Bloom has that protean, energetic play of mind which is supreme in Mulligan, and which even Stephen is forced to envy. It is a capacity to change the self according to circumstances—a supremely Ulyssean capacity—which is set in strong contrast to Stephen's stiff posing. And yet we never suspect that hollowness in Bloom which we soon learn to recognize in Mulligan. Mulligan's overtures to Stephen—"I'm the only one that knows what you are. Why don't you trust me?"—are perhaps at first convincing, but on a second reading they seem only another selection from his costume wardrobe. We never suspect Bloom of this kind of shamming, because Joyce makes clear early on the touchstones of Bloom's life, the anchoring points which give stability to his other, errant thoughts. Those touchstones are instances of

familial love—of his parents, his wife, and his children. Those
affections have wrought havoc in Bloom's life, but more than anything else they give to his character a sense of fixed bearings. It is
this sense of constancy beneath the contradictory flickerings of his
mind which makes of Bloom the realization of what Stephen sought
in "Proteus": the enduring self persisting beneath phenomenal
change.

Bloom combines opposite qualities because his mind operates in
cyclical patterns; and in this he differs very strongly from Stephen.
For Stephen, process is linear, always moving toward some
terminus. Seeing the dead dog on the beach, he thinks, "Dogskull,
dogsniff, eyes on the ground, moves to one great goal. Ah, poor
dogsbody. Here lies poor dogsbody's body" (46). When de-
pressed, Stephen sees life and history as a march toward death,
while in his more hopeful moments he thinks in the opposite—but
still linear—terms of progression and fulfillment. Bloom, on the
other hand, sees cycles, repetitions, alternations between good and
bad. The very circularity of his journey outward from 7 Eccles
Street in the morning and back at night typifies the cyclical patterns
he experiences and perceives. Instead of seeing life as progression,
he sees it as a finely adjusted economy, the birth of Mrs. Purefoy's
baby exactly corresponding to the death of Paddy Dignam. This
vision gives to Bloom's consciousness its characteristic pendulum
swings, from total futility to the philosophic shrug of patience and
stoicism.

Bloom is also self-contradictory, though, because he has the
inconsistencies of a man immediately engaged in sensory experience.
Here again, the contrast with Stephen is considerable. In general,
Stephen's thoughts rule over his experience, while Bloom's experience predominates over his thoughts. Stephen is prone to establish
an intellectual and imaginative framework into which he inserts
whatever experience comes his way. If the experience is not relevant
to the thought, then he excludes it; there are, especially in "Proteus," lengthy passages in Stephen's thought which take place *in
vacuo*, undisturbed by any sensory input. Even though he is trying
to force himself to a keener awareness of the particulars of experience, Stephen's basic tendency is strongly deductive. Bloom is much
more at the mercy of his senses. His thought-patterns are free from

his immediate sensory experiences only for very short periods. An inductive thinker, he is most likely to move from the concrete to the abstract. His mnemonic devices are examples of this way of thinking. So is his effort to instruct Molly: "Better remind her of the word: metempsychosis. An example would be better. An example" (65). He is curious about abstractions such as scientific laws (the conduction of heat, the laws of falling bodies), but the curiosity springs directly out of empirical observation. Moreover, when he does try to follow a line of reasoning from the specific to the general, he often falters along the way. What Richard Ellmann has nicely termed "Bloomisms"—instances of a fact scrupulously but incorrectly remembered—frequently crop up when Bloom tries to find a general law to explain a specific instance. Thus, for example, he reflects on the cat's whiskers:

> Wonder is it true if you clip them they can't mouse after. Why? They shine in the dark, perhaps, the tips. Or kind of feelers in the dark, perhaps. (56)

Or again:

> Where was the chap I saw in that picture somewhere? Ah, in the dead sea, floating on his back, reading a book with a parasol open. Couldn't sink if you tried: so thick with salt. Because the weight of the water, no, the weight of the body in the water is equal to the weight of the. Or is it the volume is equal of the weight? It's a law something like that. (72)

Occasionally, Bloom wins through and reaches the general law; just as often, he does not. And when, starting from the opposite extreme, he attempts to give concrete definition to an abstract principle such as "love" or "nation," he is lost at once.[1]

This simple but radical difference between Stephen and Bloom accounts for a great deal of the divergence between their streams

---

1. In 1912, Joyce, then in Trieste, delivered two lectures—one on Defoe and one on Blake. As a number of critics have observed, the two eighteenth-century writers symbolize the two poles of Joyce's art: the scrupulous empiricism of Defoe and the sovereign imaginative power of Blake. The two writers also correspond to the two heroes of *Ulysses*: Stephen, who seeks imaginative control over the world and who frequently quotes Blake, and Bloom, who is hypnotized by concrete detail and who once brought Molly a copy of *Moll Flanders*.

of consciousness. The genius of Stephen's stream of consciousness
is that a central idea draws together examples like a magnet; his
intellect sweeps over the available material and royally chooses the
details which may serve his purpose. Bloom's stream of consciousness is more purely an association of ideas—scraps of reflection and
memory shaped and diverted by a series of sensory incidents. Two
examples will show the difference. First, Stephen on the beach:

> A bloated carcass of a dog lay lolled on bladderwrack. Before him the
> gunwale of a boat, sunk in sand. *Un coche ensablé,* Louis Veuillot called
> Gautier's prose. These heavy sands are language tide and wind have
> silted here. And there, the stoneheaps of dead builders, a warren of
> weasel rats. (44)

The distinctive quality of this passage is its cluster of images
around one central idea, the idea rendered in *ensablé*. That idea
exists at the center of Stephen's mental process for the moment,
and every allusion he makes, even everything which enters his
consciousness as a thing *seen* is related to that idea. To this, compare Bloom idly reading the hoardings:

> Hello. *Leah* tonight: Mrs Bandman Palmer. Like to see her in that
> again. *Hamlet* she played last night. Male impersonator. Perhaps he
> was a woman. Why Ophelia committed suicide? Poor papa! (76)

The concatenation of ideas leading from *Leah* to his father's suicide is witty—especially "Perhaps he was a woman. Why Ophelia
committed suicide?" But Bloom is too immersed in the particulars
of his thought to foresee the movement of his mind toward the
death of his father, one of those traumatic memories he is usually at
pains to avoid. Once he has led himself into that trap, he must cast
about for some new associative train as an escape:

> Mr Bloom went round the corner and passed the drooping nags of
> the hazard. No use thinking of it any more. Nosebag time. Wish I
> hadn't met that M'Coy fellow. (76)

Bloom's plight is that his mind is at the mercy of its own associations. He is too close to the particularized content of his own

thought to have any true idea of its shape or any warning of its direction. Bloom's strength is that he can so readily create for himself a new associative train as an escape from the traps into which his thoughts lead him.

This immersion in detail is at once Bloom's damnation and his salvation. His very closeness to the physical world robs him of his ability to conceptualize his own fate and thereby redirect it effectively. (Stephen, in contrast, might say with Yawn what Joyce is supposed to have said to Jung: "I can psoakoonaloose myself any time I want" [*FW*, 522].) At the end of each day Bloom can regard his own problems with equanimity, but he cannot clearly foresee the possibility of ever escaping them. And yet this inability (which is also a refusal) to conceptualize also accounts for Bloom's suppleness and humanity. His very lack of doctrine allows him to respond to each particular with fresh eyes. Deprived of Stephen's shaping vision, he has a less exclusive way of seeing the world.

## "Calypso"

If Stephen's first three chapters show the young hero in the process of maturing, "almosting it," Bloom's first three chapters show a consciousness already formed. The question of possible change is urgent in Stephen's chapters, but the question of Bloom's ability to change is not even a prominent issue until much further along in the book. The maturity of Bloom's consciousness requires a different strategy of presentation, and that strategy is reflected in the structural relation of his first three chapters. In *Ulysses on the Liffey,* Richard Ellmann has suggested that Joyce consistently groups his chapters in triads, the third chapter in each triad resolving the conflicts established in the first two.[2] Ellmann has seized upon what is indisputably a triadic pattern in Joyce's work, but he has mistaken a tendency for a hard-and-fast rule. Stephen's first three chapters perfectly illustrate Ellmann's thesis; Bloom's do not. Stephen's chapters show a young mind working toward and

2. Richard Ellmann, *Ulysses on the Liffey* (New York: Oxford University Press, 1972) pp. 1–2. Ellmann's contention that each third chapter is a climactic episode was anticipated by Foster Damon, "The Odyssey in Dublin," *James Joyce: Two Decades of Criticism,* ed. Seon Givens (New York: Vanguard Press, 1963), p. 211.

achieving a tenuous conclusion. Bloom's show something like the reverse. "Calypso" shows us the essential Mr. Bloom, his contradictory qualities in exact equilibrium; then "Lotus-eaters" and "Hades" begin the lengthy process of dissection, dramatizing first his tendency toward fantasy and then his intense fidelity to the here and now. No other chapter sees Bloom so neutrally and so wholly as "Calypso." If other chapters have more impact, their intensity comes from a more confined point of view.

The very opening of "Calypso" is indicative of the chapter's special status in the book: "Mr Leopold Bloom ate with relish the inner organs of beasts and fowls." This is rather different from "Stately, plump Buck Mulligan came from the stairhead, bearing a bowl of lather on which a mirror and razor lay crossed." Both passages are third-person narration, but the description of Bloom, with its privileged information on Bloom's habitual actions, is different—it is, in fact, unique in the book. This is an old-fashioned narrative voice (compare "Emma Woodhouse, handsome, clever, and rich . . ."), serene in its unquestioned knowledge of its subject. Not again until "Ithaca"—and then in a very different form—will Joyce supply this kind of privileged information unfiltered through the character's own perceptions. This steady, self-confident prose is appropriate for "Calypso": it corresponds to the evenly balanced view of Bloom which the chapter presents. The style assures us—falsely, as it turns out—that we can know Bloom in the same way that we know Maggie Tulliver or Arthur Clennam. Only gradually does it become clear, in the course of the ensuing chapters, that our only way of knowing Bloom is Stephen's way of knowing the world in "Proteus"—by assimilating the information which comes to us refracted through Joyce's various narrative media.

The Bloom of "Calypso" is, as it were, an overture to the various Blooms which the succeeding chapters offer. The whole man is here, but unaffected by the distorting perspectives of the later chapters. The most salient quality about the Bloom of "Calypso" is his easy combination of opposites.[3] The chapter opens

3. Marilyn French has recently made much the same point about Bloom's combinations of opposites. See *The Book as World* (Cambridge, Mass.: Harvard University Press, 1976) pp. 84–85.

with fresh morning thoughts and ends with a thought of death: "Poor Dignam!" It is poised between eating and defecation, between the East as the beginning and as the end of all things. Offal is nourishment—"a fine tang of faintly scented urine"—and the genitals symbolize death—"the grey sunken cunt of the world." More pervasively, Bloom is persistently characterized by a double consciousness, as he triangulates upon a given subject with two different thoughts. Here is his early-morning conversation with the cat:

> —Milk for the pussens, he said.
> —Mrkgnao! the cat cried.
> They call them stupid. They understand what we say better than we understand them. She understands all she wants to. Vindictive too. Wonder what I look like to her. Height of a tower? No, she can jump me.
> —Afraid of the chickens, she is, he said mockingly. Afraid of the chookchooks. I never saw such a stupid pussens as the pussens.
> Cruel. Her nature. Curious mice never squeal. Seem to like it.
> —Mrkrgnao! the cat said loudly. (55)

The conversation with the cat is typical of Bloom's sensory involvements throughout the day. There is a childlike quality in Bloom's words to the cat, but also a reserve and a clinical scrutiny as he thinks of the cat's animal sadism. This sustained duality of response is the very center of Bloom's character.

Probably the clearest example of the pattern of dual responses in "Calypso" occurs as Bloom is returning from the butcher's and thinking about the East. Here, if anywhere, is the full portrayal of a pattern of consciousness which we will see repeated many times during the day. (The passage, indeed, is something of a set piece, an encapsulation of Bloom's moods. Its centrality is at least tacitly understood by the critics: it seems impossible to write about "Calypso" without discussing this reverie.) Throughout the novel, the essential Mr. Bloom feels drawn toward some ideal conception (sexual, utopian, paradisiacal), until some observed or remembered detail brings him plummeting down, usually into a feeling of profound loneliness; then yet another of his observations reestablishes the norm and—in a nice phrase from "Circe"—"Bloom plodges forward again" (474). This emotional rhythm begins in "Calypso" when the notice of the Mideastern planting company, the sunlight, and the morning air induce in Bloom a lotus-land vision: "Silvered powdered olivetrees. Quiet long days: pruning ripening" (60). Then two details—the cloud covering the sun and an old woman crossing the street—send him into an emotional dip: "Dead: an old woman's: the grey sunken cunt of the world" (61). What is most interesting is the spectacle of Bloom regaining his equilibrium at the end of this rhythmic cycle:

> Grey horror seared his flesh. Folding the page into his pocket he turned into Eccles Street, hurrying homeward. Cold oils slid along his veins, chilling his blood: age crusting him with a salt cloak. Well, I am here now. Morning mouth bad images. Got up wrong side of the bed. Must begin again those Sandow's exercises. On the hands down. Blotchy brown brick houses. Number eighty still unlet. Why is that? Valuation is only twenty-eight. Towers, Battersby, North, MacArthur: parlour windows plastered with bills. Plasters on a sore eye. To smell the gentle smoke of tea, fume of the pan, sizzling butter. Be near her ample bed-warmed flesh. Yes, yes.
>
> Quick warm sunlight came running from Berkeley Road, swiftly, in slim sandals, along the brightening footpath. Runs, she runs to meet me, a girl with gold hair on the wind. (61)

The reasons for Bloom's recovery are various: he rationalizes the cause of depression ("Morning mouth bad images"); he wills his recovery ("Got up wrong side of the bed. Must begin again those Sandow's exercises"—as if he actually gets up again and starts the day anew); he falls back upon his usual interest in facts and things ("Number eighty still unlet. Why is that?"); and finally he invokes what sensuous enjoyments there are to be had at 7 Eccles Street ("the gentle smoke of tea . . . her ample bedwarmed flesh"). This is ultimately Bloomian. His forces in momentary disarray, they rapidly reassert themselves—rationality, empiricism, sensuousness—at first atomistically and then fully, monolithically: "Yes, yes."

Bloom, we might say, has mentally prepared himself for the reappearance of the sun, and when that occurs, the old woman crossing the street has been replaced in Bloom's imagination by

the Milly-like girl running to meet him. The imagined figure of
the girl is the clue which shows the relation between this down-
and-up pattern of response and the conditions of Bloom's life.
Upset by the sight of an old woman (Molly, we recall, is pre-
cariously poised, still young enough to resemble the girl of the
early days with Bloom but already beginning to show the first signs
of age), Bloom works his way through to a vision of his daughter
who is for both Molly and Bloom a reminder of youth.

The mental rhythm of this scene in "Calypso" is the prototype
for many moments later in the day. The pattern of Bloom's hallucinations in "Circe" is directly continuous with this rhythm of
inflation-depression-recovery. The progression of feeling in "Nausicaa" points to the sexual nature of the pattern, leading from
excited fantasy through post-coital dumps and back to a mediate
plateau. In the heated argument in "Cyclops," even though our
point of view is outside Bloom's mind, we can see the same pattern.
Bloom first rises to an almost uncharacteristic fervor ("I'm talking
about injustice, says Bloom"), flags as he recognizes the futility of
his utopianism ("But it's no use, says he. Force, hatred, history, all
that"), then levels off and resumes his practicality ("Love, says
Bloom. I mean the opposite of hatred. I must go now, says he to
John Wyse" [332–33]).

Bloom operates by a kind of internal gyroscope. He tilts alternately toward one extreme or the other, but his internal economy
always rights the balance. Bloom does not really avoid extremes,
as Stephen does in recoiling first from Mulligan and then from Mr.
Deasy. Instead, Bloom *includes* both extremes of a given polarity
and therefore is completely prey to neither.

## "Lotus-eaters"

In "Lotus-eaters" and "Hades," Joyce begins to break down
the wholeness of Bloom's character, to isolate and focus upon its
extremes. Joyce has not yet begun to subject Bloom to the distortions of style which open up new perspectives on him. He does,
however, place Bloom in dramatic situations which elicit from him
very one-sided responses.

"Lotus-eaters" is the first chapter in *Ulysses* to be organized around a Homeric episode of temptation. (The other two major Homeric temptation scenes are "Sirens" and "Circe.") Ulysses and Bloom have rather different reactions to the temptations offered them. Through prudence, divine assistance, or sheer good luck, Ulysses usually avoids the snares set for him. Bloom's resistance is never so clear-cut. His truest resemblance to Ulysses centers in Ulysses's strategy in sailing by the sirens. Homer's Ulysses is able to have his cake and eat it too in the sirens episode: he experiences the deep and sensuous thrill of the sirens' songs and yet remains free of them. Similarly, Bloom often yields spiritually to temptation before he escapes its influence. He skirts safely past the lotus-eaters, the sirens, and Circe, but not without first indulging in their dangerous delights.

"Lotus-eaters" is patterned upon this alternation of surrender and resistance. Bloom is at once lotus-eater and celibate (even though, as he realizes, celibacy carries with it its own form of narcosis). He effortlessly resists the most pervasive Dublin drugs— he is never more disinterestedly skeptical than in his critique of religion in this chapter—but he has his own paradisiacal fantasies into which he often retreats. To overstress Bloom's alert skepticism and resistance to temptation (as, for example, Richard Ellmann does) is thus to miss exactly half the chapter.

Bloom has little trouble resisting the more public forms of narcosis which paralyze his fellow citizens. His long standing as an outsider gives him a natural immunity to the enervation of religion or boozy fellowship, and his outsider's prudence makes him critical of the Dubliners' betting mania. Much of his sturdy independence comes simply from his exclusion. As he reflects on the worshipers in All Hallows, for example, he is aware that their torpid peace comes in part from the communal nature of Christianity: "Then feel all like one family party, same in the theatre, all in the same swim. They do. I'm sure of that. Not so lonely" (81). That last, distanced "Not so lonely" registers both the strength and the cost of Bloom's outside position. He shrewdly notes how religion satisfies his fellow citizens' longing for community, but he thereby rules out that option for himself. This is the "I feel so lonely" Bloom of "Sirens." And yet it is obvious that this kind of wistfulness does not predominate in "Lotus-eaters."

His desire for companionship is only brief, and he is actually irritated the two times when an acquaintance strikes up a conversation: "M'Coy. Get rid of him quickly" (73); and of Bantam Lyons: "Better leave him the paper and get shut of him" (85). These are the thoughts of a mental onanist, annoyed at the interruption of his fantasy.

We will learn most about Bloom, then, not by admiring those moments when he safely avoids Dublin's lotuses—such avoidance is actually quite easy for him—but in examining those moments when he gives in to the pleasures of his own fantasy world. As we might expect of Bloom, there is always a double consciousness about his fantasies—always a flicker of common sense or humor around even his most gratifying dreams. His major fantasy in the chapter centers upon his correspondence with Martha Clifford, but even in his thoughts about Martha there is a strong antidote of common sense:

> Could meet one Sunday after the rosary. Thank you: not having any.
> Usual love scrimmage. Then running round corners. Bad as a row with
> Molly. Cigar has a cooling effect. Narcotic. Go further next time.
> Naughty boy: punish: afraid of words, of course. Brutal, why not? Try
> it anyhow. A bit at a time. (78)

Bloom fantasizes, but the thought always hovers near that the fantasy is just that—a dream which will not survive the touch of reality. He sets the thought at a distance by coolly classifying it ("Usual love scrimmage"). Then, in one of Joyce's nicest touches, Bloom thinks of subduing the effects of this drug by resorting to another ("Cigar has a cooling effect. Narcotic"). But once he has marked off the boundaries of the fantasy, he allows it to go on existing within the confines of that special, closed-off place: "Go further next time. . . . Try it anyhow. A bit at a time."

Bloom thus eats his own kind of lotus. He enjoys various paradises, but always with the saving consciousness that the paradises are false. And this strategy of containment is true of all of Bloom's "temptations" during the day: his surrender to fantasy always contains its own antidote. In creating his own small moments of pleasure, he is aware of their ephemeral or chimerical nature, so that when the bubble inevitably bursts, he accepts it with a phil-

osophical shrug. Lotuses of various kinds—religion, betting, bar-
room companionship, nationalism—are a way of life for Bloom's
fellow citizens. His own are small moments of respite, necessary
for the recollection and reintegration of his forces.

## "Hades"

In Prospect Cemetery, Bloom stands by the grave of Paddy
Dignam and thinks: "Chinese cemeteries with giant poppies growing produce the best opium" (108). Bloom's stray reflection suggests how "Hades" is the mirror image of "Lotus-eaters." Death
is itself a powerful opiate for the living and, as Joyce dramatizes
from "The Sisters" onward, is more insidious than the generally
socialized opiates of "Lotus-eaters." The narcotic power of the
very subject of death is evident in the stifling piety in which both
Church and society swaddle the naked fact. "Daren't joke about the
dead for two years at least," Bloom thinks, and then caps the
thought with a Bloomism: *"De mortuis nil nisi prius"* (109).
Simon Dedalus exhibits this required reverence in a subtler form:

> —Her grave is over there, Jack, Mr Dedalus said. I'll soon be
> stretched beside her. Let Him take me whenever He likes.
> Breaking down, he began to weep to himself quietly, stumbling a
> little in his walk. Mr Power took his arm.
> —She's better where she is, he said kindly.
> —I suppose so, Mr Dedalus said with a weak gasp. I suppose she is
> in heaven if there is a heaven. (105)

The moment is perfectly rendered (Joyce knew his Flaubert).
Dedalus's grief and Power's kindness are real enough, but they
are cheapened and falsified by the bromidic expressions which death
requires. There is an evasion here which is of a piece with the
shallow, boozy sentiment of "Sirens."

If the drug of death stifles because it falsifies response, it can
also have the more terrible effect of heightening emotion, creating
an obsession. This is the effect of death which Bloom thinks of near
the end of the chapter:

Poor papa too. The love that kills. And even scraping up the earth at night with a lantern like that case I read of to get at fresh buried females or even putrefied with running gravesores. Give you the creeps after a bit. I will appear to you after death. You will see my ghost after death. My ghost will haunt you after death. (114-15)

Rudolph Virag—"poor papa"—did indeed have the love that kills, for he committed suicide out of love for his dead wife. But Virag is not a unique instance of the love that kills: both Bloom and Stephen are haunted, paralyzed by their love of the dead. This is the most terrible opiate in all of *Ulysses:* the living are drugged by their allegiance to the dead. If Joyce's mythic vision has the archetypes of the past surviving into the present, his characters carry about with them their own ghosts from the past.

There is one other major instance in "Hades" of the brooding presence of the dead; it is to be found in that predominating mood of Joyce's Dublin, the shabby-genteel recollection of better days. In the *Portrait,* Stephen described to Cranly the many professions of Simon Dedalus: "A medical student, an oarsman, a tenor, an amateur actor, a shouting politician, a small landlord, a small investor, a drinker, a good fellow, a story teller, somebody's secretary, something in a distillery, a taxgatherer, a bankrupt and at present a praiser of his own past" (*PA,* 241). Simon is a synecdoche for his city, which lives on the memories of its dead patriots, dead tenors, and dead journalists. Such memories are especially prominent in "Hades," as the carriage ride to the cemetery becomes a tour through the city of the dead. For perhaps no other novel so meticulously lists the statues of a city—in this chapter, Sir Philip Crampton's bust and the long line of statues up the center of O'Connell Street: the Liberator (Daniel O'Connell), Sir John Gray, Nelson, Father Mathew, the foundation-stone for Parnell's monument. (Elsewhere in the book are the statues of Tom Moore, Grattan, Goldsmith, and, outside Dublin, Michelangelo's Moses.) And the procession of monuments does not stop with the journey: the graves of both O'Connell and Parnell are in Prospect Cemetery. The statues and graves are signs of that essential element of Dublin life: the enervating allegiance to a past which is glorious but dead.

These are the attitudes which surround Bloom in "Hades"—and which to some extent envelop him as well, for he is certainly not immune to the call of his own dead, his mother, father, and son. And, beyond this, death is potentially even more chilling to Bloom's atheistic mind than to his Catholic fellow Dubliners. Bloom thinks of a corpse as "meat gone bad" (114), because that is for him the totality of death's meaning for the dead. Bloom's secular mind does not seriously consider the idea of an afterlife, and so he must face death as the end of all things. "Hades" thus exactly complements "Lotus-eaters," as the two chapters split up the unitary self of "Calypso." "Lotus-eaters" singles out and exaggerates the balmy, paradisiacal visions of the East which Bloom imagined in "Calypso." "Hades" tempts him to submit to the countervailing, wasteland vision: "A barren land, bare waste. Vulcanic lake, the dead sea: no fish, weedless, sunk deep in the earth" (61).

Bloom's confrontation with death in "Hades" is prolonged and honest, but when he leaves the cemetery he is calm, even—after his encounter with Menton—perky. The key to his rebound and his opting for life is not to be found in any one attitude, but (as was the case earlier in "Calypso") in a number of atomistic assertions which gradually gain in strength. Only at the end of the chapter can Bloom say, fully and convincingly: "They are not going to get me this innings. Warm beds: warm fullblooded life" (115). The true center of Bloom is in those small triumphs of insight which slowly mount toward the chapter's triumphant ending.

Look first at one of Bloom's most grisly reflections on decomposition:

> I daresay the soil would be quite fat with corpse manure, bones, flesh, nails, charnelhouses. Dreadful. Turning green and pink, decomposing. Rot quick in damp earth. The lean old ones tougher. Then a kind of a tallowy kind of a cheesy. Then begin to get black, treacle oozing out of them. Then dried up. Deathmoths. Of course the cells or whatever they are go on living. Changing about. Live for ever practically. Nothing to feed on feed on themselves. (108–109)

Bloom begins with the gardener's particular interest in cemeteries—a thought which seems subliminally continuous with the idea of

manuring the garden in "Calypso." "Dreadful," Bloom thinks; but
his empirical curiosity has been set in motion and leads him rapidly
("Then . . . Then . . . Then") through the stages of the body's
decomposition. And when he is through, he has been brought back
to the self-generating process already implicit in "corpse manure":
"Changing about. Live for ever practically" (109). Out of death
comes life. Such a conclusion about death is commonplace; what is
extraordinary is the childlike curiosity by which Bloom rediscovers
and revitalizes the commonplace.

Although Bloom's thoughts at the cemetery are grisly, there are
no moments of terror, few even of strong disgust. For the most
part, he has an easy control over the idea of death: Paddy Dignam,
after all, was only a slight acquaintance. Since he is not overwhelmed by the immediacy of grief, Bloom's thoughts hit on either
side of his subject and avoid any actual confrontation with deep
anxiety. On one hand—as we have just seen—he seizes upon individual details which usurp his entire attention and push out of his
mind the more general concern from which the details spring. Or,
at the other extreme, Bloom may lapse into a dejected fatalism
which is as much a dodge as a recognition: he falls into an easy
pessimism which lessens specific evils by lumping them together into
one vision of bleakness. Some of this variety of response is clear in
a passage in which Bloom thinks of death as the end of all human
affection:

> People talk about you a bit: forget you. Don't forget to pray for him.
> Remember him in your prayers. Even Parnell. Ivy day dying out. Then
> they follow: dropping into a hole one after the other.
> We are praying now for the repose of his soul. Hoping you're well
> and not in hell. Nice change of air. Out of the fryingpan of life into
> the fire of purgatory.
> Does he ever think of the hole waiting for himself? They say you do
> when you shiver in the sun. Someone walking over it. Callboy's warning.
> Near you. Mine over there towards Finglas, the plot I bought. Mamma
> poor mamma, and little Rudy. (111)

Bloom's thoughts here have a hidden logic which revolves around
the conflict between "People talk about you a bit: forget you" and
Bloom's refusal to forget: "Mamma poor mamma, and little

Rudy." The uneasy disparity between the two thoughts is registered
in the short burst of wit satirizing ritualistic means of remembering: "Hoping you're well and not in hell." The rapid alternation of
somber acceptance, satire, and grief suggests the kind of equilibrium
of consciousness which Bloom achieves in "Hades." He gives death
its due—at moments he even celebrates death as a part of the
natural cycle—but this large vision is exactly balanced by Bloom's
acknowledgment of individual grief. Incapable of formulating a
consistent philosophical consolation, Bloom by his self-contradictions incorporates death into his vision, into his very way of life.

Such is Bloom's considerable achievement in "Hades"; but Joyce
makes us aware of the definite limits of that achievement. Bloom's
mental victory over death contrasts with the most painful facts of
his own life, the deaths of his father and son, just as his defense of
love later in the book contrasts with his traumatized relations with
his wife. This is Bloom's paradoxical dilemma in the novel: he is
the apostle of a compassionate humanity, but he is incapable of
benefiting from his own creed. Nowhere is Bloom's baffled dilemma
clearer than in his thoughts about Queen Victoria just after he
arrives at the cemetery:

> Widowhood not the thing since the old queen died. Drawn on a gun-
> carriage. Victoria and Albert. Frogmore memorial mourning. But in the
> end she put a few violets in her bonnet. Vain in her heart of hearts. All
> for a shadow. Consort not even a king. Her son was the substance.
> Something new to hope for not like the past she wanted back, waiting.
> It never comes. One must go first: alone under the ground: and lie no
> more in her warm bed. (102)

Bloom is able to sympathize with the old queen but he is unable to
follow her example. For Bloom, to look forward to the future is
to be reminded of the past—the death of his son Rudy. Cut off
from continuity with either past or future, Bloom is unable to
participate in the very processes of Nature to which he gives intellectual and emotional assent.

This same dilemma is summed up in one of Bloom's thoughts
late in the chapter: "Drowning they say is the pleasantest. See your
whole life in a flash. But being brought back to life no" (114). The
strong contrast with Stephen's fear of drowning is obvious: the
best death for Bloom would be total submersion in the flux which

is his comfort and Stephen's dread. And yet: "But being brought
back to life no." This touches upon Bloom's weakest point. In spite
of his resounding affirmation of life over death; in spite of his
feeling that a visit to the cemetery gives him a "second wind. New
lease of life" (109); in spite of his cyclical view that "It's the
blood sinking in the earth gives new life" (108), there are strict
limits to Bloom's powers of resurrection. He is (before his meeting
with Stephen, at any rate) incapable of confronting his own personal traumas and of reemerging fully into the life around him.

Bloom's first three chapters establish the large scope of his
character. His very assurance of an established identity gives him a
large freedom of movement; he has a long tether and so can
wander into extremes of mental behavior before coming back to
the solid resting points within himself. This tendency to wander,
moreover, is self-correcting. "Lotus-eaters" dramatizes Bloom's
tendency toward fantasy, but his fantasies always have the ballast
of shrewd common sense. "Hades" dramatizes Bloom's down-to-
earth, empirical nature, but he is saved from his own purely
mechanistic views by affection, humor, and a partial evasion of
death's ultimate power over him and his family. Bloom's first three
chapters thus reveal a man of myriad strategies, alternately
aggressive and retiring in his thoughts, whose mercurial changes
work to protect the foundation stones of his life—a very strong
love of his family and a vaguer general compassion.

And yet these first three chapters also set very definite limits to
Bloom's character. Both his fantasies and his empirical curiosity
are, in the most trying moments, dodges, escapes from the crisis of
self-confrontation. This is obviously the case with his fantasies: the
letters to Martha are blatant examples of avoidance and substitution. And when Bloom is under the greatest psychological pressure,
his empiricism is just as evasive. In such moments, he seizes upon a
physical detail which will distract his thoughts from that knot of
feeling which consists of Rudy, Molly, and Boylan. One especially
clear instance of this diversionary attention to detail occurs on the
way to the cemetery, as Bloom sees Boylan from the carriage:

> Mr Bloom reviewed the nails of his left hand, then those of his right
> hand. The nails, yes. Is there anything more in him that they she sees?
> Fascination. Worst man in Dublin. That keeps him alive. They some-

times feel what a person is. Instinct. But a type like that. My nails. I am
just looking at them: well pared. And after: thinking alone. Body
getting a bit softy. I would notice that from remembering. What causes
that I suppose the skin can't contract quickly enough when the flesh falls
off. But the shape is there. The shape is there still. Shoulders. Hips.
Plump. Night of the dance dressing. Shift stuck between the cheeks
behind.

He clasped his hands between his knees and, satisfied, sent his vacant
glance over their faces. (92)

Bloom attempts to wrest attention away from Molly and Boylan
and to relocate it somewhere else, anyplace else. When his review
of his nails fails to distract him, he forces himself to forget his
wife's adultery by singlemindedly concentrating on her body. It is
an especially clear example of Bloom's drugging himself through
attention to the specific.

Bloom, then, is not simply attracted to the phenomenal world.
At his most painful moments, he is psychologically addicted to it,
since it serves as his chief refuge from revolutionizing thought. He
is in this respect the precise opposite of Stephen, who suffers a
kind of spiritual anemia from being so removed from Bloom's
world. Stephen is incomplete because he has only mental solutions
to his problems; he can only *imagine* his desired commitment to the
world. Bloom is incomplete because his nature is so completely subdued to what it works in. Immersed in the physical world, he is
incapable of a depersonalized distance from himself, and so he cannot grasp even the nature of his own dilemma. Both men need a
salvific assistance from some person beyond themselves if they are
to overcome the imprisonment of their respective mental sets.

In Stephen's chapters, and even more in Bloom's, Joyce celebrates the mind's ability to construct the simulacrum of a world. He
also delimits the mind's triumphs by suggesting the horror and the
tedium of the mind as a closed system which works by its own laws
and resists the painful readjustment of those laws.

*Chapter III*

# The Worst Hours
# of the Day

Bloom's great strength lies in the rhythm of his personality which his first three chapters clearly establish. The systole and diastole of his character make him the strongest fantasist and the strongest realist of the three major characters. Stated in terms of Joyce's sexual mythology, Bloom has both the masculine ability to create his own world and the feminine ability to identify with the world as it is. He would not really understand Gabriel Conroy's crisis at the end of "The Dead," because for Bloom such a moment is not usually a crisis. The passage from a tight sense of identity to an ego-less identification with the world is usually an easy thing for Bloom. The rhythm of integration-disintegration-reintegration is, indeed, one of his defining characteristics. He is therefore more various than either Stephen or Molly. His discriminating consciousness gives order to the flux of things, but he seldom loses the awareness that the order he creates is inferior to, because imposed upon, the flux.

But there come moments when the relation between intellect and brute matter fails. At such times, the need for meaning coexists, rather than alternates, with the overriding perception of meaninglessness, and Bloom's consciousness breaks or retreats under the strain. In particular, this is true of "Lestrygonians," "Sirens," and "Nausicaa." Although markedly different in tone, these three

chapters offer much the same perspective on Bloom: no longer resisting, he succumbs to the vision of himself as mere integer, undistinguished by personality. Catching Bloom at low points of vitality, these three chapters represent his consciousness at rock
bottom.

When thus isolated, these three chapters reveal a constant perspective upon Bloom in the middle chapters of *Ulysses* ("Lestrygonians" is the eighth, "Nausicaa" the thirteenth). Even while
Joyce's imposed stylistic distortions begin to crowd out the fundamental style of the book's opening, these three chapters still convey
Bloom's stream of consciousness to us in a surprisingly undistorted
form. Such is clearly the case in "Lestrygonians," which contains
only minimal stylistic distortion. In "Sirens," one of the most
radically "stylized" chapters, there are many passages of Bloom's
straightforward stream of consciousness; and even when his stream
of consciousness is subjected to the chapter's distortions, the effect
actually *emphasizes* rather than leads away from the clipped, asso-
ciational quality of Bloom's thought:

> Why do you call me naught? You naughty too? O, Mairy lost the pin
> of her. Bye for today. Yes, yes, will tell you. Want to. To keep it up.
> Call me that other. Other world she wrote. (279)

And in "Nausicaa" Joyce returns to a virtually pure form of
Bloom's stream of consciousness. In these middle chapters, Bloom's
thought itself remains our one surest touchstone.

If there is constancy in these three chapters—the constancy of
the rhythm of Bloom's own thought—there is also progression. As
Bloom's day proceeds, he becomes more and more frazzled. (In
spite of the book's insistence upon the typical, the quotidian, surely
we cannot consider June 16 to be truly "typical." Attendance at a
funeral, an argument which stops just short of physical violence, a
visit to a destitute widow and her children, all accompanied by the
thought of Molly's adultery, quite possibly her first consummated
extramarital adventure—Ulysses himself might have had trouble
bearing up under this.) And as Bloom becomes more and more
frazzled, his pendulum swings between lotus-land and wasteland
become more and more extreme. In particular, as Bloom anticipates,

arrives at, and then looks back upon the four o'clock meeting between Molly and Boylan, his alternate visions of sexuality—the
idealized paradise and the reductive "reality"—move further and
further apart. In "Lestrygonians," he is caught between the paradisiacal memory of Molly on Howth Head and the reality of Boylan
outside the museum. In "Sirens," at the crucial hour, the tension
within Bloom's mind is well-nigh unbearable, and he devises the
psychological strategy which is explored more fully in "Circe": he
vicariously participates in the adultery itself. These are terrible,
strained hours for Bloom, and, very significantly, it is in these two
chapters that he makes his only conscious, if very tentative, approaches to the idea of returning to Molly. Until the climax of
"Circe," these two chapters, because of the very pain they inflict
upon Bloom, bring about his closest approach to self-confrontation.
In "Nausicaa" the strain is gone—not because Bloom has resolved
anything, but because the tension between the idealized and the
reductive is broken by Bloom's masturbation. The paradisiacal
Bloom—the Bloom, that is, who longs for the happy days with
Molly but who is unwilling to make the effort to regain those days—
subsides, and the wry, empiricist Bloom remains. In his post-coital
lethargy, Bloom achieves a bogus calm: sexually satisfied, he can
accept with relative indifference Molly's infidelity.

These three chapters contain all of Bloom's evasive strategies:
his flight from Boylan, his letter to Martha, his vicarious participation in the adultery, his masturbation. If we accept as unchangeable
*données* the permanence of Bloom's inability to have sex with
Molly and his deep-seated fear of suffering the death of another
child, these dodges and evasions are actually victories, victories
which consist in sidestepping and thwarting the dragon that cannot
be slain. But there are clear hints of the possibility of change in
Bloom, even if they are muted and rejected by Bloom himself.
Earlier critics of *Ulysses* such as Wilson or Tindall made too much
of these hints and predicted the certainty of change. More recent
critics, Ellmann and French for example, have pronounced the
reader's concern with such change naïve and have seen such hints of
change in Bloom as so many of Joyce's means of "teasing" the
reader into hoping for a happy ending. But the book clearly points
us in both directions. It celebrates Bloom's comic-pathetic victories

of evasion. It also points to the ultimate inadequacy of the evasions themselves—and to Bloom's underlying awareness of their inadequacy. And, significantly, the evasions seem most inadequate, most clearly defeats rather than victories in "Nausicaa," the last chapter before Bloom finally meets Stephen.

## "Lestrygonians"

"Lestrygonians" is Bloom's "Proteus."[1] In no other chapter does he so consistently regard himself as a mere object drifting in the stream of the world's process. The chapter is, perhaps, what Bloom calls it, "the worst hour of the day"—for Bloom is completely overpowered by the vision of life senselessly flowing toward death. His tendency toward the reductive vision runs wild here, with little of his usual sensuous luxuriating to counterbalance it.

Bloom's weariness and disgust are only augmented by the spectacle of the people passing before him. Dublin at this hour seems populated by madmen and eccentrics, typified by Denis Breen and Cashel Boyle O'Connor Fitzmaurice Tisdall Farrell. Russell passes, speaking words which are just this side of madness: "Of the two-headed octopus, one of whose heads is the head upon which the ends of the world have forgotten to come while the other speaks with a Scottish accent . . . " (165). And John Howard Parnell passes, leading Bloom to reflect that all of the Parnell family are "a little bit touched" (165).

John Howard Parnell is also typical of "Lestrygonians" in another way. He is, as Bloom reflects, a woefully inadequate successor of his great brother. In "Lestrygonians," the world seems to be running down, and the present is only a sad reflection of the past. Mrs. Breen, for example, seems to Bloom to have only a shabby resemblance to her former self: "Same blue serge dress she had two years ago, the nap bleaching. Seen its best days . . . . Shabby genteel. She used to be a tasty dresser" (158). More painfully, Bloom recalls the old days with Molly and finds the present

1. Erwin R. Steinberg lists many of the "Proteus"-"Lestrygonians" correspondences in " 'Lestrygonians' a Pale Shadow of 'Proteus'?" *Modern Fiction Studies*, xv (1969), 73–86. His argument is repeated in *The Stream of Consciousness and Beyond in "Ulysses"* (Pittsburgh: University of Pittsburgh Press, 1973), pp. 65–88.

wanting: "Me. And me now" (176). Like Stephen in "Proteus," Bloom in "Lestrygonians" sees history as a series of empty roles. More acutely than Stephen, Bloom intuits a gradual loss of energy as one role gives way to the next.

Like Stephen, Bloom has a characteristic vocabulary for describing his perception of change. For example:

> Mr Bloom moved forward raising his troubled eyes. Think no more about that. After one. Timeball on the ballast office is down. Dunsink time. Fascinating little book that is of sir Robert Ball's. Parallax. I never exactly understood. There's a priest. Could ask him. Par it's Greek: parallel, parallax. Met him pikehoses she called it till I told her about the transmigration. O rocks! (154)

Such is Bloom's vocabulary for describing time and change, and it is a wholly adequate one. But whereas Stephen carefully marshals his terms and brings them to bear upon the subject of change, Bloom's words merely drift through his mind—even though they precisely define the problems which he struggles unsuccessfully to formulate. For example, he has no apparent consciousness (as Stephen would) of the relevance of "Dunsink time"—which he corrects a few pages later: "Now that I come to think of it, that ball falls at Greenwich time" (167)—to his thoughts. And yet this is a metaphor for the essential theme of "Lestrygonians": how to impose some order, however arbitrary, upon the undifferentiated flow of time. Neither, obviously, is Bloom aware of the meaning of "parallax," but the word is perhaps the best term in the book for defining the time problems of both Stephen and Bloom. "Parallax" denotes the observable difference in the direction of a heavenly body when viewed from two different points on the earth. As a recurrent motif, it suggests first the duality of vision the book offers through Bloom and Stephen; second, it suggests the attempts of both Stephen and Bloom to triangulate upon an abiding self from two different points in time. (Compare Bloom's "Me. And me now" with Stephen's "I am another now and yet the same.") Finally, there is "metempsychosis," Molly's "met him pikehoses." Like "parallax," this is one of the book's multivalent motifs which applies to a wide number of situations. Most broadly, "metempsychosis" describes mythic parallels themselves: the past is reincar-

nated in the present. But the word also applies to Bloom's and
Stephen's conceptions of selfhood. For the self also passes through
its distinct phases, from incarnation to incarnation. Bloom's problem in "Lestrygonians," like Stephen's in "Proteus," is that the
self seems to consist *only* of its manifestations, its serial incarna-
tions, with no underlying sense of endurance. At the very worst
hour of the day, Bloom, like Stephen, feels the baleful temptation of
Mulliganism.

Joyce thus gives Bloom a critical vocabulary which defines his
problem, but Bloom is incapable of putting it to use. This is not
simply a difference of intellect; it is also a difference of vision.
Whereas Stephen constantly seeks the permanence which lies beyond change, Bloom is held by the perception of sheer process itself.
Many times in "Lestrygonians," Bloom's vision has its own acute-
ness, in its concentration upon a nightmarish energy, powerful,
blind, pointless ("Cityful passing away, other cityful coming . . ."
[164]). This is one side of Bloom, distilled to its very essence, and
opposed to Stephen's romantic individualism. Bloom is conscious
only of change itself and of the ultimate nullity of the individual.
At his lowest energy levels, Bloom anticipates that somber historical
vision which accompanies the gaiety of *Finnegans Wake:* all that
endures are the historical cycles themselves; the individuals within
the cycles are interchangeable integers.

Once, Bloom does come startlingly close to Stephen's terminology and conceptions, but then he veers away again without confronting the issue:

> I was happier then. Or was that I? Or am I now I? Twentyeight I
> was. She twentythree when we left Lombard street west something
> changed. Could never like it again after Rudy. Can't bring back time.
> Like holding water in your hand. Would you go back to then? Just
> beginning then. Would you? Are you not happy in your home, you poor
> little naughty boy? Wants to sew on buttons for me. I must answer.
> Write it in the library. (168)

The phraseology—"Or was that I? Or am I now I?"—is actually
much more typical of Stephen than of Bloom, in its attempt to
define the self in time. For a moment, Bloom consciously registers

the cluster of emotions that he usually scrupulously avoids: he compares the happy past and the somber present, remembers the death of Rudy, and even thinks of going "back to then." But he catches himself in the act and diverts his thoughts to Martha, his substitute for going "back to then," and the moment of self-recognition passes.

Either through choice or through inability, then, Bloom fails intellectually to locate himself in relation to the flow of time. And yet he does have experiences in "Lestrygonians" which, existentially rather than intellectually, ratify his sense of selfhood. One such experience occurs as he sits in Davy Byrne's pub:

> Stuck on the pane two flies buzzed, stuck.
> Glowing wine on his palate lingered swallowed. Crushing in the winepress grapes of Burgundy. Sun's heat it is. Seems to a secret touch telling me memory . . . . (175)

This is the closest thing to a Proustian moment in *Ulysses,* a moment of involuntary memory so intense as to join the Bloom of 1904 directly with the Bloom of 1888. And, of course, the event recalled is the most magical event in *Ulysses,* Molly's acceptance of Bloom, with which the book closes. The prose of the passage is still recognizably Bloom's, but the disturbed syntax is a sign of the memory's source in the unconscious. (The emergence of a submerged sensation from the depths is further suggested by a phrase within this passage: "Fields of undersea, the lines faint brown in grass, buried cities.") Moreover, Bloom lingers over the scene with an unaccustomed absorption: in the very wholeness of the sensation he approaches Molly's free and unmediated form of memory. The drop after the recollection is very clear, as Bloom reenters sequential time—"Me. And me now"—but for an instant the past has been brought directly into the present. In stressing the survival of the past, Bloom's moment of memory repudiates the feeling, strong in "Lestrygonians," that his life has been a series of disconnected shells. And the *content* of the memory—Molly's free offer of herself—makes the same point that we learn from Molly herself much later: the happiness of the past is not necessarily lost forever.

The blissful moment of memory in Davy Byrne's ratifies Bloom's connection with his own past and even suggests the continuing availability of that past. Through memory Bloom momentarily experiences that unity of self which Stephen describes in the next chapter: "But I, entelechy, form of forms, am I by memory because under everchanging forms" (189). The memory in Davy Byrne's shows Bloom's unconscious experience of his own perduring selfhood within time.

Another moment, the near-encounter with Boylan at the end of the chapter, shows Bloom at the very limit of his resources but still capable of defining himself, not in time but in the *nebeneinander* world of space. (Stephen too, we noticed earlier in "Proteus," attempted a definition of himself first in time and then in space.) The recording of the flight from Boylan (183), let it be said in passing, is wonderful writing. Bloom is tense and anxious as he feigns a serious search through his pockets—"Handker. *Freeman*. Where did I? Ah, yes. Trousers. Purse. Potato. Where did I?"— but he does succeed in holding off disaster. His attention to detail, which is usually a small diversionary action, here becomes Bloom's only means of reinforcing his crumbling, panic-stricken ego. We are reminded of Beckett's tramps—Molloy and especially Malone— who anticipate an inventory of their earthly possessions as their last worldly act. For Bloom, as for Malone, that frantic inventory is the self's last-ditch effort to assure itself of its own reality.

The two moments I have singled out—the memory of Howth and the flight from Boylan—are both brilliant expositions of Bloom's mind in his hours of greatest need. Operating under extreme pressure at one of the worst hours of the day, Bloom's dual responses to the world—established in "Calypso"—are greatly heightened. The memory of Howth is the very archetype of Bloom's wish for Paradise, and the flight from Boylan shows Bloom's diversionary attention to detail in its purest form in the book. Just when Bloom is consciously experiencing the nightmare world of internal discontinuities in Davy Byrne's, his unconscious rears itself up to reestablish the continuity of memory, the thread running between and uniting the various selves Bloom has been. Similarly, just when Bloom is consciously regarding the world as a collection of so many drifting, disconnected objects, the chance encounter with Boylan forces him to concentrate with furious intensity upon a few of those objects and to keep his composure by locating himself strictly in relation to them.

I have stressed Bloom's small victories in "Lestrygonians," but they are, of course, skin-of-the-teeth victories. There is no doubt that the chapter is more insistent upon the forces which attack Bloom's sense of himself than upon Bloom's resistance to those forces. It is also true that Bloom fails to profit from his small victories. We seldom feel (as we frequently do in the case of Stephen) that Bloom uses his experiences as steppingstones toward some solution to his problems. But even when that is said, "Lestrygonians" still offers the portrait of a man who (again like Beckett's Molloy) crawls forward when he cannot walk. Even at the worst hour of the day, he dumbly experiences a sense of his own integral selfhood which Stephen can only intellectually project.

## "Sirens"

"Sirens" is one of those chapters which, in its form, stands as an epitome of *Ulysses* as a whole. Designed as a complex fugue, the chapter is a particular instance of the musical organization of the entire book. The various characters enter the Ormond bar, one by one, each of them bringing with him his theme, and the intertwining of these themes is in great part the "music" of "Sirens." This presentation of characters as musical themes is not confined to "Sirens." When Bloom sees Boylan he thinks: "It is. Third time. Coincidence" (263). "Coincidence," that important Bloom-word (which he uses again later in the chapter: "*Martha* it is. Coincidence" [275]) is here expressive of a musical relationship: the sounding of two themes at once. Within Bloom's mind, as well as within the book's pattern, Boylan—or Lenehan or Simon Dedalus—is a theme played in counterpoint to the thousand other associative clusters within *Ulysses*.

Bloom's problem in the chapter is that of keeping the Boylan-theme in its place; it is four o'clock, and that trenchant rendition of "Love's Old Sweet Song" which is about to take place at 7 Eccles Street threatens to become the only melody within Bloom's mind. There is no possibility within the chapter that Bloom will take decisive action to oust Boylan; such an action becomes even

vaguely possible only after the meeting with Stephen. All that
Bloom can do is attempt to keep the tune going in his mind and
assert against the Boylan-theme what he always asserts against it—
that is, whatever he can.

If the fugue of sorrow is played within Bloom's mind, there is a
larger fugue within the chapter of which Bloom himself is one of
the themes: the fugue of statement and counterstatement which
takes place between the Ormond bar, where Dedalus and Dollard
sing their songs, and the adjoining restaurant section where Bloom
sits with Richie Goulding. This is the dialogue, which takes many
forms elsewhere in the book, between the gregarious community of
Dublin males and Bloom the outsider. And this is maybe the best—
or at least the most typifying—representation in all *Ulysses* of the
Dublin men, its focus upon their pathetic fellowship in a bar as
they stand around the coffin of the piano and sing their songs of
loss (lost love and lost chances against the English) whose very
sentiment is an anodyne. This exposition of a boozy, tired, and
tawdry sentimentality is one of Joyce's great modes: "Sirens" is
the continuation of "Ivy Day in the Committee Room" and of the
scene of Stephen's trip to Cork with his father in Chapter II of the
*Portrait.* (Later in *Ulysses,* we can see Stephen himself falling into
the same manner, even if more cerebrally and more self-consciously,
in "Oxen of the Sun.")

Over against the theme of the male Dublin community stands—
or sits—Leopold Bloom. His reaction to the singing is a complex
version of his reaction to most of the opiates of Dublin (such as
those in "Lotus-eaters"). Here the Homeric parallel is especially
enlightening, not for this chapter alone but for Bloom's reaction to
"temptation" throughout the day. Homer's Ulysses puts beeswax
into the ears of his men so that they will be deaf to the ravishing
songs of the sirens. He then has himself tied to the mast so that he
will be able to hear the singing but will not be able to fling himself
overboard. Ulysses, notice, enjoys to the full the thrill of the sirens'
songs, but he does not have to pay the price for his enjoyment. And
this is Bloom's usual strategy as well: he is never completely immune to the temptations of voyeurism, masochism, or the beguiling
sense of his own futility, but he never has to pay the full price because he is never fully committed to any one of these subordinate

tendencies within his whole character. Thus within "Sirens" Bloom
yields to the siren-song of sentimental self-pity ("I feel so lonely")
but then reacts against his own yielding by criticizing false sentiment
itself.

Underlying both the musical statement in the Ormond bar and
Bloom's counterstatement is the siren-theme itself. This theme, of
the fatal attraction toward the concealed source of one's own
destruction, provides the radical metaphor of the chapter. In
Bloom's mind the Blessed Virgin is herself a siren: "Bluerobed,
white under, come to me. . . . All comely virgins. That brings
those rakes of fellows in: her white" (259–60). Later, Bloom
thinks again of religion as a deceptive trap: "Latin again. That
holds them like birdlime" (284). Simon Dedalus flatteringly chides
Miss Douce for "Tempting poor simple males" (261), in words
which contribute to the half-gallant, half-frustrated tone of the
coy flirtations in the bar. Bloom's thought calls to mind the bone-
strewn coast of the sirens' island when he reflects upon the smile
of the shopgirl who sells him his writing paper: "Think you're the
only pebble on the beach? Does that to all. For men" (264). Ben
Dollard makes Bloom a victim of the sirens when he recalls the
night he had to borrow a pair of trousers from Bloom: "I knew he
was on the rocks" (268). And Dollard's own song, "The Croppy
Boy," is an instance of the siren-theme, as it describes the croppy
boy lured to his death by an English soldier disguised as a
benevolent Catholic priest.

We should notice two qualities of Bloom's mind as he reflects
upon various instances of sirens. First, Bloom is aware of sirens
*as sirens*. He knows that the shopgirl's smile means nothing, and he
is aware of the part that sexual longing may play in Mariolatry.
Bloom is never blind to the nature of temptation, even if he yields
to it; if he does not always keep himself lashed to the mast, he
always has the mast in the back of his mind as a point of repair.
The second quality to note is Bloom's tendency to make of the
siren-theme a metaphor for the economy of human life. His perception of particular instances of fatal attraction leads him to the
larger vision of a world so constituted that bodily hungers lead the
victim unwittingly toward his destruction. He thinks, for example,
of Ben Dollard's fall from prosperity:

Failed to the tune of ten thousand pounds. Now in the Iveagh home.
Cubicle number so and so. Number one Bass did that for him. . . .
   Ruin them. Wreck their lives. Then build them cubicles to end their
days in. Hushaby. Lullaby. Die, dog. Little dog, die. (283)

Bloom sees in the nature of things an inherent cruelty which makes
men like rats that ravin down their proper bane. There is a perception of cruelty also in Bloom's thought about Simon Dedalus
(and here the sex roles of the siren-story are reversed, so that
Simon is the fatal siren and May the victim): "Wore out his wife:
now sings" (274). But Bloom's fullest expression of the sirens'
cruelty as a universal principle has to do with the tragedy of his
own life:

Thou lost one. All songs on that theme. Yet more Bloom stretched his
string. Cruel it seems. Let people get fond of each other: lure them on.
Then tear asunder. (277)

Beneath this series of thoughts lies the central trauma of Bloom's
life: his love of Molly lured him on to the catastrophe of his
son's death and the sorrowful aftermath of the subsequent years.
   Miss Douce gives another turn to the siren-theme when she sees
(or fancies that she sees) the honorable Gerald Ward gaze at her
from his carriage in the viceregal cavalcade: "He's killed looking
back" (257). The act of looking back is itself central to the
chapter, as Simon Dedalus sings of a lost youthful love and Ben
Dollard sings of a lost heroic past. All the characters in the
Ormond brood over the pathos of lost time, in part because the
very songs and song titles which hang in the air like a heavy perfume evoke all the sorrows of transience: "When first I saw that
form endearing," "All is lost now," "The Last Rose of Summer."
Other details insist upon the passage of time: Dollard is "Big
Benben" (257); Miss Douce snaps her elastic garter in a routine
known as *Sonnez la cloche*!; Boylan wears socks with "skyblue
clocks" on them (282).
   Bloom, of course, is aware of time lost because it is four o'clock,
the trysting hour of Boylan and Molly. What is most terrible here
is that the tryst is itself a sirens' island for Bloom: he wishes to
avoid thinking of it, but at the same time he is also drawn to it,

fascinated by it. Only in "Circe" does Joyce make as clear as he does here Bloom's participation in Molly's adultery. In spite of his "Wish they'd sing more. Keep my mind off" (280), Bloom furtively keeps his mind on Molly and Blazes and finds in the music a means of participating in their intercourse: "Tenderness it welled: slow, swelling. Full it throbbed. That's the chat. Ha, give! Take! Throb, a throb, a pulsing proud erect" (274). This is Bloom's masochism at its most neurotic and intense, passing over into actual identification with Molly and Boylan. And yet it is facile to say simply that Bloom secretly sanctions Molly's affair and wishes for its continuance. If his desire not to think of Molly and Blazes seems at times a dodge, a cover for his true desire to play the voyeur, in the end the real dodge is this voyeurism itself. Bloom's identification with Boylan is his last line of defense against the dreaded confrontation with the problem of returning to a full sexual relationship with Molly.

The idea of renewed sex with Molly constitutes the true zone of disaster in Bloom's mind—a territory so intimidating that he enters it directly only twice during the day—once in "Lestrygonians" and again here in "Sirens." At the very worst hours of the day, his defenses frayed, Bloom is forced to face the unfaceable, but even then he shies away from it after only a moment. In "Sirens" the moment comes as he listens to Dollard singing "The Croppy Boy":

> All gone. All fallen. At the siege of Ross his father, at Gorey all his brothers fell. To Wexford, we are the boys of Wexford, he would. Last of his name and race.
> I too, last my race. Milly young student. Well, my fault perhaps. No son. Rudy. Too late now. Or if not? If not? If still?
> He bore no hate.
> Hate. Love. Those are names. Rudy. Soon I am old. (285)

The moment appears and is then gone. All that it establishes is a vague possibility which is still not dead after ten years.

Throughout the chapter, Bloom plays Ulysses's game of listening to the songs and yet avoiding disaster, of thinking and not thinking. Early on, as he is buying his letter paper, he sees Boylan, and his thought becomes as staccato and tense as it was when he saw Boylan at the end of "Lestrygonians": "Follow. Risk it. Go quick. At four. Near now. Out" (264). "Risk it": a confrontation seems imminent, but Bloom takes evasive action as he goes into the restaurant of the Ormond instead of the bar: "Avoid. . . . See, not be seen" (265). Bloom is willing and not willing to encounter Boylan: *Vorrei e non vorrei.*

Once he is in the Ormond, Bloom acts out another part of the Homeric parallel—but with a difference—as he twists around his fingers the elastic band which held together his letter paper. The allusion is to the tying of Ulysses to the mast: "Yet too much happy bores. He stretched more, more. Are you not happy in your? Twang. It snapped" (277). The snapping of the band is simultaneous with the snapping of the tension within Bloom's mind. The phrase from Martha's letter ("Are you not happy in your home you poor little naughty boy?") destroys that balance between stoicism and self-pity which has dominated Bloom's four o'clock thoughts. Bloom thus goes Ulysses one better. Ulysses enjoyed the songs even as he remained tied to the mast. Bloom actually breaks the securing ropes and indulges more thoroughly in temptation than Ulysses did, for the hand that breaks free from the elastic band goes on to write the letter to Martha.

The writing of the letter to Martha is one of those moments in *Ulysses* when—as in the flight from Boylan—Bloom's very weakness is imbued with strength, so that even amid the direst disaster we are reminded of Bloom's prodigious powers of recovery:

> Bloom mur: best references. But Henry wrote: it will excite me. You know now. In haste. Henry. Greek ee. Better add postscript. What is he playing now? Improvising intermezzo. P. S. The rum tum tum. How will you pun? You punish me? Crooked skirt swinging, whack by. Tell me I want to. Know. O. Course if I didn't I wouldn't ask. La la la ree. Trails off there sad in minor. Why minor sad? Sign H. They like sad tail at end. P. P. S. La la la ree. I feel so sad today. La ree. So lonely. Dee. (280)

(Another wonderful passage.) The conflict between Bloom's murmuring and Henry's writing is a witty instance of the counterpoint between Bloom's public and private selves. But more important is the counterpoint toward the end of the passage, in which the very expression of sadness in the letter brings about a resurgence of Bloom's recuperative powers. The moment of inquiring curiosity ("Why minor sad?") and the self-conscious strategy of flirtation ("They like sad tail at end") signal the general rousing of spirits evidenced in Bloom's humming—all this, while the letter passes into self-abasement and self-pity. A passage such as this is a triumphant justification of musical form in "Sirens."

With the writing of the letter to Martha, Bloom hits bottom— and begins his reascent. (It is on the way back up that, no longer identifying with Boylan, he hesitantly touches upon the idea of returning to Molly.) His recovery is even helped along by circumstance. Bloom's self-pity was abetted by Simon's singing of the aria from *Martha,* but Dollard's patriotic song has less of an immediate appeal for Bloom—the glories of the Irish past have no strong hold over his imagination—and he chooses a moment near the end of Dollard's song to make his departure. "Glad I avoided" (287), he thinks, as he steers safely around the group of drinkers and singers. He again uses his tactics of avoidance once he is out in the street and sees the whore of the lane.

In the open air, Bloom reasserts himself as he scrutinizes and criticizes the experience he has just passed through. Of the whole atmosphere of sentimental singing, he thinks: "Cowley, he stunts himself with it; kind of drunkenness. . . . Thinking strictly prohibited" (288). This is the Bloom of "Lotus-eaters," gazing with dispassionate interest upon alien forms of drug-taking. In a humorously irreverent moment, Bloom even goes on to criticize the croppy boy of Dollard's song for having been deceived by the soldier disguised as a priest: "All the same he must have been a bit of a natural not to see it was a yeoman cap" (290). Bloom, it is clear, would never have been taken in by such a transparent ruse.

The chapter closes with two more episodes of counterpoint. One of these is Bloom's fart as he reads Robert Emmet's last words on a portrait in the window of Lionel Marks's antique shop. The irony here is not Bloom's by intention (he is interested only in speculating whether his gas comes from the Burgundy or the cider he has drunk) but exclusively Joyce's. Bloom's fart is Joyce's own comment upon the flatulence of modern Irish patriotism as it manifests itself in places such as the Ormond bar. The moment here at the end of "Sirens" recalls the similarly flatulent salutes to Parnell as the corks fly out of the heated bottles of stout in "Ivy Day in the Committee Room": "Pok!"

An even more telling counterpoint takes place back in the bar. Beginning just over halfway through the chapter, the "Tap" of the blind stripling's cane has been heard as an increasingly insistent motif, as he heads back toward the Ormond to retrieve his tuning fork. The last time we see the drinkers in the bar, the blind stripling has arrived and stands before them:

> Tip. An unseeing stripling stood in the door. He saw not bronze. He saw not gold. Nor Ben nor Bob nor Tom nor Si nor George nor tanks nor Richie nor Pat. Hee hee hee hee. He did not see. (290–91)

Seldom is Joyce's irony so simple and so clear. The drinkers in the bar have been applauding the sentiments of grief and sorrow, and here stands the thing itself, the reality of suffering which is the fatal coast which the unwary forget under the spell of the sirens' song.

The two scenes which end "Sirens"—the appearance of the blind stripling and Bloom's breaking wind as he reads Robert Emmet's last words—are both scenes of ironic counterpoint, and they operate in counterpoint with one another. They very clearly reveal the kind of superiority Bloom has to most of his fellow Dubliners, the superiority of humane skepticism to the false humaneness of sentiment. (It was Bloom, we remember, who assisted the blind stripling earlier in the day.) Indeed, this superiority is to be revealed *in excelsis* in the next chapter, "Cyclops," in which Bloom combats bigotry, the concomitant of false sentiment. (Were *Ulysses* about the American South, "Sirens" and "Cyclops" would link the Good Old Boys with the Ku Klux Klan.)

But if Bloom achieves in "Sirens" the quiet moral victory over his fellow citizens which is his a hundred times during the day, his struggle with himself ends in a standoff. At the very worst hours of the day, Bloom's victory is one of simply existing, of sailing past the sirens' island which his own mind and his own actions create. The most perplexing passage in "Sirens" reflects this plight of Bloom's; it is a sudden intrusion of Stephen's words from "Scylla and Charybdis" (202) into this Bloom-chapter:

Music hath charms Shakespeare said. Quotations every day in the
year. To be or not to be. Wisdom while you wait.
In Gerard's rosery of Fetter lane he walks, greyed-auburn. One life
is all. One body. Do. But do.
Done anyhow. Postal order stamp. (280)

This sequence (Bloom's thought of Shakespeare—Stephen's Shakespeare who counsels himself, "Do. But do"—Bloom's "Done anyhow") establishes a counterpoint, not between the parts of "Sirens"
but between "Sirens" and another section of the book. And by
comparing Bloom to the traumatized and unfulfilled Shakespeare
of Stephen's theory, this passage underlines the limitations of
Bloom's victory over his own thoughts at four o'clock. Bloom's victory is one of "Do. But do"—a victory gained by occupying his
mind in a frenzy of evasive activity. The very skill at evasion leads
to a triumph of sorts—a triumph over the sorrow of the moment—
but the strategy of evasion makes less likely any final victory in
his relations with Molly. At the very worst hours of the day,
Bloom's victories take place within the parameters of failure which
he himself has established.

## "Nausicaa"

Even more than "Wandering Rocks," which is widely recognized
as a pivotal chapter, "Nausicaa" is a major turning point in
*Ulysses*. Situated between the threatened violence of "Cyclops" and
the muzzy chaos of "Oxen of the Sun," "Nausicaa" shows Bloom's
relaxation between the two most trying assaults he experiences during the day. (One's sense of the chapter as a respite is increased by
Bloom's recollection of his visit to the widow Dignam, which took
place immediately after his departure from Barney Kiernan's.)
Moreover, "Nausicaa" is the last chapter under the old dispensation, before the meeting of Stephen and Bloom; it provides the transition between Bloom as loner and Bloom as friend. And we say
virtually the same thing when we say that the chapter is also the
transition between day and night, for Stephen's and Bloom's experiences together all take place at night, when discrete identities relax
and even merge with one another. Finally, "Nausicaa" is the first of

the closing chapters to look back upon the day in a retrospective kind of arrangement ("Circe" and "Ithaca" are the other two main examples). Bloom, in fact, explicitly sums up the day's events in "Nausicaa": "Long day I've had. Martha, the bath, funeral, house of keys, museum with those goddesses, Dedalus' song. Then that bawler in Barney Kiernan's" (380).

"Nausicaa" is a stopping place in the book, a place for summing up. It is the most static of Bloom's chapters (in spite of his very kinetic relation to Gerty). In the atmosphere of twilight calm, Bloom's wanderings temporarily cease, and the "art" of the chapter, relevant for once, is the static art of painting. In Bloom's half of the chapter, moreover, Joyce reverts completely to the earlier stream-of-consciousness narration, and we are given one final, still tableau of Bloom's character before the plunge into the murk of the succeeding chapters.

As the chapter pauses, it does more than sum up Bloom: it also creates a static network of correspondences among all the major characters. Both Bloom and Stephen lounge along Sandymount Strand and observe a young woman; young Stephen stands in relation to mature Bloom as Gerty stands in relation to Molly; and Bloom, who drifts off to sleep in a post-orgasmic lull, antici-pates Molly's drifting off to sleep at the end of the book. Joyce even recapitulates in infant form the conflict between Stephen and Mulligan:

> Boys will be boys and our two twins were no exception to this golden rule. The apple of discord was a certain castle of sand which Master Jacky had built and Master Tommy would have it right go wrong that it was to be architecturally improved by a frontdoor like the Martello tower had. But if Master Tommy was headstrong Master Jacky was selfwilled too and, true to the maxim that every little Irishman's house is his castle, he fell upon his hated rival and to such purpose that the wouldbe assailant came to grief and (alas to relate!) the coveted castle too. (347)

The implied analogy between the Caffrey twins and Stephen-Mulligan is an instance of a recurrent theme in the chapter. There is a finite number of human patterns of behavior: the young only mime the patterns of the elders, and the elders only repeat patterns established in youth. Nothing changes; the young grow up to repeat the lives of the old. That is a somber statement of the theme of *Finnegans Wake*, and it is the theme of "Nausicaa" as well.[2] There is little that is consoling in the chapter's presentation of enduring patterns. Instead, the chapter conveys the sad picture of a world in which there is no new input of energy: processes repeat themselves without any possibility of significant change. It is for this reason that I call "Nausicaa" the last chapter under the old dispensation and one of Bloom's worst hours of the day (even though *he* doesn't consider it one of the worst). Nowhere else in the book does Bloom's mood of acceptance pass over so completely into a shrug of surrender. This is not a surrender to ample bedwarmed flesh or to warm fullblooded life; it is, indeed, a mockery of that. It is a surrender to the closed system of the self and, analogously, to the closed system of a universe which progresses only by means of unprogressive repetition. Nowhere are we more aware of Bloom's need of Stephen—and Stephen's concern with progressive change—than in this chapter just before their meeting.

We can best enter the chapter by exploring some of the relations which Joyce establishes between characters. First of all, Gerty resembles Stephen in a number of ways. Stephen is twenty-two now; Gerty will be twenty-two in November (352). Gerty's lameness sets her apart from Edy Boardman and Cissy Caffrey in much the same way that Stephen's emotional trauma sets him apart from companions such as Mulligan and Lynch. Both Gerty and Stephen avoid their companions, and in both cases this proud aloofness is in great part a defensive reaction. So far does Joyce extend the comparison that he even has both Stephen and Gerty quote St. Thomas Aquinas on Sandymount Strand (47, 360). But most significantly, both Stephen and Gerty lounge on the beach at once longing for and fearing a sexual involvement:

> Touch me. Soft eyes. Soft soft soft hand. I am lonely here. O, touch me soon, now. What is that word known to all men? I am quiet here alone. Sad too. Touch, touch me. (49)

2. "Nausicaa" anticipates Book II, Chapter i of *Finnegans Wake*, "The Mime of Mick, Nick, and the Maggies." The half-innocent, half-knowing movement of children toward sexual awareness was for Joyce the supreme instance of repetitive pattern, the young beginning to mime the old.

> The old love was waiting, waiting with little white hands stretched out, with blue appealing eyes. Heart of mine! She would follow her dream of love, the dictates of her heart that told her he was her all in all, the only man in all the world for her for love was the master guide. Nothing else mattered. Come what might she would be wild, untrammelled, free. (364–65)

The difference in tone between these two passages is considerable; the difference in situation is small. Both Stephen and Gerty hover about the fringes of experience, their words at once an expression of and a defense against their emotional needs.

Compared to Bloom and Molly, Stephen and Gerty are not only younger characters; they are also attenuated characters. If there has been a loss of energy between Homer's Greece and Joyce's Dublin, or even between Parnell's Dublin and Bloom's, an analogous loss has taken place between the generations within *Ulysses*. The loss is like that registered in two books roughly contemporaneous with *Ulysses: The Rainbow* and *To the Lighthouse*. There has been a gain in cerebral powers (Gerty's imagination is, in a debased way, as "literary" as Stephen's) but at the expense of immediate experience. This falling-off of energy between generations contributes to the entropic climate of "Nausicaa."

A second implied comparison is that between Bloom and Stephen. In *A Portrait of the Artist* and again in "Proteus," Stephen gazes at a woman on the beach and notices in particular her "skirties." The description of Bloom's voyeurism recalls both of Stephen's earlier scenes:

> At it again? A fair unsullied soul had called to him and, wretch that he was, how had he answered? An utter cad he had been. He of all men! But there was an infinite store of mercy in those eyes, for him too a word of pardon even though he had erred and sinned and wandered. (367)

As Richard Ellmann has pointed out, Bloom's attraction to Gerty is a "parody" of Stephen's attraction to the girl on the beach in the *Portrait*. Echoes from the *Portrait* are fairly clear (they are not as close, however, as one's ear at first leads one to expect): "A fair unsullied soul had called to him . . ." (*Portrait:* "A wild angel

had appeared to him . . .") ; "even though he had erred and
sinned and wandered" (*Portrait:* "To live, to err, to fall, to triumph, to recreate life out of life!).[3]

The passage I have quoted is a particular instance of a problem
which, I suspect, most readers experience during the course of
"Nausicaa": there is "irony" or "parody" aplenty, one feels, but
directed against what? Here, it seems to me, the effect of the
parody is destructive to an extent rare in *Ulysses,* as it operates to
cut away the positions of both Bloom and Stephen. Bloom's reaction to Gerty brings down to earth Stephen's more highfalutin
reactions to the women in the *Portrait* and "Proteus" and isolates
the sexual nature of encounters which Stephen mythifies and
aggrandizes. But Stephen is able to give those encounters significance, even if he is tiresome in his tendency to do so. Bloom, more
capable of seeing such an encounter as *simply* an encounter, refuses
the comfort—as well as the salvation—of Stephen's grasping after
significance: "Sad about her lame of course but must be on your
guard not to feel too much pity. They take advantage" (p. 377).
This is one of those instances when Joyce's parody is almost totally
destructive in its double-edged power. It reminds us at once of the
fatuity of adolescence and the futility of maturity.

There is another event in "Nausicaa" which draws a strong
comparison between Bloom and Stephen. Earlier in the day, Stephen attempted to locate and define himself on this beach by writing
a poem. Before leaving, Bloom also tries his hand at composition.
With a stick, he scratches in the sand the message "I. AM. A."
Then: "He flung his wooden pen away. The stick fell in silted sand,
stuck" (382). Bloom's writing in the sand directly recalls Stephen's
writing of his poem: compare the attempt at composition, the
attendant attempt at self-conceptualization ("Bend, see my face
there . . ."), even Bloom's exclamation as he writes, "O, those
transparent!" which is reminiscent of Stephen's concern with
Aristotle's diaphane.[4] But in every way the force of the similarity

---

3. Ellmann, *James Joyce* (New York: Oxford University Press, 1959) pp. 370n., 385.
Fritz Senn has pointed out further correspondences between the two scenes. See "Nausicaa,"
*James Joyce's "Ulysses,"* ed. Clive Hart and David Hayman (Berkeley: University of
California Press, 1974), pp. 285–86.
4. Kenner has an extensive treatment of Bloom's writing in the sand. See *Dublin's
Joyce,* Beacon Paperbacks (Boston: Beacon Press, 1962) pp. 201–204.

underlines the contrast between the two men. For Stephen, art is
an act of self-exploration which ends in self-knowledge. For Bloom,
the act of self-knowledge is incomplete: I AM A . . . . The
expression is completed only by Bloom's gesture of throwing the
stick into the sand, and the resultant message anticipates Molly's
words later in "Circe": "O Poldy, Poldy, you are a poor old stick
in the mud! Go and see life. See the wide world" (440). A stick in
the mud suggests the kind of stasis which "Nausicaa" typifies: a
stasis of paralysis and inaction. Bloom's perception of protean
change is less panic-stricken than Stephen's but it runs deeper; and
with a reflection on the fading of all things, Bloom subsides once
more into a meditation upon the cosmic cycles which contain him
and deprive him of meaning.

The correspondences among characters in "Nausicaa" are not
simply situational (a man sees a woman on the beach); in numerous small ways they grow out of the very texture of the prose. Take
as an example one of Gerty's passages:

> She gazed out towards the distant sea. It was like the paintings that man
> used to do on the pavement with all the coloured chalks and such a pity
> too leaving them there to be all blotted out, the evening and the clouds
> coming out and the Bailey light on Howth and to hear the music like
> that and the perfume of those incense they burned in the church like a
> kind of waft. (357)

Two small details link Gerty to other characters. The phrasing
("She gazed out towards the distant sea . . .") once again recalls
Stephen's girl on the beach in *Portrait* ("A girl stood before him in
midstream, alone and still, gazing out to sea"); and her synesthetic
mingling of "the music" and "the perfume of those incense" suggests Molly, who is similarly surrounded—in Bloom's mind and
her own—by associations of music and perfume.

Two of Gerty's thoughts in this passage deserve more attention.
First, she looks at Howth—and "dear old Howth" dominates this
chapter from the first paragraph on. Howth is the Eden of *Ulysses,*
the scene of Molly's acceptance of Bloom and the source of the
single most redeeming memory for both Bloom and Molly. It
stands in the background of "Nausicaa" as the place of achieved

love, a reminder of possibilities in the past which the two characters on the beach at once adumbrate and mock. Of equal importance is Gerty's memory of the pavement artist whose chalk drawings are so soon effaced. Gerty's reflections on art (like Bloom's incomplete attempt to define himself through writing in the sand) state the countertruth to the truth which Stephen at least tentatively discovered in "Proteus": if Stephen's poem suggests the possibility of an art whose superior stasis is derived from an awareness of cyclical change, Gerty and Bloom think of art as a part of that process, as transient as the creating artist himself.

The correspondences among characters in "Nausicaa" do not suggest the endurance of vital archetypal patterns of human experience, as such correspondences usually do in *Ulysses*. Instead, they show the characters operating mechanistically, like so many automata controlled by the universal force which Bloom calls "magnetism." A voyeuristic man and an exhibitionistic girl sight one another; at a considerable distance they go through their charade; and they part. This is straight out of Ionesco. This sense of predictable, controlled behavior is further reinforced by the very placement of "Nausicaa." Joyce has juxtaposed Gerty, the only major female consciousness other than Molly, to the Nameless One, the narrator of the preceding chapter, which is the most aggressively "male" chapter in *Ulysses*.[5] The connection between "Nausicaa" and "Cyclops" is strengthened by an otherwise trivial detail: Gerty's "grandfather Giltrap" is the owner of the Citizen's companion, Garryowen. The juxtaposition of male and female chapters reveals a damning picture of sexuality. The Nameless One and his fellow males elsewhere in the book linger over sexuality with an obsessive leer which suggests their own sexual insecurity. Gerty approaches and avoids the subject of sex in a way that makes her their mirror image. The pairing of "Cyclops" and "Nausicaa" makes clear the most pervasive evil in *Ulysses*, the absolute separation between the feckless man and the abandoned and impoverished woman.

It is useful to compare "Cyclops" and "Nausicaa" in another

---

5. French has also mentioned this juxtaposition of male and female chapters in *The Book as World* (Cambridge, Mass.: Harvard University Press, 1976) pp. 156–57.

way. In "Cyclops," Bloom is the focus of the chapter's stereoscopic vision. The two narrative voices—the Nameless One and the "gigantic" voice—offer two points of view on Bloom, but neither succeeds in describing him. "Cyclops" increases our respect for the indefinable complexities of personality. In "Nausicaa," on the other hand, Bloom *is* one of the two opposed points of view, unable to break beyond his limited boundaries. If "Cyclops" impresses us with Bloom's suppleness and variety, "Nausicaa" gives us a picture—a static "portrait," in terms of the chapter's art—of a man who has surrendered to his own self-imposed limitations.

The peculiarly fated quality of Bloom's thoughts is especially clear once we have noticed the final large pattern of analogy between characters in the chapter: that between Bloom and Molly. Both Bloom in "Nausicaa" and Molly in "Penelope" are drifting off to sleep, and as they do so their thoughts take place in the context of recent infidelity. They share several highly charged images: Milly's maturing, Mulvey's kiss, the proposal on Howth. Both of them think of the opposite sex as a kind of undifferentiated "they"; and in both, this refusal to discriminate coexists with a precarious but abiding emotional fidelity to the other.

But if Bloom and Molly frequently think of the opposite sex simply as "they," they do so for very different reasons. Molly looks down on men with affectionate condescension; to her they seem similar because they all act with the same childlike predictability. Bloom depersonalizes women because they seem to him agents of the natural order. Like Stephen in "Proteus," Bloom relates women to the moon; more than this, he thinks of them in terms of the laws of a haphazardly controlled universe: "They believe in chance because like themselves" (369). "Still there's destiny in it, falling in love" (373). This idea of destiny marks Bloom's greatest divergence from Molly's monologue in "Penelope." It is part and parcel of the difference between them that Bloom—the Bloom of "Nausicaa"—conceives of the world as ineluctably determined while Molly shrewdly imagines new, unexplored possibilities.

Bloom has a clear motive for envisioning the world as determined by chance or destiny or "magnetism": such a view deprives him of responsibility. He therefore feels free to yield to his most basic inner temptation, the temptation to cease all effort and regard

himself as helpless, contemptible, meaningless. He holds on to this
self-conception even when the universe itself seems to be telling
him to change:

> June that was too I wooed. The year returns. History repeats itself. Ye
> crags and peaks I'm with you once again. Life, love, voyage round your
> own little world. And now? Sad about her lame of course but must be
> on your guard not to feel too much pity. They take advantage.
>
> All quiet on Howth now. The distant hills seem. Where we. The
> rhododendrons. I am a fool perhaps. He gets the plums and I the plum-
> stones. Where I come in. All that old hill has seen. Names change:
> that's all. Lovers: yum yum.
>
> Tired I feel now. Will I get up? O wait. Drained all the manhood
> out of me, little wretch. She kissed me. My youth. Never again. Only
> once it comes. Or hers. Take the train there tomorrow. No. Returning
> not the same. Like kids your second visit to a house. The new I want.
> Nothing new under the sun. (376–77)

There are two senses of "return" in this passage, one cosmic ("The
year returns. History repeats itself"), the other personal ("Never
again. Only once it comes . . . . Returning not the same"). On a
cosmic scale, Bloom intuits a process of eternal recurrence, but
within his own life he totally shies away from the possibility of a
return to the happy days, or even the possibility of taking the train
to see his daughter.

In viewing himself as an integer in a world of limited possibilities, Bloom anticipates the historical vision of *Finnegans Wake,*
and in mapping out the bounds of his dying, entropic world ("Then
if one thing stopped the whole ghesabo would stop bit by bit"
[p. 374]), he looks forward to Beckett's tramps. But the world of
*Ulysses* is a more open world, a world of more possibilities, than
the world of *Finnegans Wake* or the world of *Molloy*. Bloom's
vision of fated, repetitive cycles coexists in *Ulysses* with Molly's
more celebratory awareness of the continuing possibility of renewal; and Bloom's conception of his personal life as only a series
of events in a world of diminishing possibilities coexists with Stephen's vision—in his most hopeful moments—of a series of events
which may lead to self-knowledge and self-fulfillment. In the final
pre-Stephen chapter, Joyce has chosen to give us a portrait of

Bloom without spark or resilience, a Bloom locked within the walls
of his own psychological prison and obviously unable to break out
unassisted.

I suggested at the beginning of this study that "Telemachus"
might be considered a false or mock beginning to *Ulysses:* it opens
the book with a false Mass and introduces a spurious hero in Mulligan. "Nausicaa" might by analogy be called a false or mock
ending. Through its quiet atmosphere and its dominating image of
painting, it arrives at the stasis which Joycean art strives for, but
this is the stasis of paralysis. It is a stasis typified by Bloom's watch,
traumatized at the hour of four-thirty. This false ending seems to
bring together woman and man, but it does so only in order to
emphasize their radical isolation. It also brings together youth and
age, in a way which at first seems to recall the balanced views of
Prospero and Miranda in *The Tempest:*

> *Miranda.*                          O brave new world,
>                That has such people in't!
> *Prospero.*                         'Tis new to thee.

But whereas Prospero's melancholy wisdom surrounds and protects
Miranda's naïve innocence, Gerty's and Bloom's points of view
undercut one another. Gerty's vision of a brave new world is
pathetic because so self-deceptive, and Bloom's "The new I want.
Nothing new under the sun" is the wisdom only of futility. It is
only in the chapters that follow, beginning with "Oxen of the Sun,"
that the book heads toward its true ending, toward a more complex
confrontation between youth and age and between man and woman.

## Chapter IV

# The Outsider as Insider

## "Cyclops"

"Cyclops" is the only one of Bloom's own chapters (as distinguished from those he shares with Stephen) in which he is viewed completely externally: we have not even a glimpse of his mind's workings. By this point in the book, however, the contours of his personality have been firmly established, and a great part of our enjoyment of the chapter's comedy derives from our recognition of the "rhythms" of Bloom's mind which we have heretofore seen only from the inside. "Cyclops" is also the chapter which most persistently regards Bloom as a social being. Elsewhere in the book we see Bloom acting with polite deference toward his fellow citizens, and we occasionally hear his fellow citizens speaking of him. But here we see Bloom forced into a hostile confrontation, not with citizens but with the Citizen, who is in grotesque form the spokesman for the Community.

If Bloom's opponent is the Citizen, Bloom is the Exile. We have already noticed (in "Lotus-eaters," for example) how fundamentally the rhythms of Bloom's thought and the patterns of his behavior are controlled by his constant perception of himself as outside the mainstream of Dublin life. "Cyclops" seeks to define the relation between Exile and Community, and the result is surprising.

Since each of the Bloom chapters renders a new and unique

*vision* of Bloom, "Cyclops" is of special interest since its most prominent motif is ocular. Starting from Homer's one-eyed Cyclops and Ulysses's act of blinding him with a burning stake, Joyce has filled his chapter with details of faulty vision and metaphorical blindness. What *we* see in "Cyclops" is complex. Earlier in "Proteus," Stephen thought: "Flat I see, then think distance, near, far, flat I see, east, back. Ah, see now. Falls back suddenly, frozen in stereoscope. Click does the trick" (48). Stephen's words might be taken as the epigraph to "Cyclops," for in this chapter Bloom is subjected to a stereoscopic treatment. There are two narrators in the chapter who operate from two points of view, almost literally as two eyes. The Nameless One (as he is called later in "Circe"), friend of Joe Hynes, is the reductive impulse gone wild: he is eager to believe the worst about Bloom or about any other subject, including the Citizen. His opposite, the narrator characterized by what Joyce called "gigantism," has the reverse tendency: he sees the heroic dimension of every action and object. Thus, when viewed through the eye of this narrator, the Citizen's handkerchief becomes a "muchtreasured and intricately embroidered ancient Irish facecloth" whose embroidered scenes are "rendered more beautiful still by the waters of sorrow which have passed over them and by the rich incrustations of time" (331–32). Rich incrustations, indeed. The two narrators of "Cyclops" are the two narrative impulses of *Ulysses,* the one obsessively down-to-earth, the other highfalutin and heroic, and as usual, the truth is the added dimension, the stereoptical depth which neither eye can see alone.

Bloom is at the focus of this stereoscope. The Nameless One sees him as "the prudent member" who will not stand drinks even after his (supposed) winning bet on Throwaway, and the gigantic narrator sees him as (among other things) "the distinguished scientist Herr Professor Luitpold Blumenduft" (304). The added depth necessary for a full picture of Bloom can be supplied only by the reader. The reader's special knowledge of Bloom, in fact, makes "Cyclops" one of the strongest ethical centers of the book. We can believe in the validity of Bloom's courage and in the value of his defense of love because we have previously been made aware of the doubts and hesitancies out of which he speaks. Indeed, so forthright is the presentation of Bloom as an ethical hero and so broad is the comedy of the chapter, that it is easy to miss the subtlety of what Joyce has done. The chapter, a deft study of the relation between the exile and the society from which he is excluded, makes of Bloom the Hungarian Jew an Irish Christian.

One of the great broad comic effects of the chapter is immediately apparent: Bloom is a more thoroughgoing Christian than any of the other Dubliners in Barney Kiernan's pub. In these pages, Joyce fleshes out the Christ parallel and gives substance to the Citizen's sneer that Bloom is "a new apostle to the gentiles." Bloom paraphrases Christ (although probably unwittingly, if we remember Bloom's usual difficulty in tracking down and verifying the allusive scraps which float through his mind): "Some people, says Bloom, can see the mote in others' eyes but they can't see the beam in their own" (326).

Later, memorably, Bloom is provoked into making what amounts to his most explicit *apologia pro vita sua* in the book:

> —Are you talking about the new Jerusalem? says the citizen.
> —I'm talking about injustice, says Bloom.
> —Right, says John Wyse. Stand up to it then with force like men.
> That's an almanac picture for you. Mark for a softnosed bullet. Old lardyface standing up to the business end of a gun. Gob, he'd adorn a sweepingbrush, so he would, if he only had a nurse's apron on him. And then he collapses all of a sudden, twisting around all the opposite, as limp as a wet rag.
> —But it's no use, says he. Force, hatred, history, all that. That's not life for men and women, insult and hatred. And everybody knows that it's the very opposite of that that is really life.
> —What? asks Alf.
> —Love, says Bloom. I mean the opposite of hatred. I must go now, says he to John Wyse. (332–33)

Anyone familiar with Joyce's methods in *Ulysses*—and the sensibility displayed in all of Joyce's work—comes to suspect that the statements of value closest to Joyce's own are the statements most crowded out by irony. (R. M. Adams, recognizing this principle, has wittily remarked that Mozart clearly *must* have been Joyce's favorite composer since in *Ulysses* Mozart is so frequently mentioned in the company of third- and fourth-rate composers.) This

ironic inversion of values is nowhere more evident than in Bloom's
lame defense of love. Bloom is pathetically, comically unable to
define a principle such as love, and both the narrators quickly move
in to mock his efforts. ("Love loves to love love," the gigantic narrator intones, and then proceeds to reel off instances of the kindly
flame: "Jumbo, the elephant, loves Alice, the elephant.") But what
gives the scene its special piquancy for the reader is its stereoptical
depth. We watch Bloom as "he collapses all of a sudden, twisting
around all the opposite," and recognize that characteristic deflation
which follows any of Bloom's idealistic or utopian statements. Only
then does he defend love. Bloom too is somewhat of a Joycean
ironist: he defends "the opposite of hatred" only after he has
acknowledged the near-futility of what he is saying: "Force, hatred,
history, all that."

To complete the Christ parallel, there is the comic tour de force
of the novel, Bloom's exit from the pub:

> And says he:
> —Mendelssohn was a jew and Karl Marx and Mercadante and
> Spinoza. And the Saviour was a jew and his father was a jew. Your
> God.
> —He had no father, says Martin. That'll do now. Drive ahead.
> —Whose God? says the citizen.
> —Well, his uncle was a jew, says he. Your God was a jew. Christ
> was a jew like me.
> Gob, the citizen made a plunge back into the shop.
> —By Jesus, says he, I'll brain that bloody jewman for using the holy
> name. By Jesus, I'll crucify him so I will. Give us that biscuitbox here.
> (342)

There is no finer example in the book of Joyce's double perspective
on Bloom. The wonderful humor of "Well, his uncle was a jew" is
precisely balanced against the resounding and convincing "Christ
was a jew like me." This is Joyce's jocoserious art.

The "Christianity" of Bloom the Jew is drawn in large comic
strokes. It is perhaps less apparent at first that Bloom the Hungarian is also more Irish than the other men in the pub. He is, in
Bloom's own phrase, "more Irish than the Irish" (119). The
analogy between Bloom and Ireland arises during one of Bloom's

more flustered moments, as he attempts—with about the same measure of success as in his definition of "love"—to define "a nation" (331). One effect of his effort is to create an analogy between the individual and the national body. When Bloom defines a nation as people "living in different places," we are reminded of Bloom's Jewishness and of the Diaspora in general. ("The oldest people. Wandered far away over all the earth, captivity to captivity, multiplying, dying, being born everywhere" [61].) But if Bloom is a little Israel, he is also, as he sturdily maintains, a little Ireland. When he describes the misery of the Jews—"Plundered. Insulted. Persecuted. Taking what belongs to us by right" (332) —he is also describing the ills of Ireland. The analogy between Bloom and Ireland is made complete by the detail of the location of Barney Kiernan's pub, "8, 9 and 10 little Britain street" (340). In the bigoted atmosphere of the pub, Bloom is a little Ireland persecuted by a little Britain. The Dubliners participate in the forms of displaced aggression familiar to us from Joyce's "Counterparts": abused by the English, the Irish seek out their own victims.

Bloom's resemblance to Ireland is given added force by the Citizen, who unwittingly makes his most devastating attack on Bloom:

—The strangers, says the citizen. Our own fault. We let them come in. We brought them. The adulteress and her paramour brought the Saxon robbers here.

—Decree *nisi,* says J. J.

And Bloom letting on to be awfully deeply interested in nothing, a spider's web in the corner behind the barrel, and the citizen scowling after him and the old dog at his feet looking up to know who to bite and when.

—A dishonoured wife, says the citizen, that's what's the cause of all our misfortunes. (324)

The Citizen's reference to Eva MacMurrough, paramour of O'Rourke, Prince of Breffni, touches upon Bloom's sorest point: the idea of usurpation through adultery.[1] If Haines the Sassenach has literally usurped the Martello Tower, Boylan, the Sassenach

---

1. In "Nestor," Mr. Deasy is obsessed by the same historical event (pp. 34–35).

by analogy, is in possession of Molly's bed. The Irish expression
"strangers in our house" applies generally to the usurping English
and specifically to Boylan.

One other comment by the Citizen gives the Bloom-Ireland
analogy its finishing touches:

> Where are our missing twenty millions of Irish should be here today
> instead of four, our lost tribes? . . . Where are the Greek merchants
> that came through the pillars of Hercules, the Gibraltar now grabbed by
> the foe of mankind, with gold and Tyrian purple to sell in Wexford at
> the fair of Carmen? (326)

The Citizen's lament brings together all the major nationalities of
*Ulysses,* Greek and Jew, English and Irish. The mention of the lost
tribes, like Taylor's speech in "Aeolus," makes the Jews emblematic
of the persecuted state of the Irish, while the mention of the pillars
of Hercules once again makes of Boylan—"the foe of mankind"—
the Englishman who has usurped Molly's Gibraltar.

Bloom is thus more Christian than the Christians and more Irish
than the Irish. The monolithic point of "Cyclops" is that the outsider represents in quintessential form the society from which he
has been excluded. Like the woman in Victorian fiction or the black
man in modern American fiction, Joyce's outsider becomes the focus
of his culture. And Bloom's Irishness is maybe even more instructive
than his Christianity. Because he must always be alert and on the
defensive, Bloom keeps alive the Irish virtues which have stagnated
in his fellow countrymen: the shrewd prudence of the underdog, an
independent integrity, and above all a refusal to become implicated
in the immorality of his oppressors.

In "Telemachus" Stephen mentally transformed the old milkwoman into the "poor old woman," Ireland herself, and watched
bitterly as she spoke obsequiously to Mulligan: "Stephen listened
in scornful silence. She bows her old head to a voice that speaks to
her loudly, her bonesetter, her medicineman; me she slights" (14).
Implicit in Stephen's bitterness is his belief that he himself, although
outwardly despising things Irish, is really most faithful to the soul
of Ireland. As is very often the case, Stephen's highly self-conscious
image of himself is realized fully, but unconsciously, in Bloom; for

it is in Bloom that the Irish virtues are incarnate—and scorned by the Irish themselves.

The two narrative voices of "Cyclops"—its two "eyes"—are symptomatic of the stereoscopic view of Bloom which the entire chapter demands. Bloom in this chapter is both bumbling and heroic, both outsider and insider. Simple in its broad effects, the chapter is yet an epitome of the art of *Ulysses* in its demand upon the reader to see stereoscopically and to hold in equilibrium both the reductive and the heroic points of view. As Richard Ellmann has noted, the two narrative styles come together only in the final paragraph of the chapter: [2]

> When, lo, there came upon them all a great brightness and they beheld the chariot wherein He stood ascend to heaven. And they beheld Him in the chariot, clothed upon in the glory of the brightness, having raiment as of the sun, fair as the moon and terrible that for awe they durst not look upon Him. And there came a voice out of heaven, calling: *Elijah! Elijah!* And he answered with a main cry: *Abba! Adonai!* And they beheld Him even Him, ben Bloom Elijah, amid clouds of angels ascend to the glory of the brightness at an angle of fortyfive degrees over Donohoe's in Little Green Street like a shot off a shovel. (345)

The contrast between "having raiment as of the sun" and "like a shot off a shovel" has much the same effect as the contrast between "Well, his uncle was a jew," and "Christ was a jew like me." The Biblical grandeur and the Chaplinesque bumbling coexist, neither canceling out the other. Click does the trick.

2. Ellmann, *Ulysses on the Liffey* (New York: Oxford University Press, 1972), p. 115.

## Chapter V

# Stephen and Bloom:
# The Complicating
# of the Pattern

Consciousness in *Ulysses* is a series of mental *actions*. It may passively accept the sense-data which flow in willy-nilly, but it stamps upon those data the imprint of the perceiving, receiving mind. Although it is impossible to make too fine a distinction between the two modes, the passive and the active, we can say that Bloom is relatively open, receptive to the sensory world, while Stephen is frightened whenever his imperial intellect loses power over what his senses report to him. And yet no character's mind is truly passive very long, for *Ulysses* dramatizes consciousness as a creator, and not simply a perceiver, of order.

Throughout the first six chapters of *Ulysses,* and intermittently thereafter, the character's consciousness is itself the principle of order. These chapters present not "the world" but the world as perceived and given order by Stephen or Bloom. This is the primary form in *Ulysses:* the form of the character's consciousness. We do not forget this primary form even when we enter the bizarre stylistic mutants of the second half of the book. In fact, it is only by exercising our mnemotechnic, by remembering the rhythms and movements of the characters' minds as they are established in the opening chapters, that we are able to understand fully such later extravaganzas as "Cyclops" or "Oxen of the Sun": the depiction of Bloom from the outside in these later chapters is dependent for its effect upon our already knowing him from the inside. Our awareness of Bloom's and Stephen's essential identities permits us to recognize the familiar patterns persisting beneath the more troubled surface of the later chapters.

With a few notable exceptions, the chapters following the first six do not take their form from the consciousness of the characters. Joyce begins to introduce material which stands between us and the "reality" of plot and to insist upon a pattern which includes the characters rather than one which arises from their own modes of thinking. This larger pattern may be implicit (an organizing metaphor or parallel) or explicit (an obtrusive style which forces us to see the characters in a new way), but in either case the characters of Stephen and Bloom tend more and more to merge into a larger design which is beyond their consciousness. Here I will discuss the increasing intricacy of pattern in three of the chapters which include both Stephen and Bloom: "Aeolus," "Scylla and Charybdis," and "Circe."

## "Aeolus"

"Aeolus" is the first chapter in the novel to employ a style which has been obtrusively introduced by the author working outside the consciousnesses of his characters. Earlier chapters such as "Proteus" and "Calypso" take their form from the consciousness of the characters. The newspaper headlines of "Aeolus," on the other hand, begin a process of stylistic deformation which will culminate in chapters such as "Sirens," "Cyclops," and "Oxen of the Sun": the deformation is not grounded in the consciousness of the characters, but is imposed by the fiat of the author. Up until this point, the stream of consciousness of Stephen and Bloom has fragmented our sense of the reality of Dublin; henceforth, the novel will proceed toward a more pervasive kind of fragmentation, as each chapter seems to break apart from the whole and to take on a life of its own. One reason for the break in narration occurring just here is evident: for the first time, a chapter is divided between the consciousnesses of Stephen and Bloom. (They both appear in "Hades," but Joyce does not render Stephen's thoughts in that chapter.) Joyce begins at this point not to nudge but to bludgeon the reader, to remind him of the superior artistic consciousness not only above and beyond the work but also within it.

But although "Aeolus" is a chapter which tends, through its eccentricities, to break away from the whole, it also tends to recapitulate, to epitomize the whole. It is an example of one of the major premises of Joycean art: "When a part so ptee does duty for the holos we soon grow to use of an allforabit" (*FW*, 18–19). Most of the chapters of *Ulysses* (with some special pleading one might prove it for all) do duty for the whole, summarizing in some way the theme, form, or movement of the entire book. "Sirens" is only a very overt form of the book's musical techniques; "Cyclops" does what the book does by creating two points of view in juxtaposition, the one reductive, the other mythic; most obviously, "Circe" recapitulates all the preceding motifs in the novel. "Aeolus" performs this function through its use of the machinery of journalism. During the chapter, under the headline "Omnium Gatherum," Myles Crawford remarks: "All the talents. . . . Law, the classics . . . . Literature, the press" (135). Joyce's literature, the literature of *Ulysses* and *Finnegans Wake,* is in many ways very like the press—not least for being an omnium gatherum. The format of the newspaper, like Joyce's last two works, places great items by small indiscriminately (Sino-Soviet Split Widens/Jeffersonville Man Grows Six-pound Cucumber), often to ironic effect (Burial of Patk Dignam/Plumtree's Potted Meat). Bloom's thoughts about Monks the "dayfather" reinforce this analogy between the press and Joycean literature: "Old Monks the dayfather. Queer lot of stuff he must have put through his hands in his time: obituary notices, pubs' ads, speeches, divorce suits, found drowned" (122). Old Monks, in fact, might well serve as a model of Joyce, dayfather of June 16, 1904—for just as certain chapters recapitulate the book, so do several characters point toward the figure of the book's creator.[1]

---

1. In "Scylla and Charybdis," Stephen hypothesizes that Shakespeare refers to himself obliquely in the plays: "He has hidden his own name, a fair name, William, in the plays, a super here, a clown there, as a painter of old Italy set his face in a dark corner of his canvas" (209). Similarly, in *Ulysses* we occasionally glimpse Joyce tucked away in a dark

But such models of the book within the book would be of little account did they not offer some unique, illuminating perspective. "Aeolus" does this through the essential art of the newspaper page, which is the art of juxtaposition. "Aeolus" juxtaposes Bloom and Stephen, who do not actually meet within the chapter, and out of this juxtaposition arises a powerful metaphor for viewing the two heroes and the book itself: the metaphor of "A Pisgah Sight of Palestine." "And yet he died without having entered the land of promise," says J. J. O'Molloy of Moses (143). The idea of the barely missed goal becomes the subject around which the chapter revolves. First of all, Moses is in the chapter in overplus—in Bloom's confused memories of the Passover (122), in Professor MacHugh's mention of "the Jews in the wilderness and on the mountaintop" (131), in the two reported speeches (Seymour Bushe's and John F. Taylor's), and finally in Stephen's use of the Mosaic allusion as the title of his enigmatic "vision." The Homeric parallel also includes such a Pisgah vision: aided by the winds of Aeolus, Ulysses's ship was actually in sight of Ithaca when his men loosed the winds and sent the ship flying back to Aeolus's isle. Bloom fulfills the parallel in his efforts to arrange the ad for Keyes. At first encouraged by Myles Crawford-Aeolus, Bloom seems on the verge of success; but when he asks for "just a little puff" for Keyes, Bloom receives his rebuff: K. M. R. I. A. Finally, in a chapter of missed chances, it is notable that Bloom and Stephen only barely miss meeting each other.

The allusions to Moses are of great interest. Like Shakespeare in "Scylla and Charybdis," Moses in "Aeolus" usurps attention, and the Mosaic parallel momentarily becomes more important than the Homeric. But whereas the Shakespeare allusions radiate outward from "Scylla and Charybdis," the Moses allusions are largely confined to this one chapter. This very localized concentration of material reveals one of Joyce's methods: in one chapter he creates a network of allusion and correspondence which briefly brings the book into a new focus, then in the next he rotates the prism by one

---

corner. These small self-images are cases of Joyce's definition of all art as a transubstantiation of the artist's own life. Most of the Joyce figures seem to me simply arabesques in the book's design. See, however, my subsequent discussion in Chapter VI of W. B. Murphy in "Eumaeus."

facet to reveal another view. *Ulysses* is a magic lantern, always focused against the same screen, but there is a constant interchange of slides.

The major point of the Moses allusions is clear: they illustrate the heroism and integrity of the exile. The heart of the parallel is in the closing words of Taylor's speech:

> —*But, ladies and gentlemen, had the youthful Moses listened to and accepted that view of life, had he bowed his head and bowed his will and bowed his spirit before that arrogant admonition he would never have brought the chosen people out of their house of bondage nor followed the pillar of the cloud by day. He would never have spoken with the Eternal amid lightnings on Sinai's mountaintop nor ever have come down with the light of inspiration shining in his countenance and bearing in his arms the tables of the law, graven in the language of the outlaw.* (143)

The speech is accompanied by minimal touches of irony. Professor MacHugh, who reports the speech, interrupts it with "a dumb belch of hunger," and Lenehan adds his tired facetiousness: "A-sudden-at-the-moment-though-from-lingering-illness-often-previously-expectorated-demise . . . . And with a great future behind him" (143). But such touches leave intact what is perhaps the most straightforward defense in the book of the strength and integrity of the exile. The Moses speech bears comparison with Gabriel Conroy's afterdinner speech in "The Dead." Both speeches are rhetorically overblown, and Joyce in both cases emphasizes the speaker's lack of commitment to what he is saying. But, in context, both speeches are *true*—far truer, certainly, than the speaker realizes. Gabriel's speech describes a warmth in the Irish which he does not discover until the story's shattering crisis. MacHugh also praises the Irish, but in reality his words single out the two exiles, Bloom and Stephen.

Moses, though, died before he was able to enter the land of promise. This is the most important detail of the parallel, because it precisely defines the spiritual states of both Bloom and Stephen. In his compassionate and hardheaded way, Bloom is able to live more fully and acutely than any other character in the book; but, as in the case of Moses, one flaw holds him back from the full achievement of happiness. The trauma of his son's death keeps him forever turned toward the past, unable to face or even conceptualize a future of promise. Stephen too is stopped short of fulfillment: to use his own phrase, he is continually "almosting it." In no way is he more like Bloom than in this feeling of incompleteness, of thwarted fulfillment.

The Moses parallel thus serves as a correlative for the spiritual states of both heroes. It gives a somber but accurate description of Bloom: the pathos of his life is that he is incapable of entering fully into possession of the promised land which lies before him in his life with Molly. The parallel, though, has a second, equally relevant application which is suggested in one of the newspaper headlines: LET US HOPE (144). A Pisgah sight of Palestine augurs hope and the possibility of fulfillment and not simply the failure to reach a destination. It is this second sense of the Moses parallel which lies behind Stephen's curious parable.

Stephen's "Pisgah Sight of Palestine" is the story of Anne Kearns and Florence MacCabe, the two midwives of "Proteus," who, having climbed to the top of Nelson's Pillar, are frightened by the height and content themselves with eating their plums and spitting the pits from the top of the pillar. The story itself is a Pisgah vision: it is inconclusive, truncated. In place of a conclusion to the story, Stephen gives "a sudden loud young laugh as a close" (148). It is like his "shout of nervous laughter" at the conclusion of his nonsense riddle in "Nestor" (27). (Later, in "Scylla and Charybdis," "He laughed to free his mind from his mind's bondage" [212].) This nervous, hectic laugh, which Stephen uses as a kind of emotional punctuation, is one sign of his own incomplete state on Mount Pisgah. He seeks the ease and liberty of laughter and gaiety, but the self-mocking laughter is spasmodic and baffled.

And yet, if Stephen's story demonstrates the kind of quirky emotional stoppage which characterizes him throughout the day, it also hints at his efforts to break beyond that stoppage and enter the promised land of emotional maturity. Especially interesting are those short, telegraphic messages which Stephen sends to himself, the promptings he gives himself as he talks to the other men. "Dublin. I have much, much to learn," he says (144); and "On now. Dare it. Let there be life" (145). In both short messages Stephen seeks to overcome his own aversion toward experience. In the first, he tries to adopt a humility which is as yet foreign to his character, and in both the first and the second he betrays a doubleness which we recognize in him at many points in the book—one resolute self prodding and cajoling a second, reluctant self toward engagement in Irish life.

Once he begins his story, Stephen does dare it. He creates the reality of Dublin life in almost obsessive detail: "They buy one and fourpenceworth of brawn and four slices of panloaf at the north city dining rooms in Marlborough street from Miss Kate Collins, proprietress . . . They purchase four and twenty ripe plums from a girl at the foot of Nelson's pillar to take off the thirst of the brawn. They give two threepenny bits to the gentleman at the turnstile . . ." (145). Although earlier Stephen's "blood" was "wooed by grace of language and gesture" in J. J. O'Molloy's speech, Stephen resolutely opts for this intensely concrete form of expression. His scrupulous rhetoric is an enactment of that advice he gives himself later in "Scylla and Charybdis": "Hold to the now, the here, through which all future plunges to the past" (186). Stephen's diction and his process of composition are outgrowths of his speculations in "Proteus." If he is to know the city—both as itself and as a part of his past—he must immerse himself in its life. If he is to free himself, he must thoroughly know and understand the conditions of his bondage.

The story is almost ludicrously modest, but it is in such small attempts that we must sense the possibilities inherent in Stephen. "A Pisgah Sight of Palestine or the Parable of the Plums" tells us more about Stephen's direction as an artist than any of his other "works" in the book. Just before beginning his narrative, he says to himself, simply, "Dubliners" (145); and the story does in fact point toward the art of Joyce's own *Dubliners*. The severe realism of the style, the narrative of a failed expedition (compare, for example, "An Encounter"), and the unresolved ending are recognizably like Joyce's own stories. But most important is the title Stephen gives his story and the cluster of ideas the title conveys. "A Pisgah Sight of Palestine" suggests the present moment, rich with the possibilities for the future; it is the moment of incipience. This is the moment of Stephen, Bloom, and Molly—unfulfilled, but on the verge of possible fulfillment. It is also the crucial "moment" of the endings of all of Joyce's great works, from "The Dead" through *Finnegans Wake*. No other writer has ever more scrupulously avoided the happy ending, because no other writer has ever been more aware—and enamored—of the moment which bristles with possibilities.

As the first chapter to impose an external ordering device upon its material, "Aeolus" tells much about the art of *Ulysses*. As Joyce for the first time focuses upon the consciousnesses of both Stephen and Bloom, he creates new lenses by which to see the two men as parts of a single pattern. In this chapter the implicit pattern of the novel begins to become explicit. Most obviously, Joyce imposes the newspaper headlines and thereby calls attention to his own journalistic, juxtaposing art. But more significant is the Moses parallel which suddenly comes to life in this chapter. Having previously given us three chapters of Stephen and three of Bloom, Joyce creates a metaphor capable of describing them both. That metaphor is largely confined to this single chapter: once it has served Joyce's purposes, he returns to it only a few times. Interestingly, though, the Moses parallel makes a final appearance in the book, as a description of Bloom's consciousness shortly before he falls asleep:

> In what final satisfaction did these antagonistic sentiments and reflections, reduced to their simplest forms, converge?
>
> Satisfaction at the ubiquity in eastern and western terrestrial hemispheres, in all habitable lands and islands explored or unexplored (the land of the midnight sun, the islands of the blessed, the isles of Greece, the land of promise) of adipose posterior female hemispheres, redolent of milk and honey and of excretory sanguine and seminal warmth, reminiscent of secular families of curves of amplitude, insusceptible of moods of impression or of contrarieties of expression, expressive of mute immutable mature animality. (734)

It is the jocoserious culmination of the book: the man lured by, fearful of, devoted to the woman's "mute immutable mature animality." It is Moses gazing upon "the land of promise . . . redolent of milk and honey."

## "Scylla and Charybdis"

The library scene in "Scylla and Charybdis" is Stephen's most triumphant hour in the novel. His erudition is more impressive than in "Proteus" because more sustained; there are marked signs of maturity and self-understanding in his silent remarks to himself; and he convincingly protects his own integrity against the jibes and assaults of his listeners. This last point is important: Joyce has his young hero shine against the foil of his listeners' snobbery and hauteur, and thereby gives substance to Stephen's sometimes paranoid feelings of exclusion. As a vindication of the persecuted hero, "Scylla and Charybdis" is Stephen's "Cyclops." But although the chapter is Stephen's best hour—his most promising and his wisest—it is also by indirection a description of the nobility of Bloom. Even more forcefully and pervasively than "Aeolus," "Scylla and Charybdis" creates an intricate web of analogy between Bloom and Stephen which is as central to the book as the Homeric parallel. That analogy, of course, is Stephen's Shakespeare theory.

Like most things in *Ulysses*, the Shakespeare theory is presented to us as a tessellated surface, but the underlying argument is not hard to grasp. A short summary of its main points will be helpful. According to Stephen, the self-confidence of the young Shakespeare was severely shaken by hotblooded Anne Hathaway, eight years his senior, who seduced him and forced him into marriage. The original wound was exacerbated years later, when Anne committed adultery with two of Shakespeare's brothers, Edmund and Richard (whose names, Stephen ingeniously points out, Shakespeare confers upon two of his arch-villains). Shakespeare's obsession with these facts can be seen everywhere in his works, especially in his driven concern with the themes of lust and adultery.

Like other biographical critics of Shakespeare, Stephen takes *Hamlet* as the central parable of Shakespeare's soul. He associates Shakespeare, however, not with the young prince, but with the ghost of King Hamlet, whose part Shakespeare actually played. Like King Hamlet, Shakespeare sought relief from the purgatory of his own thoughts by turning to his son. Since Shakespeare's bodily son Hamnet was dead, he sought solace in a son of his soul, his created son Prince Hamlet. Stephen's thought here is elliptical, but it is the single most important hypothesis of his argument: Shakespeare, whose immense wisdom was flawed and almost destroyed by one cankering obsession, sought some means to transmit his wisdom purged of the obsession. Deprived of the bodily son who might have been the recipient of his wisdom, Shakespeare sought to externalize and rid himself of his obsession through his art. But Stephen's psychologizing is not so facile as to say that the imperfections of an artist's life are totally overcome in his art. Shakespeare's psychological wound, Stephen insists, was never totally healed, even through his art. There is a feeling of reconciliation in the last plays as the weary and suffering old man finds solace in his daughter—Marina, Perdita, Miranda—just as Shakespeare found solace in the birth of his granddaughter. Some comfort, yes, but Stephen's Shakespeare dies still driven, still unsatisfied.

The sheer complexity of the Shakespeare theory's ramifications is one of the most beautiful things in *Ulysses*. First of all there are Stephen's motives, and the most obvious of these is the sheer desire to dazzle and impress. His theory is a cunningly contrived piece of rhetoric by which he seeks to captivate his audience—AE especially, but also Magee. "Make them accomplices," he admonishes himself as he begins his narrative (188); and later, more blatantly, "Flatter. Rarely. But flatter" (208). His narrative strategies are manifold. He puts his Jesuit education to work ("Composition of place. Ignatius Loyola, make haste to help me!" [188]); he is willing once to stoop to flattery; and on occasion he is willing to distort the truth to support his claims. After telling his listeners of a star which appeared at Shakespeare's birth, he warns himself, "Don't tell them he was nine years old when it was quenched" (210). But what is most impressive in his rhetoric is his ability to marshal and weave together his material. He is able to store away facts and ideas—just as he stores away library slips for jotting down thoughts—and then to bring forth a detail when it is needed for his argument. In "Aeolus," for example, he heard Professor MacHugh's anecdote about Antisthenes, and in "Scylla and Charybdis" he repeats the story at its appropriate place (148, 201). We have already noticed this thought-pattern, which distinguishes Stephen's consciousness from Bloom's: a paragraph of

Stephen's speech or thought is a collection of allusions which have clustered around one *idée-mère* like pins around a magnet.

Stephen's jealous guarding and reworking of what he has seen and heard and said reminds us of Joyce himself (and of his assertion, implicit in *Ulysses,* explicit in *Finnegans Wake,* that all art is plagiarism, a repetition of what has already been said). But Stephen also sees this same process at work in Shakespeare, a writer who "stole" the material for all but one of his plays. Stephen cites Shakespeare's extensive use of sources and places even more emphasis on what he sees as Shakespeare's cynical use of whatever topical material fell in his way:

> All events brought grist to his mill. Shylock chimes with the jewbaiting that followed the hanging and quartering of the queen's leech Lopez, his jew's heart being plucked forth while the sheeny was yet alive: *Hamlet* and *Macbeth* with the coming to the throne of a Scotch philophaster with a turn for witchroasting. The lost armada is his jeer in *Love's Labour Lost.* . . . (204–205)

Stephen's Shakespeare is in great part Stephen's self-image—a projection both of what he is now and of what he wishes to be in the future. In the description of Shakespeare's use of whatever came to hand, we recognize Stephen's own methods of "composition"—his poem in "Proteus," his parable in "Aeolus," even the Shakespeare theory itself. All events bring grist to Stephen's mill. But Shakespeare made such use of his material because he was so closely and vitally involved in his world; he lived as well as wrote. This acting and suffering Shakespeare is the complex focus of Stephen's hopes and fears for his own future.

This concern with Shakespeare the man and with the relation between the whole man and the artist is the greatest merit of the Shakespeare theory. S. L. Goldberg has written masterfully of Stephen's theory and has pointed out its giant step beyond the aesthetic theory which Stephen presents in the *Portrait:* in *Ulysses* Stephen considers the relation between an artist's life and his work, a relationship which he entirely ignored in the *Portrait.*[2] In the

---

2. See in particular Chapter III of Goldberg's *The Classical Temper* (New York: Barnes and Noble, 1961).

earlier work, Stephen's disquisition is sharply divided into two halves. First, the artist as perceiver incorporates the object; then, at the opposite end of the creative process, the artist establishes himself in relation to his work. What Stephen omits is the creative process itself: the aesthetic theory of the *Portrait* is not invalid, but incomplete. In "Scylla and Charybdis" the focus is upon the creative act and upon the artist, not as a perceiving automaton but as a suffering human being. So far has Stephen retreated from pure aestheticism that he runs the danger of not distinguishing life from art at all. (His movement away from one extreme to the dangers of the other suggests Ulysses's ship passing between Scylla and Charybdis.) Nevertheless, Stephen's gain between *Portrait* and *Ulysses* is obvious. He is no longer insistent upon a hermetic world of art divorced from the mundanities of the artist's life. Instead, art has become for Stephen an instrument of self-understanding whereby the artist probes again and again into himself to clarify his own soul and his relation to the world. Only through self-knowledge can the artist come to know and create a world. Stephen has arrived at essentially the view of art which is later practiced by Shem:

> this Esuan Menschavik and the first till last alshemist wrote over every square inch of the only foolscap available, his own body, till by its corrosive sublimation one continuous present tense integument slowly unfolded all marryvoising moodmoulded cyclewheeling history (thereby, he said, reflecting from his own individual person life unlivable, trans-accidentated through the slow fires of consciousness into a dividual chaos, perilous, potent, common to allflesh, human only, mortal) . . . . (*FW*, 185–86)

Stephen's Shakespeare theory is impressive as a parable of the relation between an artist's life and his work, but he gives the theory another meaning of which his listeners cannot be aware: the theory becomes Stephen's program for his own hopes. Stephen's feeling of identification with Shakespeare is apparent early on, as he gives his special definition of a ghost: "One who has faded into impalpability, through death, through absence, through change of manners. Elizabethan London lay as far from Stratford as corrupt Paris lies from virgin Dublin" (188). The implication of the analogy between London–Stratford and Paris–Dublin is obvious. Shakespeare's alienation is also Stephen's; both have returned to reconcile themselves with their pasts. And yet Stephen is not truly in Shakespeare's condition, and the difference between their two cases transforms Stephen's somber tale of Shakespeare into a hopeful vision for himself. The crucial difference lies in Stephen's remarks about fatherhood.

Stephen insists, perhaps more firmly than on any other point, that Shakespeare is to be identified with Hamlet *père,* not Hamlet *fils.* Shakespeare was not the son in the play, says Stephen, because when he wrote the play he had no father:

> No. The corpse of John Shakespeare does not walk the night. From hour to hour it rots and rots. He rests, disarmed of fatherhood, having devised that mystical estate upon his son. Boccaccio's Calandrino was the first and last man who felt himself with child. Fatherhood, in the sense of conscious begetting, is unknown to man. It is a mystical estate, an apostolic succession, from only begetter to only begotten . . . .
> —What links them in nature? An instant of blind rut.
> Am I father? If I were?
> Shrunken uncertain hand.
> —Sabellius, the African, subtlest heresiarch of all the beasts of the field, held that the Father was Himself His Own Son. The bulldog of Aquin, with whom no word shall be impossible, refutes him. (207–208)

A part of Stephen's fervid insistence can be traced directly to his attempts to dissociate himself from his own father. (Even in the midst of his insistence, however, he is assailed: "Am I father? If I were?") The Sabellian heresy, which proclaims the absolute identity of Father and Son, is therefore particularly repugnant to Stephen since, as it applies to his own case, it predicts the failure of the son to become dissociated from the father. Stephen's insistence that John Shakespeare lies dead is one of his strongest statements of transcendence: the son can achieve absolute freedom from the father-past.

If this were all Stephen meant by fatherhood, he would be caught in a blatant contradiction: while the account of Shakespeare's life would seem to argue for the persistence of the past, the comments on fatherhood would seem to deny that persistence. Actually,

Stephen is aware of the opposed ideas and (again like Ulysses between Scylla and Charybdis) is steering between them. They are
resolved in a train of thought which brings to a conclusion ideas
which have been in conflict since the *Telemachia.* Early in the
chapter, Stephen remembers that he owes money to AE and devises
an ingenious argument for escaping payment:

> Wait. Five months. Molecules all change. I am other I now. Other I
> got pound.
> Buzz. Buzz.
> But I, entelechy, form of forms, am I by memory because under
> everchanging forms.
> I that sinned and prayed and fasted.
> A child Conmee saved from pandies.
> I, I and I. I.
> A. E. I. O. U. (189–90)

Stephen's thoughts here seem at first only a digression, a leftover
scrap from his ruminations in the opening chapters of the book.
But his concern with a perduring self as opposed to a succession of
transient successive selves states in different terms the relation at
the heart of the Shakespeare theory: the relation between the past
which persists and the past which is left behind. And, finally, the
two sets of terms come together, in the passage which most clearly
illuminates Stephen's motives in concocting his theory:

> —As we, or mother Dana, weave and unweave our bodies, Stephen
> said, from day to day, their molecules shuttled to and fro, so does the
> artist weave and unweave his image. And as the mole on my right breast
> is where it was when I was born, though all my body has been woven of
> new stuff time after time, so through the ghost of the unquiet father the
> image of the unliving son looks forth. In the intense instant of imagina-
> tion, when the mind, Shelley says, is a fading coal, that which I was
> is that which I am and that which in possibility I may come to be.
> So in the future, the sister of the past, I may see myself as I sit here now
> but by reflection from that which then I shall be. (194)

Insofar as the theory applies to Stephen, this is the *clou* of his
argument (although his listeners, understandably, fail to see the
relevance of what he says: "Yes, Mr Best said youngly, I feel

Hamlet quite young"). The terms "father" and "son" have been applied to phases of the self. Just as Shakespeare-King Hamlet attempted to transmit his wisdom, purged of its obsession, to a son, so does Stephen's present self, "the unquiet father," look forward to fulfillment in a future self, "the unliving son." Stephen overcomes the pessimism of his own theory by making himself both the father whose wisdom is paralyzed and trammeled by anguish and the son who finally benefits from that wisdom.

The deepest current of Stephen's thought in this chapter lies beneath the Shakespeare theory, even beneath his private applications of the theory to himself. Here, in a kind of telegraphic communication with himself (which we noticed earlier in "Aeolus"), the motives which lie behind his farfetched theory are apparent in their most primitive form. Above all, he urges upon himself a wise passiveness, a willingness not so much to encounter experience as to be washed over by it. After the adolescent arrogance of the *Portrait,* Stephen wishes to float within experience rather than confront it aggressively. These terse messages to himself gain in force when taken in the aggregate. After describing Anne Hathaway's seduction of Shakespeare, he asks himself: "And my turn? When?" (191). Later, there is a cluster of such thoughts as he leaves the library with Mulligan: "Wait to be wooed and won" (210). "Speech, speech. But act. Act speech. They mock to try you. Act. Be acted on" (211). "Life is many days. This will end" (214). In Stephen's words a weary resignation is balanced against an almost wistful longing to be taken by and included within experience. This is the very kernel of Stephen Dedalus.

One last message from Stephen to himself is worth noticing: "See this. Remember" (192). Here is the potential artist telling himself to write the work we are reading: it is as if Stephen-Joyce were storing away material for *Ulysses.* The self-reference is not at all gratuitous. As we have already seen, Stephen looks forward to that day when he can look back upon his past with complete equanimity and understanding. Here in the library he already anticipates that hypothetical future self which may be capable of writing *Ulysses.* "So through the ghost of the unquiet father the image of the unliving son looks forth." Two other comments in the chapter look forward to the composition of *Ulysses.* First, Magee reports: "Our national epic has yet to be written, Dr Sigerson says" (192). And, later, Mulligan quotes Yeats's review of a book by Lady Gregory, but the remark applies more fully to Joyce's own book: "The most beautiful book that has come out of our country in my time. One thinks of Homer" (216). (Earlier in the day, Myles Crawford virtually demanded that Stephen write *Ulysses:* "I want you to write something for me, he said. Something with a bite in it. . . . Put us all into it, damn its soul" [135].) If Stephen looks forward toward his own maturity, Joyce sanctions that hope by hints which anticipate the book we are reading.

We are interested in Stephen and his theory, however, not simply because they point toward the composition of *Ulysses.* (Cleanth Brooks has rightly complained of the criticism which praises *Ulysses* simply because the book anticipates its own composition.)[3] More important are Stephen's exploration of the artist's state and his inquiry into the economy of life and art. Moreover, the theory operates dramatically in the book—far more dramatically, certainly, than the theory in the *Portrait*—to characterize Stephen and to show his "almostness," that state of incipience and nervous anticipation which poises him on the verge of possible fulfillment. Already it is apparent that the Shakespeare theory is one of the most mobile and flexible metaphors in the book for the description of Stephen. But the theory has its applications—outside Stephen's consciousness, of course—to Bloom as well, so that the theory, like the earlier Moses parallel, becomes an all-encompassing network which recapitulates all the major relationships of the book.

In "Lestrygonians," the chapter immediately preceding "Scylla and Charybdis," Bloom muses on poetry:

> That is how poets write, the similar sounds. But then Shakespeare has no rhymes: blank verse. The flow of the language it is. The thoughts. Solemn.
>
> *Hamlet, I am thy father's spirit*
> *Doomed for a certain time to walk the earth.* (152)

3. Cleanth Brooks, "Joyce's *Ulysses:* Symbolic Poem, Biography or Novel?" *Imagined Worlds: Essays on Some English Novels and Novelists in Honour of John Butt,* ed. Maynard Mack and Ian Gregor (London: Methuen, 1968), p. 438.

Bloom's slightly inaccurate quotation of King Hamlet establishes an obvious contrast to Stephen, who throughout the day identifies himself with the Prince. In terms of his theory, Stephen hopes to gain wisdom from the paralyzed past; Bloom is the embodiment of the paralyzed wisdom itself. Stephen manages first to compare himself to a fated, agonized Shakespeare and then to imagine himself avoiding Shakespeare's fate; Bloom represents that fate.

Bloom, then, actually resembles the Shakespeare Stephen describes far more than Stephen himself does. Like Shakespeare, Bloom was overborne by a dominant woman. Bloom remains deferential to her, although he is happier in this dominated state than was Stephen's Shakespeare. In both men, the original deference to the wife is compounded by knowledge of the wife's adultery. Shakespeare's Hamnet died and so he created a Hamlet to whom he might transmit his knowledge. Bloom's son is dead, and Bloom comes, in the course of the day, to look upon Stephen as his lost Rudy. Finally, Shakespeare toward the end of his life felt some rejuvenation at the birth of his granddaughter. Bloom feels a love for Milly which is closely related to his memories of Molly. As Stephen says of Shakespeare, "Will any man love the daughter if he has not loved the mother?" (195).

These resemblances of circumstance create the strongest kind of parallel between Bloom and Shakespeare. Even more impressive are the Bloom-Shakespeare resemblances which crop up in the very texture of Stephen's descriptions. For example:

> Belief in himself has been untimely killed. He was overborne in a cornfield first (ryefield, I should say) and he will never be a victor in his own eyes after nor play victoriously the game of laugh and lie down. Assumed dongiovannism will not save him. No later undoing will undo the first undoing. The tusk of the boar has wounded him there where love lies ableeding. If the shrew is worsted yet there remains to her woman's invisible weapon. There is, I feel in the words, some goad of the flesh driving him into a new passion, a darker shadow of the first, darkening even his own understanding of himself. A [like] fate awaits him and the two rages commingle in a whirlpool.[4]

4. *Ulysses*, p. 196. Robert Kellogg in his article in *James Joyce's "Ulysses,"* ed. Hart and Hayman (Berkeley: University of California Press, 1974) p. 171n., calls attention to the misprint in the 1961 edition of "life" for "like."

This is a fair example of the effects of the prose in this chapter. It is a tissue of Stephen's own allusions and, beyond that, a tissue of allusions of which Stephen cannot be aware. "The tusk of the boar," for example, is Stephen's reference to Adonis, but it also recalls Ulysses's wound, just as the two rages commingling in a whirlpool suggest the Homeric Charybdis. While describing his version of Shakespeare, Stephen is also describing Homer's Ulysses—and, in several important phrases, Joyce's Ulysses as well. "Assumed dongiovannism will not save him": we recall not only Bloom's frequent references to *Don Giovanni* but also his halfhearted philanderings which only exacerbate the thoughts from which he is trying to escape. But perhaps the most important phrase in the passage is the one taken from the *Maynooth Catechism:* "darkening even his own understanding of himself." The phrase applies variously to Shakespeare, Stephen, and Bloom. Self-understanding is for Stephen the highest good and the greatest hope for the future: it is the ultimate act of the imperial self contemplating and comprehending all the selves it has been. It is the doom of Stephen's Shakespeare and of Bloom to be locked within their obsessions, incapable of that final, liberating act of self-knowledge.

So, while Stephen imagines himself escaping Shakespeare's fate through a future act of self-understanding, Bloom remains on the same level with Shakespeare (bizarre phrase!), haunted and unfulfilled:

> Ravisher and ravished, what he would but would not, go with him from Lucrece's bluecircled ivory globes to Imogen's breast, bare, with its mole cinquespotted. He goes back, weary of the creation he has piled up to hide him from himself, an old dog licking an old sore. But, because loss is his gain, he passes on towards eternity in undiminished personality, untaught by the wisdom he has written or by the laws he has revealed.
> (197)

"Ravisher and ravished, what he would but would not": this is the quintessence of Bloom's fate. The phrase suggests Bloom's latent masochism and his habitual approach and withdrawal (with an echo of *Vorrei e non vorrei,* the words from *Don Giovanni* which, in misquoted form, preoccupy Bloom throughout the day)—in a word, his entrapment in a psychological prison he cannot see beyond. "Untaught by the wisdom he has written or by the laws he has revealed": the phrase pinpoints the weary pathos of Bloom's life. He is a man so blocked by his one obsession that he is incapable of the distance which would be necessary for him to draw conclusions from his own experience. Like Moses, he shows the way, but is unable himself to enter the promised land.

The Shakespeare theory shows Joyce's structural art at one of its peaks. As *Finnegans Wake* amply demonstrates, Joyce at his most inspired is inclined to create an archetypal story into which he may insert the most various of particular examples, from Adam and Eve to Humpty Dumpty. The Shakespeare theory works in this way in *Ulysses:* Stephen's mind-boggling account of Shakespeare's life comes to serve not only as a universal parable of the artist but also as a story flexible enough to illustrate the potentialities of all the major characters of the book.

The very title of "Scylla and Charybdis" has this same multivalence. I have already suggested how Stephen's form of argument frequently resembles a hazardous nautical passage through dangerous straits. There are, though, a number of other analogues of Scylla and Charybdis. Early in the chapter, for example, Stephen comments to himself, "Between the Saxon smile and yankee yawp. The devil and the deep sea" (187). This is a very minor instance of Scylla and Charybdis, but worth some study. "The Saxon smile" recalls Stephen's thought as he looks at Haines at the end of "Telemachus": "Horn of a bull, hoof of a horse, smile of a Saxon" (23). (He is thinking of three proverbially untrustworthy things.) The "yankee yawp" is almost certainly a reference to Whitman's line, "I sound my barbaric yawp over the roofs of the world" (*Song of Myself,* 51). Mulligan is the robust bard who quotes Whitman in "Telemachus" ("Do I contradict myself? Very well then, I contradict myself"). Just before launching out on his theory, then, Stephen is constructing one of his characteristic dichotomies: he locates himself between oppressive Haines and mercurial Malachi. Intensely conscious of his own language, he sees himself between the oppressive language of the Saxon and the barbaric chaos of the American. This is the linguistic version of the dichotomy Stephen has sensed all day, between oppressive stasis and protean mutability.

But the Saxon smile and the yankee yawp are only minor versions of Scylla and Charybdis: they are instances of the way in which Joyce's radical metaphors often crop up in unexpected nooks and corners. The major use of Scylla and Charybdis is closer to the central issue of the chapter. Frank Budgen reports that Joyce saw Plato and Aristotle as the Scylla and Charybdis of the chapter.[5] But this analogy seems questionable. Stephen's Aristotelianism is neither Scylla nor Charybdis but the *tertium quid,* the middle course between the two extremes. Stanley Sultan and Richard Ellmann are certainly right in suggesting that the two poles are AE and Mulligan.[6] AE is the Platonist of the chapter, with his dictum that "Art has to reveal to us ideas, formless spiritual essences" (185). Specifically, he is the whirlpool Charybdis: Stephen thinks of him as "Gulfer of souls, engulfer" (192). Like a whirlpool, he is capable of reversing his direction and contradicting his own ideas. His combination of aestheticism and love of the land, for example, leads him into confusions of which he seems unaware. On one hand, ". . . France produces the finest flower of corruption in Mallarmé but the desirable life is revealed only to the poor of heart, the life of Homer's Phæacians" (187). But, whirlpool that he is, he can quickly shift his preferences and scorn the poor of heart: "As for living, our servants can do that for us, Villiers de l'Isle has said" (189). Opposed to AE's Platonism is Mulligan's mockery, the worldly cynicism which Stephen risks in avoiding AE's whirlpool.

Stephen's opposition to AE is clear. Against AE's insistence upon formless spiritual essences, Stephen mentally makes his rebuttal:

Unsheathe your dagger definitions. Horseness is the whatness of allhorse. Streams of tendency and eons they worship. God: noise in the street: very peripatetic. Space: what you damn well have to see. Through spaces smaller than red globules of man's blood they creepycrawl after Blake's buttocks into eternity of which this vegetable world is but a

---

5. Frank Budgen, *James Joyce and the Making of "Ulysses"* (Bloomington: Indiana University Press, 1960), p. 107.

6. Stanley Sultan, *The Argument of "Ulysses"* (Columbus: Ohio State University Press, 1964), pp. 151–53, and Ellmann, *Ulysses on the Liffey* (New York: Oxford University Press, 1972) p. 83.

shadow. Hold to the now, the here, through which all future plunges
to the past. (186)

Stephen is arguing not only against AE's ideas, but also against
his own tendency toward Platonism in the *Portrait*. Then, when
Mulligan enters, Stephen is thrown into immediate disarray, for
Mulligan is the dangerous extreme Stephen risks in avoiding AE:
"Hast thou found me, O mine enemy?" (197). Stephen is disturbed not simply because he finds Mulligan unlikable but also
because Mulligan represents a dangerous parody of his own
thoughts. While Stephen insists upon the intimate relation of life
and art, Mulligan totally destroys the distinction itself. We are
again reminded of the air of the '90's which hangs about Mulligan:
his dandyish dress, his love of paradox, and above all his treatment
of life as a series of poses. Mulligan's life *is* his art—or rather his
artifice, for Mulligan trivializes art, making of it a narcissistic appeal for applause. After Mulligan's poem on masturbation, Stephen
thinks, "Jest on. Know thyself" (216). His wit exactly places
Mulligan. If the ideal of Stephen's art is self-knowledge, the ideal
of Mulligan's is carnal self-knowledge, narcissistic and masturbatory. Stephen's androgynous artist, acting and acted upon,
becomes Mulligan's self-abuser.

Leaving the library, Stephen is fretting under the burden of
Mulligan's mockery when his path crosses Bloom's for the third
time:

> Part. The moment is now. Where then? If Socrates leave his house
> today, if Judas go forth tonight. Why? That lies in space which I in
> time must come to, ineluctably.
> My will: his will that fronts me. Seas between.
> A man passed out between them, bowing, greeting.
> —Good day again, Buck Mulligan said.
> The portico.
> Here I watched the birds for augury. Aengus of the birds. They go,
> they come. Last night I flew. Easily flew. Men wondered. Street of
> harlots after. A creamfruit melon he held to me. In. You will see. (217)

It is a highly symbolic meeting. Stephen, dissatisfied with the parody
of his own self standing beside him, thinks of Maeterlinck's

description of the soul encountering its own embodiment, and simultaneously he sees Bloom pass. (The Maeterlinck allusion, the mention of augury, and Stephen's memory of his dream all strongly foreshadow the encounter of Bloom and Stephen later in the book, in the "street of harlots.") Standing apart with "seas between" them, Mulligan and Stephen themselves become Scylla and Charybdis, as Bloom-Ulysses carefully steers his course between them. It is a very nice dramatization of Bloom's centrist position in the book. Both ravisher and ravished, both man and woman, Bloom passes between—and combines within himself—Stephen's rigid integrity and Mulligan's protean fluidity.

## "Circe"

"Aeolus" and "Scylla and Charybdis" are beautiful examples of chapters which unite Bloom and Stephen by creating large analogies capable of containing and describing them both. It is a part of the complexity of *Ulysses* that each such analogy or ordering matrix states in different terms the relation between the two men. "Aeolus" proclaims their essential similarity: they both resemble Moses as they hold to their own creeds in an oppressed land, and both of them stand atop Mount Pisgah, stopped just short of fulfillment. "Scylla and Charybdis" emphasizes their complementarity: Bloom resembles King Hamlet, whose wisdom is darkened by one obsessive thought, while Stephen projects a future for himself as a successful Prince Hamlet, the heir of that wisdom.

"Circe," that extraordinary chapter, does not create anything like a Moses parallel or Shakespeare theory; it is too multifarious for that. Instead, it flays the two men and lays bare the deepest motive forces which impel them throughout the day. Most specifically, "Circe" reveals the two men's contrasted relationships to the feared, dominant woman. The chapter makes clear that equation which runs throughout *Ulysses:* a man's relation to women equals his relation to experience. And, indeed, the respective reactions of Bloom and Stephen to their haunting women accurately summarize their characters as a whole: Bloom willingly, cravenly capitulates while Stephen angrily rebels.

There are two issues to deal with before we enter the nightmare of "Circe." The first concerns the nature of the chapter's "hallu-cinations." I shall use this not entirely adequate term to describe the several surreal sequences experienced by Bloom and Stephen, those clearly nonnaturalistic sequences which irrupt into the pal-pable streets of Dublin. Sometimes the break between the natural-istic and the surreal is clear-cut: Bloom's extended utopian fantasy (478ff.) is triggered by Zoe's saying "Make a stump speech out of it." Just as often, there is a blending of the two levels: at the top of page 527, the stage direction indicates that Bella Cohen enters the parlor of the brothel. Naturalistic dialogue elsewhere in the chapter assures us that Bella has indeed entered the room, but it is highly doubtful that she actually wears (as the same stage direction instructs) a keeper ring, sign of her authority over Circe's mena-gerie. On page 554, this hallucination winds down but it does not abruptly stop. "You'll know me the next time," Bella tells Bloom. In the "real" parlor, Bella is telling Bloom that he has been gazing at her longer than convention allows, even in a brothel. In the short period of Bloom's distracted gaze—five seconds? ten?—the entire sequence of Bella, Bello, and the nymph has unfolded. Even now, though, the sequence continues for five more speeches before Bella makes another "naturalistic" speech—"Which of you was playing the dead march from *Saul*?" (555)—and the entire hallucination recedes.

Bella's "You'll know me the next time" is a very useful hint. The "hallucinations" are like those extensive dreams which we later realize must have taken place in an incredibly short time. And this intense compression of psychic events is not confined to the dream-ing state. In "Nausicaa" Bloom thinks of his watch, stopped at 4:30:

Was that just when he, she?
O, he did. Into her. She did. Done.
Ah! (370)

This stream-of-consciousness passage is in fact a kind of shorthand for the Molly-Boylan episode in "Circe." Stream-of-consciousness narration pretends to register thought in approximately the length of time the thought would occupy. "Circe," with its elaborate stage directions, ignores the lapsed time of thought but allows for the succession of images which stream-of-consciousness narration cannot completely convey.

Still, the expressionistic technique of "Circe" can no more give us the thing itself, the very stuff of human thought and feeling, than can stream-of-consciousness narration; "Circe," indeed, does not even make such a claim. The expressive equipment of "Circe," for all that it reveals, reminds us that thought and feeling can be bodied forth only through more-or-less imperfect media. "Circe" summarizes virtually all the motifs of *Ulysses* because, like the mind, it can use as expressive means only what it already contains within itself; it therefore combs back through the events of the day and uses whatever paraphernalia it finds there to body forth the characters' inner dramas. The *rhythm* of each hallucinatory sequence actually occurs within the chapter; the bodying forth of that rhythm is self-consciously, ludicrously outrageous. It is in "Circe" that Stephen proposes a language of gesture which would render visible "the first entelechy, the structural rhythm" (432), but "Circe" itself refutes Stephen's proposal of a "pure" language. The chapter reveals the deepest truths about Stephen and Bloom by means of the vilest objects and crudest noises in the street.

There is another matter which requires short preliminary discussion: the question of whether the characters—and Bloom in particular—*change* within the chapter. In short, I propose that Bloom does change, if only minimally. The nightmare of "Circe" is not randomly placed; it occurs just when some inchoate feeling toward Stephen has begun to roil about in Bloom. The notion of actually having a son—a notion which Bloom has defended himself against all day—is so revolutionizing a thought as to necessitate the overturning of all the psychological barricades which Bloom has so painstakingly constructed. The series of hallucinations within "Circe" moves progressively through each of these defenses and leaves the field of force within his mind definitely altered. One does not expect much more from a single day.

So much for the preliminaries. We can now enter this masterpiece within a masterpiece by considering the nature of Bloom's powers of self-preservation, his *moly*.

Earlier, in discussing "Calypso," I suggested that Joyce presents in that chapter a sketch of Bloom the whole man, who makes a small version of the coming day's odyssey (the trip to the pork-butcher's and back) and who contains within himself a balance of attitudes which the later chapters sort out and test under extreme conditions. Each of the subsequent Bloom-chapters is thus something of a bath in corrosive acid, a trial of Bloom's stuff, a test which consists in the subjection of his total personality to one of his own subsidiary neuroses. At the worst hours of the day these tests end in standoffs; more often, Bloom the "allroundman" (235) and "unconquered hero" (264) wins his comic, skin-of-the-teeth victories.

We can account for Bloom's victories over himself in part by appealing to the finely adjusted economy of his nature, in which each of his qualities is precisely balanced by its opposite. Thus Bloom is empiricist and fantasist, sympathetically open and furtively guarded, utopian and nihilistic. His stream of consciousness is a constant dialogue between such contraries. We might also appeal, as an explanation of Bloom's allroundness, to those qualities of love which more than anything else give his life a sense of fixed bearings. He orders his life around familial love, and his day is punctuated by acts of charity and compassion. S. L. Goldberg and Richard Ellmann have both spoken eloquently of love itself as the stabilizing center of Bloom's character.

But there is something in Bloom more essential than his many-sidedness or his capacity for love. There is, to adopt and distort Robert Langbaum's phrase, a "mystery of identity" about Bloom, a depth of character which goes further than the eye can see, a mysterious vitality of being which Joyce refuses to define even when, as in "Ithaca," the motive behind Joyce's methods seems to be entirely that of accounting and analyzing.[7] This unknowable quality within Bloom's character is perhaps nearer the surface in "Circe" than anywhere else in the book. It is conveyed in part through—but is by no means confined to—his freemasonry. Freemasonry, with its connotations of secret orders and rites of initiation, becomes a metaphor for the secret reserves of energy Bloom is able to draw upon. Nosey Flynn, of all people, contributes to this

---

7. See Robert Langbaum, "The Mysteries of Identity," in *The Modern Spirit*, Galaxy Books (New York: Oxford University Press, 1970), pp. 164–84.

air of mystery when, in "Lestrygonians," he speaks with evident awe of Bloom and the Masons (177–78). Bloom's memory of his Jewish father and his sketchily defined relationship with Jewish friends such as Citron, Mastiansky, and Mesias create much the same impression. We know, from ample evidence given throughout the day, that Bloom's actual knowledge of Judaism is slight—only a little greater than his comically scant knowledge of Catholicism. Nevertheless, an exotic aura of the Middle East, first evoked in "Calypso," hangs about Bloom; and the other characters—most notably the anti-Semitic Dubliners but also Stephen Dedalus—have a belief in Jewish wisdom and power.

Bloom's freemasonry and Jewishness are, in "Circe," only instances of something deeper. Like Bloom's potato, which represents his bond to the maternal past (another of those mysterious areas of experience within Bloom which we know very little about), these details of character serve as synecdoches for that Bloomian power to reach into the depths of his own character and rescue himself in his hours of need. Bloom's version of the magical *moly*— the herb Hermes gave Ulysses as a protection against Circe's charms—is not a specific talisman (although it can be symbolized as the talismanic potato). His moly is his deep and unconscious converse with his whole nature.

The language I have used in trying to define this deep level which Joyce points toward in Bloom's being may seem unnecessarily vague, but this level of being is as indefinable and ungraspable as Lawrence's states of blood-consciousness. A major difference between the two writers lies in their presentation of this deep self. Lawrence frequently attempts to describe the unconscious self directly, either through an account of its dark movements or through an evocation by metaphor. Joyce, the creator of the epiphany and the artist of the unspoken, never attempts explicit description; he meticulously assembles thousands of particular details and molds them around a central identity which the details point toward and suggest but do not name. It is this central, unfathomable identity which Stephen the lapsed Catholic still pays homage to by calling it the soul.

"Circe" is a full-scale attack upon this mysterious identity, carried out by all the forces which threaten to alienate Bloom from his own nature. The attack begins early on in the chapter, as Bloom, like Ulysses, enters the scene in pursuit of his fellows who have already been enchanted by Circe. In the opening stage direction, Joyce describes the "danger signals" alongside the tramsiding at the entrance to nighttown. Bloom's first significant encounters in the chapter are with danger signals—psychological monitors and censors who warn him away from descent further into the depths of nighttown and the unconscious. Bloom's danger signals are three: his father, his mother, and his wife. They are all ineffectual. For all his love of his father, Bloom takes much of Rudolph's paternal advice as ill-informed and old-fashioned. In one of the most amusing metamorphoses of "Circe," Bloom becomes a young Oxford student shrugging off his father's Yiddish-accented paternal advice (438). Rudolph carries on a fairly lengthy conversation with his son, but Ellen Bloom appears only for a moment. Similarly, during the day as a whole, Bloom does not think of "poor mamma" very often or in very specific terms; she is not nearly as powerful a force in Bloom's mind as Rudolph is. The psychology of this suppression of the mother becomes clear in this scene from "Circe." Just when Bloom assumes the shamefaced attitude of a naughty boy in response to his mother's exclamations, Ellen Bloom becomes Molly, calling, "(*Sharply.*) Poldy!" (439). The image of Molly in Bloom's mind has almost completely subsumed the image of the mother. (Later, however, in a very interesting moment, Bloom will again have a distant recollection of his mother.) If Rudolph and Ellen are ineffective danger signals, Molly actually encourages Bloom to go further into nighttown. Far from angry, she is amused at Bloom's sortie: "O Poldy, Poldy, you are a poor old stick in the mud! Go and see life. See the wide world" (440). Thus do the protective authority figures within Bloom's mind work eventually to encourage his self-abasement.

Parents and wife stand at the entrance to nighttown, ineffectual in warning Bloom away. The figure who actually ushers him into the whore district is Mrs. Breen. She is precisely the appropriate person to take on this role, for she is not only Mrs. Breen; she is also "Josie Powell that was, prettiest deb in Dublin" (444). She stands at the boundary in Bloom's mind between daytime and nighttime; she is at once the respectable woman he meets on the streets of Dublin and the former sweetheart whom Bloom once thought of in sexual terms. She ushers Bloom from the decorous world into the world of bawds and whores. (The ungraduated division between respectability and whorishness is premonitory of the fantasies to come. It is typical of Bloom—and even more typical of his society.) As Bloom strolls along with Mrs. Breen, the first signs of deep unsettlement begin to appear in him, as he is uncertain whether to apologize for his presence in nighttown or to indulge with her in coy and flirtatious memories of the past. And another ambivalence begins to appear in Bloom which the chapter will later explore in depth: in a passage continuous with his appraising glance at her shabby hat in "Lestrygonians," Bloom falls into a highly "feminine" speech pattern which is one of the first signs in "Circe" of Bloom the "womanly man": "Because it didn't suit you one quarter as well as the other ducky little tammy toque with the bird of paradise wing in it . . ." (449).

Bloom's dispersal of identity during his conversation with Mrs. Breen prepares for the first major hallucination of the chapter. It is important here not to lose touch with whatever concrete reality there is in "Circe." Mr. Leopold Bloom, respectable citizen and *paterfamilias,* is in the red-light district of Dublin, in pursuit of a young man for reasons of which he himself is not completely aware. He is troubled at the idea of being seen here, and his vague apprehensions make him nervous and jumpy. When the two night watch approach, they add to his embarrassment, and the passage from embarrassment to deep-felt guilt is swift. The two watch come up to Bloom muttering the words, "Bloom. Of Bloom. For Bloom. Bloom" (453). This is a declension of Bloom's name—and there is a pun both in the notion of "declining" (as Bloom travels psychologically into the nether regions) and in the accusative case with which their declension ends (since Bloom feels himself accused). Henceforth the "Circe" chapter is to be a fantastical declining of Bloom's name and identity, an extraction of many cases from the nominative "Bloom."

A figurative declension of his name, in fact, begins at once, as the watch demand: "Come. Name and address" (455). This demand that Bloom identify and locate himself heightens that uncertainty (which first appeared in his conversation with Mrs.

Breen) as to which identity, which face, he should present to the world: "I have forgotten for the moment. . . . Dr Bloom, Leopold, dental surgeon. You have heard of von Bloom Pasha. . . . Henry Flower. . . . Bloom. The change of name Virag" (455). Bloom's unease here is interestingly similar to Stephen's memory of his paranoid fear of the police in Paris:

> Yes, used to carry punched tickets to prove an alibi if they arrested you for murder somewhere. Justice. On the night of the seventeenth of February 1904 the prisoner was seen by two witnesses. Other fellow did it: other me. Hat, tie, overcoat, nose. *Lui, c'est moi.* (41)

Both men have a vague dread of uniformed officials, and both men become rattled when these authority figures demand that they identify themselves. Under the pressure of this demand, the two men's conscious self-conceptions disperse into a bewildering, protean multiplicity: *Lui, c'est moi.*

In Bloom's case, the awareness of his many selves quickly becomes the guilty recognition of his clandestine and furtive lives. The ensuing hallucination—Bloom's first full-scale self-dramatization in the chapter—revolves around this polymorphous identity. "Leading a quadruple existence!" exclaims Mr. Philip Beaufoy. "Street angel and house devil" (460). Bloom's many-sidedness, his great source of strength during the daylight hours, is thus also his major torment (as it will be in all his major hallucinations in the chapter), as each of these subterranean existences surfaces and threatens to usurp entirely Bloom's sense of his own selfhood.

The nature of Bloom's many selves within this lengthy hallucination is predominantly sexual. Various women come forward to accuse him of philandering. Some of these accusations—most notably Martha's and Mary Driscoll's—clearly have a basis in actual events. But the most revealing accusations are made by those women who seem half-created by Bloom's own obsessed imagination. Prominent among these is Mrs. Yelverton Barry, the society lady:

> He wrote me an anonymous letter . . . signed James Lovebirch . . . . I deeply inflamed him, he said. He made improper overtures to me to misconduct myself at half past four p. m. on the following Thursday,

Dunsink time. He offered to send me through the post a work of fiction
by Monsieur Paul de Kock, entitled *The Girl with the Three Pairs of
Stays.* (465)

Mrs. Barry is a fusion of Molly herself (who commits adultery at
half past four on Thursday) and the domineering women from the
pornographic books Molly and Bloom read, such as *Sweets of Sin*
or the works of James Lovebirch and Paul de Kock. (Both the
woman in *Sweets of Sin* and Mrs. Barry wear a "sable-trimmed"
garment.) Bloom's creation of Mrs. Barry is his first major
attempt within the chapter to confront his central sexual dilemma.
He recreates Molly in the form of Mrs. Barry and then has Mrs.
Barry spurn his sexual advances. But this, of course, is not a confrontation at all: it is Bloom's projection of a powerful and sadistic woman who will satisfy his masochistic sense of sexual worthlessness. Bloom's dilemma within this sequence of scenes arises
not simply from his consciousness of guilt, but more deeply from
the *need* to experience guilt and punishment. Thus Bloom readily
accedes to his own flagellation: "(*His eyes closing, quails expec-
tantly.*) Here? (*He squirms.*) Again! (*He pants cringing.*) I love
the danger" (467).

Like all of the major hallucinations, this one mounts quickly to
the point of Bloom's complete destruction. The underlying logic of
the destruction and Bloom's escape from it can be clarified by strik-
ingly similar scenes from two other hallucinatory writers, Kafka
and Dickens. Kafka's brilliant short story "The Judgment" has
much the same movement and rhythm as the fantasies in "Circe."
In that story, Georg Bendemann, a conventional young bourgeois,
prepares to tell his aging and bedridden father of his forthcoming
marriage. But since marriage is the sign of the son's maturity and
therefore a sign of his usurping his father's position as the dominant male, Georg witnesses and then accedes to his father's wrathful accusation that he is a faithless and worthless son. The story
ends as Georg willingly follows his father's command that he
throw himself from a bridge. Georg Bendemann is, like Bloom,
willing, even eager, to throw off his stable, conventional demeanor
and accept his guilt-ridden image of himself. A scene which is
perhaps even closer to the logic of "Circe" is in *Great Expectations,*

the scene of Pip's confrontation with Orlick, his furtive alter ego. Orlick ties Pip to a ladder and then reveals that he was the assailant who struck Pip's sister years ago—an act for which Pip himself felt unaccountably guilty. It is a scene of revelation, as Pip gazes upon his own repressed hatred. But Pip does not suffer death at Orlick's hands, as Orlick threatens. Three young men, Herbert Pocket, Startop, and Trabb's boy, rush to the rescue, and the nightmare is dispersed. The rescue of Pip is not fortuitous; for, in the context of this scene, the three young men are as much projections of Pip's nature as Orlick is. If Orlick is representative of Pip's repressed hatred, the three young men are representative of Pip's fundamental decency and his saving self-awareness. In this scene, Dickens acknowledges the power of the dark forces, but he stops short of the masochistic temptation to define the self entirely in terms of its repressions.

Bloom's escape from his masochistic fantasy has the same psychological contours as the scene from Dickens. Bloom's masochism is a tendency, not a definition of his whole self. When it threatens complete dominance, he reaches out to clutch any scrap of self-esteem he can lay his hands on. He appeals to his recent feeding of the dog and to his attendance at Paddy Dignam's funeral, and these two small acts of goodness are enough to restore his balanced view of himself. The hallucination is dispelled. *"All recedes. Bloom plodges forward again"* (474).

Certainly nothing is resolved within the scope of this first major hallucination; as is the case throughout the day, Bloom does not respond directly to the central issue in his traumatic self-encounters so much as he changes the subject and reaffirms his identity on other grounds. We thus arrive again at two ways of viewing Bloom— and I do not think that Joyce gives us the evidence to decide upon one view as definitely more convincing than the other. On one hand, we may logically look at Bloom as a man traumatized so severely and so long that he will probably never act to change the premises of his life. His heroism consists in his ability to go through life with a keen and even refined sensuous enjoyment and with a compassionate but wary appreciation of human behavior—yet always subject to the attacks of his own neuroses which he must somehow evade. This is no mean view of heroism in the modern novel. On the other hand, we may look upon him as a man held back from self-fulfillment by one flaw which he must overcome if his life is to be considered truly successful. This latter reading obviously puts great emphasis upon the meeting with Stephen. These two readings of Bloom's character are by no means mutually exclusive, but they do occasionally come into conflict—especially in that Bloom's momentary victories in fending off any consideration of the problems surrounding his marriage make less likely any final solution of those problems. There is much the same ambivalence surrounding Bloom's more extensive hallucinations. Each of them is a separate test of his ability to respond and cope; Bloom is in a real sense successful in merely surviving each of his inner temptations. But, clearly, we may also look upon the *series* of hallucinations as a unified psychological process working toward some end, and even toward some ultimate solution. It is the latter possibility that I want to follow for the rest of the chapter. There is in fact a thread of continuity between the hallucinations: Bloom's increasingly intimate encounters with the dominating woman. Like certain fabled rivers, this ruling obsession disappears underground for long stretches, but it insistently reappears and finally reaches its goal in Bloom's vision of a living son.

Shortly after the first major hallucination ends, Bloom meets Zoe Higgins in the street outside Bella Cohen's brothel. In an act suggesting castration, Zoe slides her hand into Bloom's pocket and takes his potato from him—and we are again reminded of Joyce's characteristic reworking of Homeric temptation scenes. Unlike Ulysses, Bloom loses his *moly* and undergoes supreme humiliation before he regains his potato and his self-control.

Zoe triggers Bloom's second major hallucination with her remark, "Go on. Make a stump speech out of it" (478). The ensuing fantasy is an outgrowth of Bloom's conception of himself as social reformer and utopian—the Bloom who proposes "a tramline . . . from the cattlemarket to the river" (478). More broadly, this entire hallucination revolves around Bloom's status as a social being and concentrates upon his alternate self-conceptions as social leader and social pariah.

Bloom's rise to power in his utopian state is swift, as he becomes "emperor president and king chairman . . . . Leopold the First"

(482). One of Bloom's royal proclamations during his rise to power at first seems curious: "We . . . announce that we have this day repudiated our former spouse and have bestowed our royal hand upon the princess Selene, the splendour of night" (483). But Bloom's proclamation is not as curious as it may seem. His vision of himself as the potent and triumphant ruler of the new Bloomusalem depends upon his psychological suppression of Molly who, in the preceding hallucination, appeared in the threatening figure of Mrs. Yelverton Barry. This suppression of the female is of great importance in the ensuing sequence.

The first sign of a threat to Bloom's power comes from the man in the macintosh: "Don't you believe a word he says. That man is Leopold M'Intosh, the notorious fireraiser. His real name is Higgins" (485). Bloom immediately takes care of this threat—"Shoot him! Dog of a christian! So much for M'Intosh!"—but M'Intosh's charge contains within it the source of Bloom's fall from the utopian heights. M'Intosh the loner, devastated by the death of a beloved woman, is himself the solitary pariah Bloom later becomes in this sequence. But what exactly is the significance of "His real name is Higgins"? Ellen Bloom's maiden name was Higgins (682) and so, interestingly, is Zoe's. M'Intosh's charge reminds Bloom of a past which is feminine and Jewish.[8] (Bloom seems to recognize the charge of Jewishness when he responds by calling M'Intosh "dog of a christian.") This hallucination, then, which began in the context of Bloom yielding up his potato (itself a momento of his mother, "poor mamma's panacea") to a woman with his mother's

---

8. The character and the genealogy of Ellen Higgins Bloom are obscure. Although she was a Catholic when Rudolph Virag Bloom married her, there is a hint that her ancestry was Jewish. In "Ithaca," Ellen Higgins is described as "second daughter of Julius Higgins (born Karoly) and Fanny Higgins (born Hegarty)" (682). Morton P. Levitt ("The Family of Bloom," *New Light on Joyce from the Dublin Symposium,* ed. Fritz Senn [Bloomington: Indiana University Press, 1972], p. 144) has suggested that Ellen's father, né Karoly, was very likely a Hungarian Jew. Ellmann in the biography makes the same assumption: "They spoke of the various Jewish families whose names were mentioned in *Ulysses,* of one with the incongruous name of Higgins, whom Joyce had related to Bloom . . ." (*James Joyce* [New York: Oxford University Press, 1959] p. 257). If Ellen Bloom was of Jewish ancestry, she at first seems symbolically the focus for Bloom's reflections upon Jewishness, since one is born Jewish only if one's mother is Jewish—but, to add a final twist, Ellen's own mother does not seem to have been Jewish. Her ancestry thus works to make even more ambivalent Bloom's attitude toward his Jewish heritage.

name, comes to center upon those qualities Bloom inherited from his mother—femaleness and Jewishness. (Zoe, incidentally, like the madame of her brothel, is a Jewess.) The underlying logic of the rest of this hallucinatory sequence is precisely the logic underlying Bloom's most utopian scene earlier in the book, his confrontation with the Citizen in "Cyclops." For in that scene too, Bloom is reviled and cast out for being womanly and Jewish.

Bloom's fall from the height of his utopian power starts in earnest during his medical examination, when Dixon proclaims, "Professor Bloom is a finished example of the new womanly man" (493) and goes on to announce, "He is about to have a baby" (494). The female, earlier suppressed in Bloom's denial of his former wife, now reappears within Bloom himself. And it is immediately after the announcement of Bloom's femaleness and the birth of the eight children from Bloom's own womb that "A Voice" mysteriously asks: "Bloom, are you the Messiah ben Joseph or ben David?" (495). This complex linkage of female and Jewish qualities in Bloom's conception of himself is expressive of his problems as a reformer. Bloom's awareness of the need for social reform arises both from the unique perspective he has as a Jewish outsider and from a sensitivity and kindness which men such as the Nameless One in "Cyclops" jeer at as womanish. And obviously Bloom's sympathetic powers are also a weakness of a sort—even if of a very praiseworthy kind—since they are founded upon an awareness of human vulnerability. The very sensitivity which causes Bloom to champion social reform also makes him despairing of the possibility of carrying the ideas through to fulfillment.

The ending of this particular hallucination thus shows Bloom willingly accepting, even craving, the defeat of his own utopian self-image. As he is transformed into the Biblical scapegoat, he "[r]ubs his hands cheerfully" and exclaims with relief, "Just like old times. Poor Bloom!" (497). This is the idealist going forward to greet his foreknown and inevitable defeat, the Messiah accepting with relish his crucifixion.

The psychological process of this hallucination is not complete until Bloom reemerges into " reality," standing with Zoe before the door of Bella Cohen's brothel. If Bloom's dilemma within this hallucination grew out of the traits he inherited from his mother, his mood immediately after is that of his father, whose reaction to Ellen Higgins Bloom's death was suicide: "I am ruined. A few pastilles of aconite. The blinds drawn. A letter. Then lie back to rest" (499). It is only when Bloom sees that Zoe, the still-living Higgins woman, is interpreting his pessimism as a personal insult that he fully recovers himself: "I am very disagreeable. You are a necessary evil. Where are you from? London?" (500). And with this leveling-off, this more than usually fatigued expression of sympathy, Bloom regains his equilibrium.

And now Bloom and Zoe enter the brothel, Circe's palace. In the ensuing pages Bloom encounters the temptations of the flesh in the form of the prostitutes—and he resists them with great ease. As in the other Homeric temptation scenes, Bloom has no trouble avoiding the usual Dublin lotuses or sirens or witch's charms. "When you come out without your gun," he comically and wistfully remarks, as he remembers that he has disarmed himself for the hunt of big game by masturbating earlier (513). Just after entering the brothel, it is true, Bloom momentarily feels attracted to the prostitutes, as he *"stands, smiling desirously, twirling his thumbs"* (511). But just at this moment Lipoti Virag, Bloom's grandfather, enters the scene; he *"wears a brown macintosh. . . . In his left eye flashes the monocle of Cashel Boyle O'Connor Fitzmaurice Tisdall Farrell"* (511). Virag, who is to rescue Bloom from any true physical desire for the prostitutes, is the quintessence of the demotic outsider, represented in *Ulysses* by the man in the macintosh, Farrell, and at times Bloom himself. It is symptomatic of the "Circe" chapter—and the nature of Bloom's character—that a man wearing a brown macintosh, who represented Bloom's weakness in the previous fantasy, should prove his strength in this.

Lipoti Virag offers to his namesake a defense against the temptations of the prostitutes, in his distanced and cynical description of their charms: "Obviously mammal in weight of bosom you remark that she has in front well to the fore two protuberances of very respectable dimensions, inclined to fall in the noonday soupplate. . ." (513). Virag is perhaps the most grotesque character in "Circe" (and he makes perhaps the most esoteric allusion in

*Ulysses*—to Rualdus Columbus, the first anatomist ever to describe the clitoris)[9], but he is a recognizable part of Bloom, who looks on with shrewd suspicion even as he feels himself drawn toward a woman. Virag is a dirty old man—"dirty" clearly, "old" because he represents Bloom's ability to remember the past: "Exercise your mnemotechnic," says Virag, and Bloom replies, "The touch of a deadhand cures" (514). By exercising his mnemotechnic, by remembering, Bloom resists that temptation of the immediate present which the prostitutes represent. And yet, typically, Bloom's assertion of one faculty engenders its contrary. Virag retires for a moment and his romantic opposite, Henry Flower, appears (517). Once again in Bloom's character each statement breeds its counterstatement.

The Virag-Henry Flower sequence is not a complicated psychological process, as were his two earlier extended hallucinations, but instead a state of suspended attitudes, leading up to the central temptation of the chapter, represented in Circe herself, Bella Cohen. What follows is the most complex of Bloom's several major hallucinations, because he is here eyeball-to-eyeball with that dominant woman he created in Mrs. Yelverton Barry and her cohorts in his first hallucination and then attempted to suppress in the second. Bloom's initial reaction, clearly, is total collapse and self-abasement: "Exuberant female. Enormously I desiderate your domination" (528). Like Ulysses's crewmen, Bloom is transformed into an animal, but animality here is a metaphor not for brute lust but for craven fear: Bloom is first "sheepish" (527), then "cowed" (528). Bella so completely dominates Bloom because she represents that overbearing and irresistible life-force to which he has the reaction throughout the day, "Will happen, yes. Prevent. Useless: can't move" (67), and which he, along with Stephen, looks upon as feminine. Bella is so powerful because she elicits in its purest form that quality which appears to some extent in all of his hallucinations —his need to retire from all endeavor and to see all of his attempts at action as futile. Bloom satisfies this need as he once again be-

---

9. Robert M. Adams tracked down this and several hundred other out-of-the-way facts in *Surface and Symbol: The Consistency of James Joyce's "Ulysses,"* Galaxy Books (New York: Oxford University Press, 1967). I do not know whether I am more astonished at Joyce's curious learning or at Adams's energetic detective work.

comes womanly, now not to give birth but to adopt a submissive and masochistic role.

The sequence with Bella is unspeakably degrading, but there is something in it necessary to Bloom's psychological wholeness. As Bella transforms Bloom into a pig, he (Bello) says, "You will fall. You are falling. On the hands down!" (531). The motif of falling, which persists throughout the chapter (for example, Bloom's stumbling as he enters the brothel), has a particular significance in the context of "On the hands down!" This latter phrase is associated with Bloom's resolve to improve himself physically: "Must begin again those Sandow's exercises. On the hands down" (61); "Must take up Sandow's exercises again. On the hands down" (435). This is a quaint but apt image, a jocoserious image, of Bloom's progress through the book and through "Circe"—not the closed pattern of fall and redemption, the *felix culpa,* but the repetitive down-and-up of push-ups. Much the same point is implicit in Bloom's physical attitude once he has been transformed into a pig: ". . . *shamming dead with eyes shut tight, trembling eyelids, bowed upon the ground in the attitude of most excellent master*" (531). Once again the language of freemasonry is suggestive of ritual: Bloom's submission before Bella is a rite of passage, a psychologically necessary self-abasement before he can confront her openly later in the chapter.

Just before Bella entered the room, Bloom heard a man leaving the brothel and believed him to be Boylan. Bloom's reaction was Semitic and Masonic:

> (*In Svengali's fur overcoat, with folded arms and Napoleonic forelock, frowns in ventriloqual exorcism with piercing eagle glance towards the door. Then, rigid, with left foot advanced, he makes a swift pass with impelling fingers and gives the sign of past master, drawing his right arm downwards from his left shoulder.*) Go, go, go, I conjure you, whoever you are. (526)

The entire episode with Bella is a frantic and imperfect attempt to complete that exorcism. As this hallucination mounts toward its climax, Bella more and more insistently reminds Bloom of Molly and Boylan. In a rapid sequence (541–44), Bloom adopts those last-resort defenses he used earlier in the very worst hours of the day, but now they are of no avail. First, Bloom for a moment considers the possibility of returning to Molly: "Moll! I forgot! Forgive! Moll! . . . We . . . Still . . ." (541). Two times before, we have seen Bloom make this tentative mental proposal to himself to return to Molly (168, 285). But Bella cruelly implies that even those thoughts of return are false in a sense, for in those moments Bloom actually wishes to return to the pre-Rudy past with Molly instead of to the Molly of the present day: "No, Leopold Bloom, all is changed by woman's will since you slept horizontal in Sleepy Hollow your night of twenty years. Return and see" (542). Bella's words prompt Bloom actually to become Rip van Winkle and to attempt to return to the dead past. What he finds upon his return is his daughter Milly: the scene recapitulates those many moments earlier in the day when Bloom's thoughts of his daughter become a medium for his reunion with Molly in the earlier days of their marriage. But the words of Milly herself destroy this attempt to return to the past: "O Papli, how old you've grown!" (542). Deprived of this alternative, Bloom is helpless before Bella's reminders of Molly's adultery, and he collapses: "My will power! Memory! I have sinned! I have suff . . ." (544). Memory is the last faculty Bloom appeals to before he is completely overwhelmed. Unable any longer to appeal to the comfort of his younger and happier days with Molly, he dissolves before the prospect of confronting the tragic present. Within a short time, Bloom will attempt to confront the present state of affairs at 7 Eccles Street, but first he has a more roundabout response to Bella.

In her penultimate, taunting speech to Bloom, Bella-Bello tells him: "I can give you a rare old wine that'll send you skipping to hell and back" (543–44). As Weldon Thornton has noticed, this is a reference to Circe's instructions to Ulysses on the means of entering and emerging from the underworld.[10] Bloom has descended into hell and he now begins his reascent. Such are Sandow's exercises cosmically conceived. Bloom ascends, in fact, to heaven, or to a pseudo-heaven, after this harrowing of his own soul, as he encounters the nymph, Bella's antitype. This wild swing from self-

10. Weldon Thornton, *Allusions in "Ulysses"* (Chapel Hill: University of North Carolina Press, 1961), p. 406. Like other Joyce critics, I am grateful for and considerably indebted to Thornton's work.

abasement to mawkish idealism is partly explained earlier by Mulligan in his medical report on Bloom: "He is prematurely bald from selfabuse, perversely idealistic in consequence . . ." (493). Bloom is a self-abuser in several senses of the term; and when borne down by Bella's dominant female power, he seeks an ideal perverse in its otherworldly unreality. Precisely this pattern underlies Bloom's earlier flight from Boylan at the end of "Lestrygonians"—toward the holy, holeless goddesses in the museum.

The source of the nymph's temptation is obvious. Unable to respond to a woman who is sexually threatening, Bloom creates an image of sexless female purity. And yet this temptation does not have a deep appeal for Bloom. The nymph exists only in a dialectical relation to Bella; Bloom creates the nymph only as a refuge, and he very soon emerges from this refuge to opt once more for the here and now. His rejection of the nymph appears first in the popping off of his trousers' button; when Bloom attempts to pursue the ideal, his pants fall down. He is more forcefully victorious when he seizes the nymph's hand, which holds the castrating knife—for both Bella and the nymph threaten to unman Bloom. And here is the crux of the Bella-nymph sequence. Bloom is capable of responding to Bella's sexual threats, but only when he transforms her into her antitype. He is capable of affirming warm fullblooded life, but he cannot completely address himself to the problems which Bella has raised in his mind. Bloom's victory here, like most of his victories, is compounded of affirmation and evasion.

It is a victory nonetheless. Bloom emerges from his experience with the nymph with that perky energy which is usually his after he has just been through one of his full emotional cycles. He retrieves his potato from Zoe and takes charge of Stephen's money. And, interestingly, he now regards Bella with that appraising scrutiny which shows that he is Lipoti Virag's true grandson: "(*Composed, regards her.*) *Passée.* Mutton dressed as lamb. Long in the tooth and superfluous hairs . . ." (554). As always, Bloom's ability to return to the world of concrete particulars allows him an escape from the specters of his unconscious.

This entire sequence, the central sequence in "Circe," is the clearest instance of Bloom's psychological activity within the chapter. Pushed toward one neurotic extreme, Bloom repeatedly creates an image of its contrary, its antitype, which saves him from the nightmare of his own history. This bouncing back and forth between extremes gives to Bloom's character its unique dynamism and its characteristic energy. But (and the operative word in any description of Bloom must be *but*) this bouncing back and forth between extremes is also a symptom of Bloom's inability to confront the neurosis in the middle. He must create Bello and the nymph because he cannot confront the reality of Molly.

The Bello-nymph sequence was Bloom's attempt to exorcise the thought of Molly and Boylan without actually confronting it. But the exorcism was unsuccessful: shortly after Bloom's emergence from that fantasy, Zoe and Florry whisper and giggle together (563), and Bloom, reminded of Miss Douce and Miss Kennedy whispering together in the Ormond bar at four o'clock, at once visualizes the adulterous meeting between Molly and Boylan. In his attempts to appease or suppress the image of the dominant woman throughout this chapter, Bloom has been moving closer to this scene. He has abased himself before the dominant woman, created an image of himself which was independent of her threatening power, and fled toward masturbatory idealism in order to escape Bella's insistence that he fully confront Molly's adultery and all it entails. Now he seems to approach the thing itself, the traumatic center—but again he sidesteps the issue. He overleaps the guilt he feels toward Molly, and the deep suffering which he himself endures, by indulging in his most extreme form of masochism: like Stephen's Shakespeare, he becomes both bawd and cuckold, as he ushers Boylan in to commit adultery with Molly. Bloom has leaped beyond his actual crisis—his inability to confront sexuality with his wife because of the death of a son—and has sought relief in the last psychological defense: vicarious participation in the adultery itself: "Show! Hide! Show! Plough her! More! Shoot!" (567).

This terribly comic and immensely pathetic scene is the only one of Bloom's major hallucinations which has no immediate resolution, no creation of an alternate psychological state which will cancel out or balance the central horror. One reason for this failure is that Bloom is here confronting not one of the subjective phases of his own consciousness, but an irreducible fact which cannot be denied—just as Stephen will shortly confront the inescapable fact of his mother's death. Bloom's fantasy ends instead in an image which suggests his paralyzed helplessness before this, the central event around which today's consciousness has been constructed:

> *Stephen and Bloom gaze in the mirror. The face of William Shakespeare, beardless, appears there, rigid in facial paralysis, crowned by the reflection of the reindeer antlered hatrack in the hall.* (567)

A paralyzed Shakespeare, untaught by the wisdom he has written or the laws he has revealed, reappears as a fit emblem for both Bloom and Stephen. Bloom's fantasy of Boylan and Molly has shown the point of blockage past which he cannot progress without some assistance from beyond the boundaries of his own mind. At the end of the chapter, prompted by his feeling for Stephen, Bloom will finally resolve this fantasy, just as Stephen's Shakespeare tried to do, by creating the necessary alternate image of his own son.

"Circe" is, of course, for the most part Bloom's chapter. He continues in this chapter to exfoliate before our eyes and to take on greater complexity and depth. Stephen, on the other hand, until quite late in the chapter is present mainly as a rapt and inward-turned voice. Up until his vision of his mother, he is perhaps more opaque to us here than anywhere else in the book. When he does speak, he treads over the ground he has already covered during the day. He is, though, very consciously repeating himself—as consciously, anyhow, as his drunkenness will allow. Indeed, in spite of his drunkenness, he is seldom in the book so intent as he is here upon transcending the limits of his own ego and, at least intellectually, grasping that condition of maturity which he has longed for through the day. Here in the street of harlots, Stephen unconsciously reaches out toward the Semitic man he dreamed of the night before.

The kernel of much of Stephen's thought in "Circe" is contained in a very rich (and very difficult) passage which he speaks just after Bloom's arrival. This is another of those passages in which many strands of the novel come together to form one central ganglion:

> The reason is because the fundamental and the dominant are separated by the greatest possible interval which . . . . (*With an effort.*) Inter-

val which. Is the greatest possible ellipse. Consistent with. The ultimate
return. The octave. Which. . . . (*Abruptly.*) What went forth to the
ends of the world to traverse not itself. God, the sun, Shakespeare, a
commercial traveller, having itself traversed in reality itself, becomes
that self. Wait a moment. Wait a second. Damn that fellow's noise in
the street. Self which it itself was ineluctably preconditioned to become.
*Ecco!* (504–505)

Just before these speeches, Stephen has said, *"Jetez la gourme.
Faut que jeunesse se passe"* (504)—"Sow your wild oats. Youth
must pass." (Later, at the end of "Eumaeus," he will sing an air,
*Youth here has End.*) Stephen's major preoccupation is with his
own initiation rite, the passage from youth to maturity. He creates
two metaphors for this passage. The first is the metaphor of the
octave—the reduplication of the same note at a higher level—a
metaphor for the generation of a new self different from yet consistent with the old. A few pages later, Stephen's alter ego, Philip
Drunk, makes the meaning of the metaphor clear: "If I could
only find out about octaves. Reduplication of personality" (518).
The octave becomes a musical version of Stephen's formulation
earlier in the day, "I am another now and yet the same" (11).
The second metaphor, more implicit, is that of the elliptical path of
a comet. Stephen is asking himself how far a comet may go without
breaking out of orbit and hurtling into space. ("Is the greatest possible ellipse. Consistent with. The ultimate return.") How far,
that is, can the personality indulge in extreme behavior before it
loses touch with its own reality? An important implication of Stephen's thought here is the fear that his current manic behavior
might take him too far, beyond the point of returning to his own
essential identity.

This concern with reduplication of personality brings Stephen
back to his teleological vision of the self's development which he
proclaimed in "Scylla and Charybdis." The self, in going forth to
encounter experience, eventually meets and becomes itself. Otherwise stated, the self, through the sheer process of living, will
realize the potential self it now contains. Stephen makes this prediction and mentions "a commercial traveller" just at the moment
when Bloom, the commercial traveler who proffers possibilities for
Stephen's future, enters the room.

Stephen's thought is further complicated by his mention of God as a being who, "having itself traversed in reality itself, becomes that self." The movement of God toward the realization of His own identity is the movement of all history toward the Apocalypse. "All history moves towards one great goal, the manifestation of God," said Mr. Deasy. "That is God," replied Stephen. "A shout in the street" (34). This dialogue from earlier in the day underlies Stephen's words as he speaks of God's movement towards self-actualization and exclaims, "Damn that fellow's noise in the street." There is a very nice depiction of Stephen's dilemma here: he is simultaneously declaring the goodness of immersion in experience, the medium of change, and irritatedly rejecting the noise in the street, the very symbol of that medium. He is expending all his intellectual energy to rise above the very process in which he believes he must immerse himself.

Stephen's consideration of the self's evolution is continuous with the imagery of the Apocalypse which immediately follows these reflections. Just after Stephen's speech, Florry—with "obese stupidity" but also with great relevance—says, "They say the last day is coming this summer" (505). Immediately, Reuben J. Antichrist and a figure named The End of the World cavort through the room. It is in this context that Stephen turns around, notices Bloom, and says, "A time, times and half a time"—a Biblical formula expressing the span of time that must pass before the Day of Judgment (506).[11] Stephen's personal Apocalypse and Day of Judgment are to come when he goes forth to meet and become the reality which is Bloom.

Stephen makes a tentative groping toward a Bloom-like experience of reduplicated personalities as he muses upon the pair of glasses he broke yesterday and the pair he broke sixteen years before on the cinder-track at Clongowes: "Must get glasses. Broke them yesterday. Sixteen years ago. Distance. The eye sees all flat. . . . Brain thinks. Near: far. Ineluctable modality of the visible" (560). Stephen's words here, an almost verbatim transcription of his thoughts on stereoscopic vision in "Proteus," describe vision which is both inward and outward and both spatial

11. *Ibid.*, p. 390.

and temporal. A temporally stereoscopic vision is one which can perceive the world from two points in time, the present and the past of, say, sixteen years ago. Put more simply, this kind of vision brings the benefit of past experience to bear upon the present—as Bloom does a thousand times during the day. A few pages later, Stephen even has one of those half-conscious intuitions (which are numerous in "Circe") of the relation between his own attempts to assimilate experience and Bloom's:

### BLOOM

(*Points to his hand.*) That weal there is an accident. Fell and cut it twenty-two years ago. I was sixteen. . . .

### STEPHEN

See? Moves to one great goal. I am twentytwo too. Sixteen years ago I twentytwo tumbled, twentytwo years ago he sixteen fell off his hobby-horse. (563)

But Stephen's description of stereoscopic vision is another of those many instances in which his conception of his own problem is in advance of his ability to act. His brain may think, "Near: far," but in fact his past experience is never far; it is always so close as to threaten to engulf him at any moment. There is good reason for him to say, *Faut que jeunesse se passe* and for him to sing, hopefully, *Youth here has End.* No author is less romantic in his descriptions of youth than Joyce. His young characters, with Stephen chief among them, need the sheer experience of living long enough for their past to fall back into a recognizable and intelligible pattern. This is not a flight from the past; it is an approximation of Proust's assertion that one must lose the past in order to regain it.

It is important to notice the placement of Stephen's and Bloom's gaze into the mirror and the reflection of the paralyzed Shakespeare. The reflection appears just after Bloom's fantasy of Molly's adultery and just before Stephen's hectic burst of activity which leads to the dancing and ends in Stephen's vision of his dead mother. The reflection of the paralyzed Shakespeare, that image of blocked and baffled creativity, is placed between the two hallucinations which describe the deepest neuroses of the two men—neuroses which the two men seem incapable of dissipating without some kind of outside help, perhaps from one another.

The woman who rises through the floor to confront Stephen is May Dedalus, but she is more than that; she is Stephen's vision of the archetypal woman. The imagery surrounding her makes her reminiscent of the woman Stephen sees and recreates in "Proteus" —the woman who represents the cycle of "Bridebed, childbed, bed of death, ghostcandled" (47–48). May Dedalus carries the trappings of the bride: "a wreath of faded orange blossoms and a torn bridal veil" (579); she reminds Stephen of the childbed and of gestation: "Years and years I loved you, O my son, my firstborn, when you lay in my womb" (581); and, needless to say, her very appearance is a visible sign of what she expresses in her hauntingly simple words: "I was once the beautiful May Goulding. I am dead" (580). There is something archetypal too in the name Joyce assigns her—not May Dedalus, but The Mother. She is the Magna Mater, the womb from which man issues and the tomb to which he returns: "All must go through it, Stephen. . . . You too. Time will come" (580). And she is another more specific but still archetypal mother: "Inexpressible was my anguish when expiring with love, grief and agony on Mount Calvary" (582). She is Mary, the Mater Dolorosa, grieving for her son.

It has frequently been noted that there is a sort of psychological seepage between Bloom and Stephen in this chapter, as one of them echoes a thought or speech belonging to the other earlier in the day.[12] This is especially true of Stephen's scene with his mother. "I pray for you in my other world," says May Dedalus (581). Her phrasing recalls Martha's slip of the pen in her letter to Bloom: "I called you naughty boy because I do not like that other world" (77). In "Hades" Bloom unknowingly gave the one possible response to May Dedalus as he thought of Martha's phrase while he stood beside Paddy Dignam's grave: "There is another world after death named hell. I do not like that other world she wrote. No more do I. Plenty to see and hear and feel yet" (115). May Dedalus echoes another of Bloom's thoughts at the cemetery when

---

12. The most obvious of these echoes have to do with the talismanic phrase Stephen reads at the bookstall in "Wandering Rocks": "*Se el yilo nebrakada femininum!*" (242). In "Circe," the phrase is echoed twice in Bloom's fantasies (440, 553).

she says, "More women than men in the world" (580). In "Hades," Bloom gazes at Mrs. Dignam and reflects, "There are more women than men in the world" (102). And finally, Stephen, frightened and panicked, tries to exorcise his mother: "The corpse-chewer! Raw head and bloody bones!" (581). Once again the phrasing is Bloom's. In "Lestrygonians," he remembers his experience at the cattle market:

> Plup. Rawhead and bloody bones. Flayed glasseyed sheep hung from their haunches, sheepsnouts bloodypapered snivelling nosejam on sawdust. (171)

None of these echoes is really very surprising—the phrases are all common enough—but in the aggregate the phrases suggest the most essential difference between Bloom and Stephen. In each of these cases, Bloom's use of the phrase is demonstrative of his ability to assimilate the experiences—death, grief, slaughter—which terrify and paralyze Stephen.

Stephen's ultimate reaction to his mother is superficially Bloomian. Rather like Bloom assuming many forms within his own fantasies, Stephen passes rapidly through a series of attitudes including Satan's *Non serviam!* (582) and Siegfried's *Nothung!* (583); but for once, Stephen the *littérateur* is almost purely the *poseur*. There is a frantic search for the right pose here (compare Bloom's similar search when he is accosted by the night watch), but Stephen's appeal is to a Mulligan-like posturing, not to any attitude derived from within. Each of Stephen's assumed attitudes, including the striking of the "chandelier," is a regression to adolescent Byronism.

Back out in the street, Stephen runs afoul of Private Carr, who insists that Stephen has insulted his girl, Cissy Caffrey. The ensuing argument is an appropriate climax to "Circe" and, indeed, to *Ulysses* as a whole. Two men argue over a dubious point of honor while the woman, the source of the squabble, stands in the background. It is a fair paradigm of the relationship between the sexes in *Ulysses*—between the feckless, bitter men and the women who wait. Like "Oxen of the Sun," this scene reminds one of Joyce's affinities to Sterne, and especially to that scene in *Tristram Shandy* in which the men—Uncle Toby, Walter Shandy, and Dr. Slop— argue obsessively and tediously while, upstairs, Mrs. Shandy is about the real business, giving birth to Tristram. The scene is also reminiscent of Mr. Deasy's paranoid insistence that women—Eve, Helen of Troy, Eva MacMurrough—are the cause of all of men's strife and war (34–35). And actually, Mr. Deasy is fairly representative of the male characters in the novel, who expend their energies in belligerent, self-assertive actions to insulate themselves from the threatening female.

Stephen, still in flight from his own threatening female, creates new images in a frantic attempt to objectify and appease his guilt. One of these is the image of Ireland herself: *"The women's heads coalesce. Old Gummy Granny in sugarloaf hat appears seated on a toadstool, the deathflower of the potato blight on her breast"* (595). This is the Poor Old Woman, that image of Ireland which Stephen in "Telemachus" projected onto the milkwoman. In her claim of allegiance from Stephen, however, Old Gummy Granny is another version of the Mater Dolorosa: "the deathflower of the potato blight on her breast" is identical with May Dedalus's cancer.

Stephen makes one final effort to rid himself of this image of the devouring mother—"The old sow that eats her farrow" (595). He creates a Black Mass, celebrated by Mulligan and Haines upon the body of another symbolic woman: *"On the altarstone Mrs Mina Purefoy, goddess of unreason, lies naked, fettered, a chalice resting on her swollen belly"* (599). This is Stephen's attempt to out-Mulligan Mulligan, but there is a vast difference between Mulligan's insouciant blasphemies and the hysterical blasphemies of the Black Mass. In his attempts to break free from the maternal past— May Dedalus, the Poor Old Woman, and Mother Church—Stephen succeeds only in creating an image of neurotic defilement.

Stephen's mental creation of the Black Mass is demonstrative of his dichotomous nature. Bloom has many sides, but Stephen has only two. "With me all or not at all," he cries in the presence of his dead mother (582), and the phrase is an index of his rigid, either/ or personality. While Bloom carries about within himself many subsidiary personalities, Stephen in "Circe" generates only two—

the bipolar Philip Drunk and Philip Sober. This rigid dualism within Stephen explains his difficulties in returning from the depths of the unconscious into the world of present and concrete reality.

Many critics have praised Stephen for the new maturity he shows in one of his remarks in these pages: "(*He taps his brow.*) But in here it is I must kill the priest and the king" (589). Certainly this remark displays a new awareness that the forces he seeks to escape are not simply external authorities but a part of the very tissue of his character. Still, one may question the wisdom of saying this in the presence of a drunk English private, whose reaction—"I'll wring the neck of any fucking bastard says a word against my bleeding fucking king" (597)—might have been anticipated. The symbolism of Private Carr's victory over Stephen is clear: in reascending from the depths of the unconscious, Stephen walks directly into the fist of the institutionalized superego.

Stephen's conscious experience in "Circe" ends with a phantasmagoric sequence of attempts to escape the mother. He is unable to make the transition between that struggle and the surface level of consciousness which contains within it an unpleasantly drunk English soldier. Bloom, on the other hand, is quite lucid in the final stages of "Circe," and his lucidity rescues not only Stephen but himself as well. Bloom's lucidity, his awareness of the reality surrounding him, has been throughout most of the chapter a form of security, a refuge from nightmare. Again and again, he has escaped from his hallucinations by fastening his attention upon the present reality surrounding him. But especially toward the end of "Circe," the relation between "reality" and "hallucination" is reversed: Bloom's actions within the concrete, "real" world have the effect of changing his unconscious image of himself. His hallucinations, as we have seen, have led finally to an impasse; but as he begins to act consciously on behalf of Stephen, he unknowingly begins to confront the central problem underlying the hallucinations. Unable, within the scope of his hallucinations, to imagine himself as a mature man, he now begins impulsively to act as a father. Only after this action, after his *experience* of the paternal role, is Bloom granted his final vision of Rudy.

First, it is Bloom who shows the proper way to bring an ashplant into contact with a chandelier:

### BLOOM

(*His hand under the lamp, pulls the chain. Pulling, the gasjet lights up a crushed mauve purple shade. He raises the ashplant.*) Only the chimney's broken. Here is all he . . .

### BELLA

(*Shrinks back and screams.*) Jesus! Don't! (584)

Poor Bloom, of course, has no intention of striking Bella with the upraised ashplant; but this vignette nevertheless has a significant resemblance to Homer's portrayal of Ulysses standing victorious over Circe. Back within the sphere of mundane action, Bloom defeats Bella by exerting powers she is apparently unaccustomed to in her clients: his care for Stephen, his shrewd business sense, and his possession of a bit of secret knowledge which he picked up earlier from Zoe and which now acts as another form of *moly:*

### BLOOM

(*Urgently.*) And if it were your own son in Oxford! (*Warningly.*) I know.

### BELLA

(*Almost speechless.*) Who are you incog? (585)

Stunned, Bella falls back before Bloom's knowledge of her son at Oxford. She is unaware that the force of Bloom's behavior arises from his corresponding care for a son. The answer to her question is that Bloom is an incognito father. The point here is not merely symbolic. Bloom has begun, finally, to act the role of the protective father which he has heretofore been unable even to imagine.

Out in the street, Bloom is more successful than Stephen in reascending from the depths of the unconscious. Like Stephen, who encounters Private Carr, Bloom encounters the institutional authorities—the watch—who ask him the same question that initiated his psychological deterioration near the beginning of the chapter: "Name and address" (603; cf. 455). But the demand now does not disturb Bloom; he is concerned with the present need to assist Stephen. It is always a happy moment for Bloom when he is able to devote himself to the particular problem at hand, and he does so now by enlisting the aid of Corny Kelleher. Kelleher has an unexpected prominence at this point in the narrative, serving as the *deus ex machina* who delivers the unconscious Stephen from the inquiries of the night watch. Both here and elsewhere in the book, he is one of those minor characters who give off an inexplicable aura of mystery (in "Wandering Rocks" he briefly stands in for Joyce himself). Robert M. Adams gives us the hint that we need for reading the significance of the character in the present scene: Kelleher in "Hades" is parallel to Charon, the mediating figure between the known world and the unknown infernal regions.[13] Kelleher ferries bodies to the cemetery, and he is in touch with the underworld of the police and with the goings-on in nighttown. He is the perfect symbolic personage to escort Stephen and Bloom back to the surface of consciousness—as if Dante and Virgil had escaped from the inferno by having Charon row them back across the Acheron.

Again embarrassed by the idea of being seen in nighttown, Bloom explains his presence to Kelleher: "Matter of fact I was just visiting an old friend of mine there, Virag . . ." (606). It is a richly suggestive alibi: Bloom has been visiting his own dead. His entire experience in "Circe" has been a confrontation with his own sense of worthlessness and futility—feelings that are epitomized for him in the memory of his father who killed himself rather than face the loneliness of life after Ellen Bloom's death. The sense of impotence and despair has been Bloom's chief inheritance from his father, and "Circe" has dramatized his ability to absorb it, to accept his own feelings of futility and yet still commit himself to the world of broken lampshades. Insofar as Bloom is able at last to accept the unhappy circumstances of his father's death, he is able to move tentatively toward the vision of himself as a father.

And so, as Corny Kelleher drives off—"I've a rendezvous in the morning. Burying the dead" (607)—Bloom and Stephen are left alone in the street. Stephen, still unconscious, murmurs words from Yeats's "Who Goes with Fergus?" and *"turns on his left side, sighing, doubling himself together"* (608). Murmuring the song his

13. Robert M. Adams, "Hades," *James Joyce's "Ulysses,"* ed. Hart and Hayman (Berkeley: University of California Press, 1974) p. 95. See also Adams's comments on Kelleher in *Surface and Symbol*, pp. 195–97.

mother asked him to sing as she lay on her deathbed, Stephen curls up in the fetal position and is at peace. The moment is reminiscent of moments in Lawrence, when the man, after having expended all his energy in demonstrating his independence of the woman, finally accedes to her power. Stephen's action here will also be Bloom's last action in the book, as he rests in bed with Molly, "the child-man weary, the manchild in the womb" (737).

Bloom stands over Stephen's prostrate body and recites fragments from the Masonic Master's oath to the Entered Apprentice:

> (*He murmurs.*) . . . swear that I will always hail, ever conceal, never reveal, any part or parts, art or arts . . . (*He murmurs.*) in the rough sands of the sea . . . a cabletow's length from the shore . . . where the tide ebbs . . . and flows . . . . (609)

This is Maturity welcoming Youth into the order—and uttering the welcome, paradoxically, just when Youth has regressed to the fetal stage. The paradox here is at the center of the initiation rite: Bloom's life is a constant dramatization of the truth that one may become reconciled to experience only by submitting to it—just as Stephen may achieve transcendence over the crippling force of his mother only by acknowledging the power of *amor matris,* subjective and objective genitive. Bloom also pays tribute to the process of submission through the phrasing of the Masonic oath. The imagery makes Bloom the drowned man himself, subdued to the element he works in.

The rite of gaining maturity through submission to process is evident also in the final psychological event of the chapter: Bloom's vision of Rudy, as he stands guard over Stephen. Bloom's vision of his son—and therefore his vision of himself as a father—is possible only after he has actually undergone the experience of protective fatherhood in his care for Stephen. This is important to understand. Bloom has not projected a filial image upon Stephen and therefore gone to the trouble of helping him. Instead, he has followed Stephen for reasons which he himself has not understood—"What am I following him for?" he asks himself very early in the chapter (452)—and now, having acted as father, he is capable of seeing himself as a father. Unable to think his way through to a logical solution to his central problems, Bloom has within "Circe" moved *through experience* toward that solution.

Once again, D. H. Lawrence, in many ways Joyce's antagonist in the modern novel, offers an interestingly analogous scene. In *Sons and Lovers,* Paul Morel forms a close bond with Baxter Dawes, the husband of Paul's lover, Clara. Both men draw strength from this relationship: Baxter is finally able to return to his wife, and Paul, at least to an extent, moves toward an acceptance of his mother's approaching death. The surrogate father-son relationship gives both men some of the strength they need to overcome their crippling fear of women. The bond between Bloom and Stephen also has its psychological basis in a fear of woman, and especially woman in her maternal aspect. Their responses to the maternal woman are so different because each of them possesses in extreme and excessive form what the other lacks. Bloom willingly capitulates to his conception of himself as a naughty boy, overborne by the power of a mature woman and incapable of a full relationship with her; Stephen hysterically and unsuccessfully resists her domination and proclaims himself independent of her power. But by the end of "Circe" there is already some sign of the resolution of this severe dichotomy. Curling up in the fetal position, Stephen unconsciously yields to the mother he has resisted all day long; and in the two chapters following "Circe" he at least begins to appreciate the value of Bloom's ability to submit. More extraordinarily, Bloom has already begun to take on some of Stephen's qualities by the end of "Circe." Through his final confrontation with Bella Cohen and through his protection of Stephen in the street, Bloom has begun to assert himself—there is none of his characteristic deference in these actions—and to assume the paternal role. Through the roundabout psychological journey of "Circe," he earns and receives a vision of his son.

## Chapter VI

# Stephen, Bloom, and Beyond: Two Cases of Mistaken Identity

The gradual tendency of *Ulysses* to move away from the character's consciousness toward a form imposed from without by the author-artificer constitutes the largest and most obvious formal movement within the book. But the movement, of course, is not simply formal: through the creation of matrices capable of containing and describing both Stephen and Bloom, Joyce stresses the complementarity, the consubstantiality, of his two heroes. Twice within the book Joyce does even more than this. He cuts away at the discrete identities of his two characters until they begin to merge into the background mass of humanity in Dublin and, even beyond this, into the background of humanity itself. By placing his characters in contexts in which it is possible to mistake one person for another, Joyce hints that Stephen and Bloom are not quite as exceptional as we may have thought and that it might have been possible to have had one of the other Dubliners as the hero, since many people on June 16 are making their own odysseys and since to an extent mythic patterns are recapitulated by everyone. Joyce never quite claims in *Ulysses* that everyone is willy-nilly a hero—there is still very definitely the dimension of moral choice in Joyce's portrayal of Bloom, as there is not in the later, more universal figure of

Earwicker—but twice Joyce at least raises that possibility. The two chapters based on mistaken identity are "Wandering Rocks" and "Eumaeus."

## "Wandering Rocks"

> Corny Kelleher closed his long daybook and glanced with his drooping eye at a pine coffinlid sentried in a corner. He pulled himself erect, went to it and, spinning it on its axle, viewed its shape and brass furnishings. (224)

Corny Kelleher's listless ease in the second section of the "Wandering Rocks" chapter corresponds to what most readers conceive of Joyce himself as doing in the chapter. Like Kelleher—who has secret knowledge of what goes on in Dublin, who is in charge of the dead in this funereal city, and who acts as the *deus ex machina* at the climax of the novel's action in "Circe"—Joyce seems to close for awhile his own "long daybook" and to spin *Ulysses* itself "on its axle, view[ing] its shape and brass furnishings."

This enigmatic chapter, which opens the second half of *Ulysses*, has elicited a fair amount of illuminating commentary, but little of it goes very far beyond the early remarks of Stuart Gilbert and Frank Budgen.[1] Basically, their information is as follows. The chapter consists of nineteen sections. Temporal relations among the sections are indicated—although in a perplexing way—by the frequent insertion of a detail from one scene of action into another. The opening and the closing sections represent the Church (Father Conmee) and the State (the viceregal cavalcade), the two orders of authority which, it seems, do little to order the lives of the Dubliners. The chapter, moreover, is marked by what appears to be a curious perversity of Joyce's: the reader must beware, lest he be led into errors concerning the identity of the characters. Thus Mr. Bloom the dentist is not our hero; the woman who thinks "Too much mystery business in it. Is he in love with that one, Marion?" (229) is not Martha Clifford, but Boylan's secretary Miss Dunne,

---

1. See the sections on "Wandering Rocks" in Gilbert's *James Joyce's "Ulysses,"* revised ed. (New York: Alfred A. Knopf, 1952) and Budgen's *James Joyce and the Making of "Ulysses"* (Bloomington: Indiana University Press, 1960).

who is reading about a mystery and a Marion in *The Woman in White;* Alderman Cowley is not Father Cowley, nor is Father Cowley a priest. Two other critics have added single valuable remarks. Foster Damon has noticed that the passage from *Cymbeline* which Stephen quotes at the end of "Scylla and Charybdis" is followed in Shakespeare's play by lines which anticipate the ensuing events of "Wandering Rocks":

> Laud we the gods,
> And let our crooked smokes climb to their nostrils
> From our blest altars. Publish we this peace
> To all our subjects. Set we forward: let
> A Roman and a British ensign wave
> Friendly together: so through Lud's town march . . . .

As Damon notes, the harmony of Rome and Britain ironically forecasts the oppression of Roman church and English state which Joyce represents in the figures of Father Conmee and Lord Dudley the viceroy.[2] Finally, William York Tindall has found a small but significant pattern within the chapter's total design: Mr. Bloom looks at a copy of "Aristotle's *Masterpiece*" (235) and Stephen looks at "the eighth and ninth books of Moses" (242). The two heroes thus grope toward one another, each of them examining a book which symbolizes the other.[3]

From these observations we can summarize what seems to be the general view of the chapter. Neither Church nor state coherently holds together the directionless wanderings of the Dubliners; instead, the citizens are engaged in random motion. If there is any order at all, it can be perceived, and in a manner constructed, only by the synthetic imagination of the reader. That imagination seizes upon the complementarity of Bloom and Stephen and, beyond this, attempts to see as a whole the city which Joyce presents as so many fragments. The unity which the imagination constructs is pitted against the formlessness of the city itself. The art of reading "Wandering Rocks" is thus the art of reading *Ulysses,* of perceiv-

---

2. Foster Damon, "The Odyssey in Dublin [and Postscript, 1947]," in *James Joyce: Two Decades of Criticism,* ed. Seon Givens (New York: Vanguard Press, 1963), p. 241.

3. William York Tindall, *A Reader's Guide to James Joyce* (New York: Farrar, Strauss, 1959), p. 181.

ing the whole organism which is at once concealed by and conveyed through surface fragmentation.

But once it has been suggested that the chapter has an imaginative order existing in counterpoint to the formless wanderings of the characters, it is still difficult to determine what that imaginative order *is*. It is, I believe, an order based on *coincidence*—one of Mr. Bloom's favorite words. There are two forms of coincidence in the chapter. There is the pervasive coincidence of event, as a detail from one section wanders into another: "Corny Kelleher sped a silent jet of hayjuice arching from his mouth while a generous white arm from a window in Eccles street flung forth a coin" (225). And there is coincidence of identity, in those moments when one character can be mistaken for another: the two Mr. Blooms, for example, or the two darkbacked men scanning books. Taking the coincidences of event, the reader may, if he wishes, reconstruct the chapter's chronology from its scattered pieces. (Clive Hart has actually done this by walking along all the routes described in the chapter and timing them.)[4] The more profitable inquiry, however, concerns the coincidences of identity, the myriad resemblances the Dubliners have to one another.

Resemblances are, of course, by no means confined to "Wandering Rocks." Throughout the day, Bloom and his fellow citizens notice that one person looks like another. Bloom, for example, thinks of Martin Cunningham: "Sympathetic human man he is. Intelligent. Like Shakespeare's face" (96). This resemblance seems fortuitous—less significant, certainly, than the resemblance Bloom and Stephen have to Shakespeare when they gaze into Bella Cohen's mirror in "Circe." A similar instance occurs early in "Aeolus," when Red Murray remarks that William Brayden looks like Christ and Bloom adds that Brayden also resembles Mario, the nineteenth-century tenor (117). Again, there seems to be an important distinction between superficial likeness and Bloom's own comic-heroic resemblance to Christ. But these apparently trivial likenesses should give us pause. It is, after all, part and parcel of Joyce's mythic method that minor resemblances frequently point toward a deep-running parallel. Cunningham's superficial resemblance to Shake-

---

4. Clive Hart, "Wandering Rocks," *James Joyce's "Ulysses,"* ed. Hart and Hayman (Berkeley: University of California Press, 1974) pp. 181–216.

speare and Brayden's to Christ raise at least the possibility that characters other than Bloom are enacting mythic patterns similar to Bloom's.

In "Proteus," Stephen considers in quite different terms this very relation between an underlying mythic reality and its multiple manifestations, when he thinks of the presence of Christ in different celebrations of the Eucharist:

> Dan Occam thought of that, invincible doctor. A misty English morning the imp hypostasis tickled his brain. Bringing his host down and kneeling he heard twine with his second bell the first bell in the transept (he is lifting his) and, rising, heard (now I am lifting) their two bells (he is kneeling) twang in diphthong. (40)

Stephen's idea of hypostasis is an instance of one of Joyce's most persistent imaginative and philosophical patterns: the enduring presence of an underlying myth which appears refracted in multiple form in the phenomenal world. Later, in the "Circe" chapter, the idea of hypostasis (in Stephen's sense of the word) is applied directly to the conception of character, when Elijah proclaims, "Florry Christ, Stephen Christ, Zoe Christ, Bloom Christ, Kitty Christ, Lynch Christ, it's up to you to sense that cosmic force" (507). In "Wandering Rocks," Joyce explores the relation of phenomenon to hypostasis, of individual identity to "that cosmic force," as he suggests that a number of characters other than Bloom participate in the universal experience—the book's "hypostasis"—which Bloom exemplifies.

It will be useful, then, to think of the mistaken identities in "Wandering Rocks" as something more than the coy attempts of Joyce to mislead the reader. As *Ulysses* pauses at its center, Joyce places Bloom in the context of the entire city, and the resulting juxtapositions establish a number of strong similarities as well as differences between Bloom and his fellow citizens. In sorting out those similarities, let us begin with a character who is generally recognized as bearing a likeness to Bloom, Tom Kernan.[5]

5. Kernan's resemblance to Bloom has been mentioned by Kenner (*Dublin's Joyce,* Beacon Paperbacks [Boston: Beacon Press, 1962] pp. 253–54), Adams (*Surface and Symbol,* p. 51n.), and Hart (*James Joyce's "Ulysses,"* ed. Hart and Hayman [Berkeley: University of California Press, 1974] p. 192). Goldberg (*The Classical Temper* [New York: Barnes and Noble, 1961] p. 123) denies that there is a significant resemblance.

Earlier in the book, in "Hades," Joyce sketched in a few brief
strokes to characterize Kernan. (He is also, of course, the major
character of "Grace" in *Dubliners*.) Tom Kernan is a pompous
man whom Martin Cunningham satirizes for his use of certain
phrases, especially "trenchant rendition" and "retrospective arrangement" (91). It is significant that Cunningham feels free to
ridicule Kernan in the funeral carriage: he considers Kernan an
outsider and therefore someone he can safely satirize among
cronies. Kernan's outsidership comes in part from his being a con-
verted Protestant—like Bloom, whom he accompanies to the grave-
side, Kernan is unfamiliar with Catholic ritual: "The others are
putting on their hats, Mr Kernan said. I suppose we can do so too"
(105). At the cemetery, Bloom obscurely feels a kinship with this
fellow outsider and sees a sign of that kinship in Kernan's eyes
(very much as he saw it in Dlugacz's in "Calypso"): "Secret eyes,
secret searching eyes. Mason, I think: not sure. Beside him again.
We are the last. In the same boat" (105).

In "Wandering Rocks," we are for a short while actually within
Kernan's mind. In this brief passage he seems more smugly self-
satisfied than Bloom, but the rhythm and tone of his thoughts increase the similarity already established in "Hades." Like Bloom,
he is a "knight of the road" (240), and he shares with Bloom at
least a rudimentary shrewdness and self-awareness necessary for
the commercial traveler. This short sampling of Kernan's stream
of consciousness provides a strong clue as to the significance of his
resemblances to Bloom: in the short space of only half a page he
three times thinks of the general idea of false appearances and mistaken identities. First he admires the second-hand coat he is wearing: "Some Kildare street club toff had it probably. John Mulligan,
the manager of the Hibernian bank, gave me a very sharp eye yesterday on Carlisle bridge as if he remembered me" (240). Kernan,
who is in many ways like Bloom, interestingly raises the question of
likeness, resemblance, disguise. His thought here is, in its modest
way, continuous with Stephen's concern with the disguises of the
self as it evolves through time, and with the more pervasive theme
of the mythic past dressed in the lowly disguise of the present.
Kernan's thoughts coincide more closely with this theme when he
remarks smugly, "Must dress the character for those fellows"
(240). Here he directly echoes one of Mulligan's remarks which

sticks in Stephen's mind as a Mulligan-leitmotif: "God, we'll simply have to dress the character" (17, 41). The echo of Mulligan is very much to the point, since it recalls Mulligan's ability—as "mercurial Malachi"—to adopt any role suitable to his audience. (Mulligan, of course, appears in "Wandering Rocks." Having disguised himself earlier in the day as Stephen's ally against Haines, he now disguises himself as Haines's against Stephen.) Finally, Kernan makes his own mistake in identifying someone: "Is that Lambert's brother over the way, Sam? What? Yes. He's as like it as damn it. No. The windscreen of that motorcar in the sun there. Just a flash like that. Damn like him" (240). Kernan's brief section thus points up in a number of ways the relation between role and essential identity. Through his own thoughts on mistaken identity he adds substantially to the chapter's dominant motif. More interestingly, through his unknowing resemblance to Bloom, he becomes for a moment another embodiment of the hero.

If Kernan is somewhat like Bloom in this chapter, that is in part because Joyce has adopted a bird's-eye view of his many characters, and the resultant distance obscures some of the more significant differences. The book-reading Bloom and Stephen, for example, *resemble* one another in their physical actions more in this chapter than anywhere else in the book. (The resemblance is even more marked in our first glimpse of Bloom. "A darkbacked figure under Merchants' arch scanned books on the hawker's car" [227]: here he is totally anonymous, indistinguishable from the other darkbacked figure.) It is also in this chapter that Lenehan says, "There's a touch of the artist about old Bloom" (235), with the effect of again blurring the sharp distinction between the two heroes. In the context of "Wandering Rocks," the otherwise commonplace observation that Bloom and Stephen are alike takes on added significance. In this chapter, their similarity is subordinate to a larger pattern of resemblance of which they are only constituent parts.

Does "Wandering Rocks," then, urge us to see each of the Dubliners as potentially the same kind of shabby hero as Bloom? Certainly the chapter goes further in that direction than does any other chapter in the book: various characters we occasionally sense to be alternate versions of Bloom—not only Kernan but also M'Coy and M'Intosh—drift through the chapter. But what of Lenehan, Father Conmee, Lord Dudley? The chapter is the focus

of what constitutes heroism in *Ulysses*. Is heroism perfectly demo-
cratic in the book—is Bloom Everyman even to the extent that *any*
other character might have been chosen as the hero? Or is Bloom a
hero because he has certain qualities of spirit which he shares with
a number, but a very limited number, of fellow citizens? We find
the answer, I believe, by examining that curious person Almidano
Artifoni.

A close look at "Wandering Rocks" reveals that there are two
sections which have no cross-references to other sections, VI and
XVII. Artifoni is in both of these sections and, interestingly, the
chapter itself closes with "the salute of Almidano Artifoni's sturdy
trousers swallowed by a closing door" (255). His progress can be
plotted with some certainty. In VI he talks with Stephen in front of
Trinity College and then dashes off in vain pursuit of the Dalkey
tram. Having missed the tram, he apparently decides to walk home.
In XVII, we catch a very brief glimpse of him as he passes Holles
Street, so he is headed in the general direction the Dalkey tram
would have taken. Finally, at the close of the chapter, he reaches
his destination, presumably his home, on Lansdowne Road.[6]

Artifoni seems an eccentric and especially noticeable detail in
the total pattern of "Wandering Rocks." His wanderings are not
"timed" by the other sections, and his final appearance gives him
an important position in the chapter's structure. His significance
becomes clear only when we recognize Joyce's allusion here: Artifoni's meeting with Stephen in section VI recalls in many details
Dante's encounter with Brunetto Latini in *Inferno*, XV. In both
cases, the younger man talks with his former teacher who gives
him kind, paternal advice. Both dialogues are in Italian. Both
interviews are concluded as the teacher runs off in haste—Brunetto
Latini to rejoin the company of the damned, Almidano Artifoni to
hail the Dalkey tram. Here are the two concluding passages:

> Then he turned about and seemed like one of those that run for the green
> cloth in the field at Verona, and he seemed not the loser among them,
> but the winner.[7]

6. Adams shows that Benedetto Palmieri, a probable model for Artifoni, did indeed live
at 14 Lansdowne Road (*Surface and Symbol*, pp. 71–72).

7. Here and in a subsequent quotation from the *Paradiso* I have used the translation of
John D. Sinclair (Oxford: Oxford University Press, 1939–1946).

Almidano Artifoni, holding up a baton of rolled music as a signal, trotted
on stout trousers after the Dalkey tram. In vain he trotted, signalling in
vain among the rout of barekneed gillies smuggling implements of music
through Trinity gates. (229)

Artifoni's baton might appear to be a musical conductor's, but it is
more appropriately a runner's. And, making his way through the
"barekneed gillies," he is like one on the field at Verona, where the
runners were naked. Although Ser Brunetto seems the winner,
Artifoni loses his race with the tram: but even here the parallel is
eventually fulfilled. While every other character in the chapter
dawdles, moves about aimlessly, or walks *toward* a destination,
Artifoni is alone in finally *reaching* his destination.

One effect of this allusion is to reinforce the parallel between
Stephen and Dante—and to give the parallel what is perhaps its
most important detail. Stephen himself is aware of his own affinity
to the Florentine exile and several times makes the comparison
explicit.[8] In "Telemachus" he thinks bitterly of Mulligan: "He
wants that key. It is mine, I paid the rent. Now I eat his salt bread"
(20). The allusion here is to Cacciaguida's prediction of Dante's
exile in *Paradiso*, XVII: "Thou shalt prove how salt is the taste
of another man's bread and how hard is the way up and down another man's stairs" (*Paradiso*, XVII, 58–60). In "Aeolus" Stephen
compares the light and beautiful rhymes of Dante to his own heavy
lines (138). And, most to the point, Stephen once thinks of Ser
Brunetto himself and quotes from *Il Tesoro*, the book which Ser
Brunetto in the *Inferno* commends to his pupil Dante: "*E quando
vede l'uomo l'attosca*. Messer Brunetto, I thank thee for the word"
(194). In other ways, Stephen closely resembles Dante—above all
in his proud aloofness and in his desire to chronicle the history and
gossip of the city from which he is (or feels himself to be) exiled.

The beauty of the allusion lies in great part in Joyce's characteristic reworking of the noble pathos of Dante's scene. Ser
Brunetto is a damned man among damned men, and yet he rises
above the torments of his existence: even in Hell, "he seemed not

8. Thornton lists the overt references to Dante in *Allusions in "Ulysses"* (Chapel Hill:
University of North Carolina Press, 1961). Howard Helsinger discusses Stephen's relation
to Dante in *Stephen Hero* and the *Portrait* in "Joyce and Dante," *ELH*, xxxv (1968).
591–605.

the loser among them but the winner." Dante's character has an integrity which transcends his place among the damned. Artifoni has the same quality, but set in a jocoserious key: in the city of the damned he behaves at first with fatherly care and then with a persistence and energy made comic by the missed tram and the sturdy trousers.

It is this plucky, unflappable comic heroism which pairs Almidano Artifoni with Bloom: they are both wandering men, stymied by comic obstacles but determined to get home. Artifoni is one kind of alien, an Italian, and Bloom is another, a Jew. (Both men even carry batons in their races through Hell. To Artifoni's "baton of rolled music" compare Bloom's "newspaper baton" [85].) Artifoni briefly serves as a father to Stephen in the afternoon; and it is a striking detail that the only place we see him between Trinity College and Lansdowne Road is Holles Street, where later Bloom will begin serving as a father to Stephen. And at Holles Street there occurs an incident which clinches the identity of Artifoni as surrogate-Ulysses, alternate Bloom. There, as Artifoni passes safely by, Cashel Boyle O'Connor Fitzmaurice Tisdall Farrell bumps into the blind stripling—in front of "Mr Bloom's dental windows" (250). Artifoni, the Ulysses figure for the moment, succeeds in bypassing the clashing rocks.

But these details of circumstance are secondary to the most important similarity between Artifoni and Bloom. Both men are unabashed and generous in their advice to Stephen—and Stephen in turn is more easy and natural with these two men than with anyone else he meets during the day. The details of the Brunetto Latini episode thus fall into place. Stephen's spiritual father lives among the damned in this city of the dead, but in his humanity the spiritual father is superior to his surroundings. Stephen, like Dante, stands on the margin and observes; Bloom and Artifoni, like Brunetto Latini, are doomed to the perpetual infernal round, but they pause to assist and advise Stephen.

The case of Almidano Artifoni helps to clarify Joyce's strategy in "Wandering Rocks." In this chapter Joyce lightly suggests the possibility in several characters of the forms of experience which his book traces more extensively in the particular characters of Leopold Bloom and Stephen Dedalus. But these possibilities are not evenly parceled out. The figures who stand out most prominently against the background of Dublin are the aliens: Bloom the Jew, Kernan the Protestant, Artifoni the Italian, Stephen the self-styled exile. They all have an alertness, a sharpness of the senses, which separates them from the drugged state of the more purely indigenous Dubliners. Even so undistinguished a figure as Kernan has a nervous energy to his stream of consciousness which is altogether lacking in the torpid, institutional thinking of a man such as Father Conmee.

The concealed pattern of "Wandering Rocks" is thus a part of the book's strong defense of the exile. It is a paradox of the chapter and of the novel as a whole that the Everyman-figures, the characters most sharply attuned to the book's underlying mythic patterns, are themselves outsiders, on the periphery of the human community. These are men who resemble the Moses of Taylor's speech in "Aeolus": in the land of the Pharaoh they keep their own faith. In fact, it is worth mentioning that the name of Moses is itself a wandering rock in the chapter. The name of Moses is cut loose from its moorings and drifts through the chapter as a reminder of the creed of the exile—in Ned Lambert's exclamation, "Mother of Moses!" (232), in "Marcus Tertius Moses' sombre office" (233), in the "Moses' beard" of old Russell the lapidary (242), and in Stephen's "eighth and ninth book of Moses" (242).

In the *Odyssey,* Circe tells Ulysses of two routes back to Ithaca— one between Scylla and Charybdis, the other through the Wandering Rocks. Paired with the preceding chapter, "Scylla and Charybdis," Joyce's own "Wandering Rocks" stands as an example of the alternative route, the route not taken.[9] "Scylla and Charybdis," containing Stephen's Shakespeare theory, dramatizes the exclusive process of driving inward, to find universal laws illustrated in the life of one man. It is the technique of *Ulysses* itself, which seeks to find in the life of a single man on a single day the totality of human myth. "Wandering Rocks," on the other hand, is panoramic: in its third-person narrative, in its naturalistic bias, and in the very scope of its portrait of the citizens of Dublin, it is the closest thing in *Ulysses* to the traditional novel. Joyce briefly pauses at the center of *Ulysses* and considers the possibility of an alternative route—

9. David Wykes has made a similar observation in "The *Odyssey* in *Ulysses," Texas Studies in Literature and Language,* x (1968), 311.

and even glances at a few of the characters who might have been
alternative heroes. Then, to the tune established by Almidano
Artifoni's music, he returns in "Sirens" to the particular case of
Mr. Bloom.

## "Eumaeus"

"Eumaeus" has not been a very popular chapter among the
critics, and the reasons for its low rank are clear: the complaint is
common that the chapter is a dead spot in which nothing happens
at great length. Walton Litz calls the chapter a failure, a glaring
example of the dangers of Joyce's imitative styles; the fatigued,
bored style of the chapter, Litz implies, is all too likely to fatigue
and bore the reader.[10] This objection is perhaps unanswerable—
unless by the answer that the style has its own exquisite humor. Two
of Joyce's greatest successors, in fact, have found the "Eumaeus"
style attractive for its attempt at precision and its conclusion in
muddledom. In *Ada,* Nabokov calls attention to the inspired ba-
nality of the "Eumaeus" style.[11] Much more pervasively, Beckett's
narrators from *Watt* onward have a close resemblance to the
"Eumaeus" narrator: they are painfully solicitous in their efforts
to convey information and woefully confused about the whole
thing.[12]

Even if the style of "Eumaeus" can be reasonably defended, the
charge remains that the chapter is an anticlimax, a disappointing
drop after the visionary ending of "Circe." But "Eumaeus" has its
own climaxes which arise from the meaningful confusions and slips
of the tongue which proliferate in the chapter. Such confusions and
slips create an interesting referential slipperiness which is surprisingly anticipatory of the drunken-dreamy shifts of identity in

10. A. Walton Litz, *The Art of James Joyce: Method and Design in "Ulysses" and
"Finnegans Wake"* (London: Oxford University Press, 1961), p. 45.
11. Vladimir Nabokov, *Ada, or Ardor: A Family Chronicle* (New York: McGraw-Hill,
1969), p. 181.
12. For an especially nice instance of the "Eumaeus" style in Beckett, see Molloy's
description of his two bad legs in the Evergreen Black Cat edition of *Three Novels by
Samuel Beckett,* p. 77. To this, compare the discussion of Corley's ancestry, *Ulysses,*
pp. 616–17.

*Finnegans Wake*. The chapter fuzzes edges and blurs distinctions to such an extent that the characters, losing their sharp outlines, mingle with the heroic or mythic figures—Ulysses, Christ, Parnell—who usually appear in *Ulysses* only in the dim background. The most significant "event" of the chapter is made possible by this merging of identities: projecting himself into the story of Parnell's affair with Kitty O'Shea, Bloom arrives at a tentative idea for resolving his own marital dilemma.

Tindall has pointed out that a recurrent situation in "Eumaeus" involves the difficulty or impossibility of determining a given character's identity.[13] What is the genealogy of Lord John Corley? Was Fitzharris/Skin-the-Goat really the driver of the car involved in the Phoenix Park murders? A look at some of these cases of confused identities will lead to some interesting discoveries about Joyce's use of mythic and historical parallels. A good place to begin is with the character of W. B. Murphy, the "redbearded bibulous individual, a portion of whose hair was greyish, a sailor, probably" (622). Tindall has pointed out that Murphy shares with Bloom the qualities of Ulysses; but in fact Murphy is, at least superficially, far more Ulyssean than Bloom.[14] Murphy is a sailor (probably) just off the threemaster *Rosevean*. He has been away from home, wife, and son for seven years. He speaks of events of ten years before (when Troy fell and when Murphy observed one Simon Dedalus's marksmanship in Stockholm). Like Ulysses, Murphy has had divine protection throughout his travels—a "pious medal" (638) and a talisman to show to the natives: "Glass. That boggles 'em. Glass" (626). But, most significantly, Murphy, one suspects, is someone else. In a chapter of false and mistaken identities, Murphy is the major example of the dubiously identified character. He himself acknowledges that he is wearing another man's clothes (630–31), and Bloom notes that the South American postcard is addressed, not to Murphy, but to one A. Boudin. Like Ulysses coming to Eumaeus's shieling, Murphy seems disguised, sailing under false colors, and like Ulysses he tells what at least seem to be tall tales. He has seen a crocodile bite an anchor and he has seen Peruvian maneaters;

13. Tindall, *A Reader's Guide to James Joyce*, p. 215.
14. *Ibid.*

but although he claims to have traveled the world over, he evades Bloom's questions about nearby Gibraltar.

As a part of the Homeric parallel, Murphy represents Odysseus Pseudangelos, the lying Ulysses who tells false stories in order to disguise his return to Ithaca.[15] He is thus a kind of alter ego to Bloom, the prudent and resourceful Ulysses. But there is more to Murphy than this. Murphy is a master tale-spinner, and Joyce compares him with a considerable number of narrators other than Ulysses. Twice (636, 659) he is called the "ancient mariner"— and the dead allusion revives at least enough to remind us that the Ancient Mariner was above all a storyteller. His initials are those of Yeats, who is referred to simply as W. B. in "Scylla and Charybdis" (188). And Stephen establishes a vague connection between Murphy and another storyteller when he remarks to Bloom, "Shakespeares were as common as Murphies" (622). Another allusion, this one made by Murphy himself, links him with the writer whom Joyce considered his major rival for supremacy in the modern novel, Proust:

> —I seen a Chinese one time, related the doughty narrator, that had little pills like putty and he put them in the water and they opened, and every pill was something different. One was a ship, another was a house, another was a flower. Cooks rats in your soup, he appetisingly added, the Chinese does. (628)

Although Joyce claimed that he never read much of Proust's work, he must inevitably have read—or had read to him—the tea and madeleine episode in *Swann's Way,* the most famous passage in Proust's novel:

> And just as the Japanese amuse themselves by filling a porcelain bowl with water and steeping in it little crumbs of paper which until then are without character or form, but, the moment they become wet, stretch themselves and bend, take on colour and distinctive shape, become flowers or houses or people, permanent and recognisable, so in that moment all the flowers in our garden and in M. Swann's park, and the water-lilies on the Vivonne and the good folk of the village and their little dwellings

15. Gilbert, *James Joyce's "Ulysses,"* p. 361.

and the parish church and the whole of Combray and of its surroundings, taking their proper shapes and growing solid, sprang into being, town and gardens alike, from my cup of tea.[16]

The echo of Proust is of especial interest, since the Proustian moment, in its bringing of the past directly into the present, contributes to one of the essential themes of "Eumaeus," the return of the past.

There is one final analogy made between Murphy and another narrator. In a chapter concerned with mysterious disguises and the possibility of revelation, perhaps Murphy's most significant act is his baring of his chest. He draws aside his shirt and thereby reveals one of the classic means of establishing identity, a tattoo.[17] Here, it would seem, the "real" Murphy is revealing himself. The tattoo is an odd assemblage of emblems: "on top of the time-honoured symbol of the mariner's hope and rest, they had a full view of the figure 16 and a young man's sideface looking frowningly rather" (631). Murphy goes on to gloss his tattoo, the art of one Antonio:

> —See here, he said, showing Antonio. There he is, cursing the mate. And there he is now, he added. The same fellow, pulling the skin with his fingers, some special knack evidently, and he laughing at a yarn.
>
> And in point of fact the young man named Antonio's livid face did actually look like forced smiling and the curious effect excited the unreserved admiration of everybody, including Skin-the-Goat who this time stretched over.
>
> —Ay, ay, sighed the sailor, looking down on his manly chest. He's gone too. Ate by sharks after. Ay, ay.
>
> He let go of the skin so that the profile resumed the normal expression of before.
>
> —Neat bit of work, longshoreman one said.
>
> —And what's the number for? loafer number two queried.
>
> —Eaten alive? a third asked the sailor.
>
> —Ay, ay, sighed again the latter personage, more cheerily this time, with some sort of a half smile, for a brief duration only, in the direction of the questioner about the number. A Greek he was. (631–32)

16. *Swann's Way*, trans. C. K. Scott Moncrieff, Modern Library Books (New York: Random House, 1956), p. 66.
17. Identification by means of a tattoo is mentioned later, p. 650.

All the details of the scene come together in one radiant image which suggests that Murphy is not only the Ancient Mariner, Yeats, Shakespeare, and Proust; he is also James Joyce. It is the very essence of Stephen's Shakespeare theory that the artist creates his work out of his own soul. James Joyce, who begins with the auto-biographical Stephen Dedalus—a young man "looking frowningly rather"—reworks his own personality to yield also Leopold Bloom, who cannot be better characterized than by the phrase "forced smiling." (In *Finnegans Wake,* Shem's creative act strongly recalls Murphy's tattoo: "this Esuan Menschavik and the first till last alshemist wrote over every square inch of the only foolscap available, his own body" [*FW,* 185].) And 16? In the next chapter it is revealed that the relation between Bloom and Stephen can be expressed as a function of the difference between their ages—sixteen years. Murphy himself, to be sure, does not spell out the meaning of his tattoo thus clearly. In response to the various questions about his tattoo, he replies only with the cryptic "A Greek he was"—just as Joyce hints at the meaning of his own work by entitling it *Ulysses.* In essence, Murphy is a witty portrait of the artist as James Joyce. He combines a pretense of self-revelation with a great deal of shamming—and more than a little concealed humor at the effect he is having on his audience.[18]

Of all the characters who briefly serve as stand-ins for Joyce himself in *Ulysses,* Murphy is by all odds the most interesting. Murphy gives off an air of fakery, but he seems the sort of fake capable of throwing off his lowly disguise and revealing a surprisingly grander true identity. Amid the woozy prose and the chameleonic identities of "Eumaeus," the shabby, crapulous figure of Murphy gives a wink and suggests that he is the representative of the archetypal narrator, the incarnation of a narrative impulse continuous from Homer to Joyce. The reader is certainly familiar with this sort of thing by now in *Ulysses:* all sorts of Dubliners bear unexpected resemblances

18. The Murphy-Joyce similarities could be extended further. Murphy, who is "a bit of a literary cove, in his own small way," "uses goggles reading" (659). At one point Bloom suspects the worst about Murphy: "He might even have done for his man, supposing it was his own case he told as people often did about others . . ." (636). This kind of displaced autobiography resembles the art of Joyce and Stephen's Shakespeare. I am indebted to Jon Megibow, a graduate student at the University of Virginia, who pointed out to me some of the Murphy-Joyce correspondences.

to other persons. (Such resemblances, as we have just seen, are part of the central meaning of "Wandering Rocks.") What is most interesting about "Eumaeus" is that the characters themselves in their fatigued condition begin to see the same sorts of resemblance.

A minor instance of such identity confusion occurs as Bloom listens to Murphy telling the Bloom-Murphy-Ulysses story of returning home. Bloom projects himself into Murphy's story and, through this means of identifying with another's plight, begins his chapter-long movement toward a plan for coping with Molly and Boylan. As Bloom listens to Murphy's story of return, he begins to think of various sorts of "return" possible for himself. At first he thinks of a Bloom-like Rip van Winkle returning home to find himself displaced (624). But soon he is musing upon another kind of return—a return to the past, a rebirth. He has the notion of taking a vacation ("constituting nothing short of a new lease of life") to "delightful sylvan spots for rejuvenation" and specifically to his and Molly's Howth, "a favourite haunt with all sorts and conditions of men, especially in the spring when young men's fancy" (627–28). In these musings upon rejuvenation there is a vague reformulation of the immediate conditions of his life going on within Bloom's mind. Such a reformulation is perhaps clearest in his surprising plan for a singing-tour with Molly:

> No, something top notch, an all star Irish cast, the Tweedy-Flower grand opera company with its own legal consort as leading lady as a sort of counterblast to the Elster Grimes and Moody-Manners, perfectly simple matter and he was quite sanguine of success, providing puffs in the local papers could be managed by some fellow with a bit of bounce who could pull the indispensable wires and thus combine business with pleasure. But who? That was the rub. (627)

This plan has the same unreal air as most of Bloom's plans for trips or business ventures; there will never be a Tweedy-Flower grand opera company. What is surprising is the organization of this hypothetical company. Bloom, not Boylan, is to be the impresario, and the "fellow with a bit of bounce who could pull the indispensable wires" has a strong resemblance to Stephen (or to Bloom's idea of Stephen), with his contacts at the newspaper office. This somewhat

daft plan is Bloom's first mental attempt to enlist Stephen in helping him to drive out the suitors.

Murphy's storytelling momentarily provides Bloom with a screen
onto which he can project his own dilemma and reach some resolution, however inadequate. This kind of projection, the substitution
of one person's story for another's, is inevitably frequent in "Eumaeus," a chapter in which neither the narrator nor the characters is
very capable of keeping one thing separate from another. The
clearest instance of this form of confusion occurs just after Bloom
has told Stephen of his encounter with the Jew-baiting Citizen.
Stephen's reply (in this, like the Citizen's angry taunts) suggests
Bloom's virtual identification with Christ: *"Ex quibus,* Stephen
mumbled in a noncommittal accent, their two or four eyes convers-
ing, *Christus* or Bloom his name is, or, after all, any other, *secundum
carnem"* (643). The reader of *Ulysses* may frequently mistake
Bloom for Christ, but until this point in the book it has not been
possible for one of the characters to do so. Stephen's linkage of
Bloom and Christ, moreover, resonates beyond "Eumaeus" and
anticipates the climactic recognition scene in "Ithaca":

> What were Stephen's and Bloom's quasisimultaneous volitional quasi-
> sensations of concealed identities?
> Visually, Stephen's: The traditional figure of hypostasis, depicted by
> Johannes Damascenus, Lentulus Romanus and Epiphanius Monachus
> as leucodermic, sesquipedalian with winedark hair.
> Auditively, Bloom's: The traditional accent of the ecstasy of catas-
> trophe. (689)[19]

The passage from "Ithaca" beautifully supplements the passage
from "Eumaeus" and suggests the continuity of an association of
ideas existent in Stephen's mind since the early hours of the day. In
"Proteus" Stephen pondered the relation between the phenomenal
world and its underlying substance. He used the word "hypostasis"
(40) to denote the underlying presence of Christ in the Eucharist.
In the same chapter, the Homeric *"oinopa ponton,* a winedark sea"

---

19. The "traditional figure of hypostasis" is Christ, and Stephen's three authorities
purportedly described His physical appearance. See Adams, *Surface and Symbol,* pp.
138–39.

(47) was a fit emblem for the flux of the phenomenal world.
Stephen's haphazard identification of Bloom with Christ in "Eumaeus" is the catalyst which fuses these two contrary conceptions—
so that when, finally, he comes closest to recognizing his spiritual
father in "Ithaca," his perception suggests the Incarnation itself.
In Bloom, Stephen glimpses the union of those qualities which, in
the opening chapters, were presented as the incompatible opposites
of Mulligan and Deasy: he has a Pisgah sight of the self capable of
maintaining its integrity even as it is immersed in the protean world.

Stephen mistakes Bloom for Christ. But the most important confusion within the syntactical murk of "Eumaeus" occurs when
Bloom mistakes himself for Parnell. Included among the many
varieties of "return" treated within "Eumaeus" is the belief that
Parnell, like other saviors, will one day reappear. "One morning
you would open the paper, the cabman affirmed, and read, *Return
of Parnell*" (648). (Earlier in the day, Mr. Power at the cemetery
alluded to this resurrection of the Chief: "Some say he is not in that
grave at all. That the coffin was filled with stones. That one day he
will come again" [112].) What Parnell's return means in the context of "Eumaeus" is quite complex. Bloom dismisses the notion that
Parnell is still alive, but he is fascinated by the myth of the Chief's
resurrection. And well he should be, for Parnell, like Murphy, is
Bloom's alter ego. Notice, for example, how clearly Parnell, like
Murphy and Bloom, resembles Ulysses:

> Of course nobody being acquainted with his movements even before,
> there was absolutely no clue as to his whereabouts which were decidedly
> of the *Alice, where art thou* order even prior to his starting to go under
> several aliases such as Fox and Stewart, so the remark which emanated
> from friend cabby might be within the bounds of possibility. Naturally
> then, it would prey on his mind as a born leader of men, which un-
> doubtedly he was, and a commanding figure, a sixfooter or at any rate
> five feet ten or eleven in his stockinged feet, whereas Messrs So-and-So
> who, though they weren't even a patch on the former man, ruled the
> roost after their redeeming features were very few and far between. It
> certainly pointed a moral, the idol with feet of clay. (649)

The analogies with Ulysses are numerous: compare Ulysses's many
disguises (Fox and Stewart), his superiority to his successors the

suitors (Messrs So-and-So), the scar on his foot (the idol with feet of clay).

An intriguing sentence—and the key to the place of Parnell in "Eumaeus"—comes shortly after the passage just quoted: "You had to come back—that haunting sense kind of drew you—to show the understudy in the title *rôle* how to" (649). Bloom is Parnell's understudy, and he projects himself into the Parnell story as thoroughly as into Murphy's account of his voyages. He is especially drawn to the memory of Parnell's affair with Kitty O'Shea, an affair which resembles his own marital situation:

> Whereas the simple fact of the case was it was simply a case of the husband not being up to the scratch with nothing in common between them beyond the name and then a real man arriving on the scene, strong to the verge of weakness, falling a victim to her siren charms and forgetting home ties. (651)

It is interesting, of course, to see Bloom sympathizing so completely with the adulterer, and we might reasonably assume that Bloom is revealing here his covert admiration of Boylan. But Bloom's participation in the Parnell story drives even deeper than that. He is sympathizing with a once-vigorous man who has now fallen into obscurity. The Parnell story is a part of a grander past—some "twenty odd years" ago (649), or, in another dimension, just before Ulysses set off for Troy. In identifying with a hero who has disappeared from the scene, Bloom is really identifying with his own former self before Rudy's death.

Bloom can continue this sympathetic identification with Parnell, however, only up to a certain point. Yes, the old Parnell was magnificent, but . . . no, it would not be wise for him to come back. Three times, in fact, Bloom pulls up short and concludes that Parnell would do well to remain dead: "he thought a return highly inadvisable, all things considered" (649); "Still, as regards return, you were a lucky dog if they didn't set the terrier at you directly you got back" (650); "And the coming back was the worst thing you ever did because it went without saying you would feel out of place as things always moved with the times" (651).

In Bloom's mind we are seeing the most intense consideration he has made all day—whether conscious or not—of returning to nor-mal sexual relations with Molly. But there is still that nagging sense of futility at the idea of becoming again his wife's vigorous lover. Then, by one of the most fortunate associations of ideas of the en-tire day (Kitty O'Shea-the king of Spain's daughter-Molly [652]), Bloom shows Molly's photograph to Stephen. Bloom is seeking help from Stephen in a newly conceived campaign against Boylan and the photograph is a lure, intended to draw Stephen to Eccles Street. The nature of Bloom's scheme emerges when he returns to the Parnell story, now with a significantly altered perspective. He dis-approves of the cabmen who make a lewd joke of Parnell's affair—

> it being a case for the two parties themselves unless it ensued that the legitimate husband happened to be a party to it owing to some anony-mous letter from the usual boy Jones, who happened to come across them at the crucial moment in a loving position locked in one another's arms drawing attention to their illicit proceedings and leading up to a domestic rumpus and the erring fair one begging forgiveness of her lord and master upon her knees and promising to sever the connection and not receive his visits any more if only the aggrieved husband would over-look the matter and let bygones be bygones, with tears in her eyes, though possibly with her tongue in her fair cheek at the same time, as quite possibly there were several others. (655)

Even though Bloom's skepticism cuts short this fantasy (but not before he imagines the amusing and very unlikely picture of Kitty-Molly as "the erring fair one begging forgiveness of her lord and master"), the shift in his thought is decisive: he now identifies, not with the adulterer, but with the victorious husband. We are on the threshold of Bloom's consciousness here, but it is nevertheless clear that he has the idea of bringing in Stephen, the "boy Jones," to serve as a practical obstacle to Molly's affair with Boylan. The plan is weak, and in the end it fails to materialize; still, it is an instance of a kind of thinking totally absent from Bloom's mind before the encounter with Stephen.

Bloom's mental participation in the Parnell story is a timid adumbration of a solution to his life-problem. Usually, when Bloom is compared to some mythic or historical personage, he is oblivious to the comparison: the point is made by the author and understood by the reader outside Bloom's consciousness. (Stephen, on the other hand, is more often aware of the parallels since he frequently makes them himself.) Here, however, Bloom *is* aware, because he has actually projected himself into the Parnell-Kitty-Captain O'Shea triangle. The Parnell parallel, like the Christ parallel earlier, has risen to the surface of the narration. The fuzzy, fatigued style of "Eumaeus" allows the distinction between realistic foreground and mythic background to waver, at times almost to disappear.

Moreover, Joyce's use of the figures of Christ and Parnell within "Eumaeus" teaches us the sort of "significance" we can expect from the meeting between Stephen and Bloom. "Eumaeus" is full of cases of mistaken identity, and certainly Bloom and Stephen mistake each other, in the chapter's bittersweet comedy of faulty communication. (Things don't get very much better even in "Ithaca.") Instead of seeing one another, each of the men sees an image which is a crystallization of his own needs. Stephen sees a secular version of the Incarnation, a man who can subdue himself to the world of Dublin and yet maintain his integrity. Bloom sees in Stephen the one thing which he himself so painfully lacks, a youthful figure for whom the future is still full of possibilities. That much each of them sees; what they do with their insights we will never know.

## Chapter VII

# Style as Obfuscation

Style, writes Proust, is a matter not of technique but of vision. Joyce, we might say, offers the antitype of that statement. Proust and Joyce set forward to encounter the predicament of modernist aesthetics in radically differing ways, although their assumptions were very much the same. Proust, discounting the possibility—and, in the end, the value—of setting forth a narrative of objective reality, committed himself to the creation of a single style which would convey his own intensely personal perspective upon reality. The creed of Proust's art is that the artist can communicate only once he has acknowledged the necessarily subjective nature of his own perceptions and has committed himself fully to the expression of that subjectivity through the creation of a personal style. Starting from similar premises, Joyce chose an opposite strategy. Since it is impossible to convey the objective world, the artist might create as many styles as possible in order to establish different perspectives upon the world which cannot be precisely fixed and codified.

As we move from story to story in *Dubliners* or from chapter to chapter in *Ulysses* (as well as the *Portrait*), we become aware of the artist as ventriloquist, projecting his voice at various pitches. It is this ventriloqual voice—or series of voices—which provides the most encompassing framework within which Stephen and Bloom are offered up to us. And, as every reader knows, in the second half of the book this voice is capable of almost completely drowning out the individual voices of the characters.

What is most troubling (or irritating) to many readers is that the style frequently seems out of joint with its subject matter. Thus, style is of such paramount importance in *Ulysses* because it frequently does *not* strike us as the inevitable fitting of words to subject matter. We become aware of style in the book, not only as the vehicle of meaning but very often as an obfuscating barrier between us and meaning. Arnold Goldman has given one of the best descriptions of this perplexing function of style in *Ulysses:*

> The theory of the "organic whole" of style and subject will not work for *Ulysses,* whose symbolic dimension (including its "styles") wars with its human dimension.
>
> *Ulysses* seems to posit a *noumenal* level which does not deny the multiplicity of phenomenal interpretive ones, but which is behind them, necessary to them inasmuch as without it, they could not exist at all.[1]

The noumenal level of the book consists of "what is really going on"; the phenomenal level is style itself, the collection of signatures we have to read if we are ever to approach any knowledge of the "what is really going on." This is the inevitable end point of Joyce's aesthetics in *Ulysses.* If Joyce's art is an art of surround, evocative of an unutterable, mysterious center, style becomes a collection of arrows pointing toward a center but reminding us that it can only point, not name. As *Ulysses* heads toward its ending, its styles move further and further away from intimate contact with the characters. One result is that by the end of "Ithaca" we are at our greatest remove from the characters; we are able to see the abstract configurations which they form and of which they are ignorant. But we are also aware (we are, I have come to think, always aware of two contradictory impulses in Joyce's work) of the severe limitations of these styles which have lost touch with their subject matter—just as, by a close analogy, we are by now impatient with the elaborate intellectual dodges by which both Stephen and Bloom rule their lives. At the end of "Ithaca" we are ready for "Penelope."

---

1. Arnold Goldman, *The Joyce Paradox* (Evanston: Northwestern University Press, 1966), p. 95. More recently, Marilyn French has made much the same argument. See note 4 below.

## "Oxen of the Sun"

No chapter in *Ulysses* presents more obvious difficulties and antagonizes more readers than "Oxen of the Sun." That spokesman for sanity, S. L. Goldberg, has little use for the chapter; and any reader who is skeptical of the achievement of *Finnegans Wake* must feel a premonitory shudder in reading some of the more overelaborated passages of "Oxen." Even those readers (such as myself) who admire the chapter for its exuberance and for the sheer wild verbal extravagance of its undertaking must sometimes, as a final resort, fall back upon a *de gustibus* argument to defend its rationale against its detractors. Before discussing the chapter's achievements, then, it will be helpful to review some of the objections (and even add a few to the list).

In his much-quoted letter to Budgen, Joyce spelled out the fetal symbolism and the stylistic progression of the chapter.[2] In this scheme, the evolution of English prose is comparable to the development of the fetus in the womb. We may accept the analogy, but only if we acknowledge that it is almost hopelessly vague. In what sense, for example, is Ruskin's prose more "developed" than Browne's? Two weaknesses of Joyce's imaginative habits and procedures in *Ulysses* are especially evident here: the purely mechanical linkage of style to subject matter and the sacrifice of the book's large pattern to the local tour de force. The fetal symbolism seems somewhat more satisfying when Joyce goes on to say in his letter that the hospital represents the womb, Bloom the spermatozoon, the nurse the ovum, and Stephen the embryo. There is some fitness, maybe, in seeing Bloom as the fertilizing agent who might help to bring about the birth of a new Stephen. And the place of Stephen in this analogy is potentially very fine indeed: he is the embryo striving to free himself from May Dedalus and Mother Church.[3] But Nurse Callan? Yes, she "her gate wide undid" to Bloom, and thus serves, I suppose, to symbolize the female organ open to Bloom (that eager spermatozoon), but her place in the symbolic scheme

2. Letter of 13 March 1920 to Frank Budgen, *Letters of James Joyce,* ed. Stuart Gilbert (New York: Viking Press, 1957), pp. 138–39.
3. The fetal symbolism is perhaps more convincing if we remember the pervasive use of the imagery of birth in the *Portrait.*

is purely local. She is there because she is needed to complete an idea, not because she grows out of any very deep level of meaning. Like the comparison of the evolution of English prose to fetal development, this analogy is imperfect. If, as Doctor Johnson said, Shakespeare was continually led astray by the fatal Cleopatra of the quibble, Joyce was always seduced by the idea of a totally systematized symbology. Nothing is more characteristic of Joyce's imaginative habits in his later works than this mechanical expansion of a metaphor for the purpose of inclusiveness: hence the organs, colors, and arts of *Ulysses;* hence also the river-names of "Anna Livia Plurabelle."

As I have already suggested, there is a problem in speaking of the chapter's styles in terms of "development." There is some hint of continuity in the persistence of the alliterative Anglo-Saxon line throughout the chapter, but this is a small thing. It is clear, I believe, that Joyce is usually more interested in miming particular authors than in developing anything like a pattern of progression or deterioration within the history of English prose. The one exception, the one "style" which reflects Joyce's idea of historical evolution, is the hodgepodge which closes the chapter. I will return later to a discussion of that section.

There is something else working against the sense of development within the chapter: Joyce's different attitudes toward and uses of the styles, varying from parody to close imitation. Sometimes, for example, Joyce uses the style mock-heroically, to describe something comically inappropriate to the content usually associated with the style. Two examples are the Bunyanesque allegory of contraception and (most comically) the Mandevillean description of a can of sardines:

> And there was a vat of silver that was moved by craft to open in the which lay strange fishes withouten heads though misbelieving men nie that this be possible thing without they see it natheless they are so. (387)

At other times, although rarely, the effect of the style is parodic; a major instance is the rather poor Dickens passage, which actually sounds like Trollope on a particularly bad day (420-21). But satirical parodies are rare; it is far more usual for Joyce to imitate the style directly. One of the best examples is the Sterne passage, in which the French phrase, the parenthetical remark describing a moment of titillation and the aposiopesis deftly recreate the atmosphere of *A Sentimental Journey*:

> *il y a deux choses* for which the innocence of our original garb, in other circumstances a breach of the proprieties, is the fittest nay, the only, garment. The first, said she (and here my pretty philosopher, as I handed her to her tilbury, to fix my attention, gently tipped with her tongue the outer chamber of my ear), the first is a bath . . . but at this point a bell tinkling in the hall cut short a discourse which promised so bravely for the enrichment of our store of knowledge. (405)

(Compare the aposiopesis which closes *A Sentimental Journey:* "So that when I stretch'd out my hand, I caught hold of the Fille de Chambre's—")

The major charges against "Oxen of the Sun," then, are twofold: the symbolic and stylistic matrices of the chapter are so complex as to hinder understanding, and the matrices themselves often seem very imperfectly related to the material they contain and describe. On the matter of the complexity itself, we have to invoke the *de gustibus* argument. The interesting question is: why does such complexity appear at this particular point in the book? It is evident that the moments of most crucial significance in *Ulysses*— the moments of emotional shifts among the major characters—are rendered through the most obfuscating prose in the book. Joyce lets us know that these shifts occur, but he does not specify them in very much detail. Thus we know in a very general way, by the end of the book, that Bloom has changed somewhat in his feelings about Rudy and Molly and that Stephen has been in some way affected by his encounter with Bloom. But we can only sense possibilities in these shifts of feeling; we cannot make confident predictions. This process of obfuscation begins in "Oxen of the Sun," the chapter in which Bloom's paternal feelings toward Stephen begin to take shape. The artistic rationale underlying this blurring and obscuring of crucial moments pays tribute to that sense of potentiality which is one of the great informing principles of the book. The relationships among the three central characters remain vague at the end of *Ulysses* because Joyce is interested there—as he is interested throughout—in projecting the myriad possibilities contained within the moment, not in pointing to one inevitable event.

The more crucial problem is that of determining the relation between the unwieldy form of "Oxen of the Sun" and the events of
the chapter. If we find unsatisfying the notion that the chapter's
styles reflect the process of fetal development, we are left then with
a series of passages much more striking for their variety than for
their consistency—and in this variety itself lies the "meaning" of
the chapter's styles. No other chapter of *Ulysses* offers such a richly
varied number of points of view upon a single subject. The chapter
is thus an equivalent of Stephen's epistemology set forth in "Proteus": just as we can know the thing in itself only through a collocation of the various phenomenal signatures we are able to read, so
we can know "substance" in *Ulysses* only through the "accidental"
stylistic refractions the author presents to us.[4] And while this
proposition is true for all books, Joyce in his later works forces us
to *experience* it in the very process of reading. "Oxen of the Sun"
is thus also a paradigm of the conception of style within *Ulysses:* in
forcing us to change perspective from paragraph to paragraph, this
chapter convinces us of the relative nature of *any* style. We are
already well on the way to *Finnegans Wake,* where Joyce remarks
of his central subject: "There extand by now one thousand and one
stories, all told, of the same" (*FW,* 5). The *Ur*-event remains
unknowable: we can understand it only through bringing together
(by a kind of parallax) the thousand-and-one versions of it the
author gives us.

I will single out one unique version of things which "Oxen of the
Sun" affords. In spite of the horseplay of the chapter—or, rather,
*because* of the horseplay—Joyce sometimes achieves a solemnity of
tone usually denied to him by his own ironic methods. Once he has
adopted the mediating persona of another century's style, he frequently exploits the legitimate resources of that style to convey a
simple and noble pathos. Here are three examples:

> Some man that wayfaring was stood by housedoor at night's oncoming.
> Of Israel's folk was that man that on earth wandering far had fared.
> Stark ruth of man his errand that him lone led till that house. (385)

---

4. See Marilyn French's similar argument, *The Book as World* (Cambridge, Mass.:
Harvard University Press, 1976) esp. pp. 10–11, 168–72.

now sir Leopold that had of his body no manchild for an heir looked upon him his friend's son and was shut up in sorrow for his forepassed happiness and as sad as he was that him failed a son of such gentle courage (for all accounted him of real parts) so grieved he also in no less measure for young Stephen for that he lived riotously with those wastrels and murdered his goods with whores. (390–91)

For through that tube he saw that he was in the land of Phenomenon where he must for a certain one day die as he was like the rest too a passing show. (395)

The alien styles allow Joyce to give to the dilemmas of Bloom and Stephen a solemnity not at all ironic or mock-heroic. These passages are epiphanic in their placement of the characters in a context of simple but powerful moral feeling—a context which is overlaid by psychological complexity elsewhere in the book, but which is nevertheless the very basis of the novel's themes.

These examples of a high and solemn style do not represent the dominant mode of the chapter, but only one of many modes. Each of the styles elicits and isolates some quality previously implicit in the characters; that picture persists for a paragraph or so and then gives way to the next. The styles thus present a montage-like sequence of narrative pictures which the reader perceives as a continuum only because he recognizes the forms of Stephen, Bloom, Mulligan, and the others persisting beneath the flickering spectacle of tenth-century solitaries, fifteenth-century knights, and eighteenth-century fops.

It is proper to say, then, that we do not so much *read* this chapter as we *translate* it. Just as each national language is capable of describing certain emotions or areas of experience with a precision which other languages can only approximate, so each style in the chapter offers some unique perspective upon the events in the hospital room—but with each style, as with each national language, we are aware that the medium is *only* a medium and that no single medium is totally adequate as an expression of the whole truth. This discrepancy between event and expression is at the very heart of the chapter. We may even begin to suspect, in fact, that the large dislocations between event and stylistic matrix, which I mentioned

earlier, are themselves functional in a chapter dominated by images
of contraception and abortion.[5]

Once we look beyond the problems of style, there are other
instances of dislocation within the chapter. There is, for example, a
very puzzling relation between symbol and event. Viewed from
a distance, the action of "Oxen of the Sun" takes place under the
aegis of two large and potent symbols, the birth of a child and the
coming of rain to end Dublin's long drought. There is undeniably
some relationship between these two symbols and the major "event"
of the chapter, the long-heralded meeting of Stephen and Bloom,
but the nature of that relationship is ambiguous. Are the symbols
predictive, in foreshadowing the forthcoming encounter and cross-
fertilization between the two heroes? Or are they instead ironic,
since they offer positive images for an encounter which does not
actually take place within the chapter? Once again, the problem
within "Oxen of the Sun" is a paradigm of a problem within
*Ulysses* as a whole. To take one of many examples: are Bloom's
successful return home and his mental slaying of the suitors signs of
a Ulyssean victory? Or is that victory cruelly parodied through
Bloom's upside-down position in Molly's bed? We are confronted
here by a disjunction between symbol and event which is not at all
uncommon in modern fiction. In *A Passage to India* or *The Sound
and the Fury*, for example, there is a similar discrepancy between
a perfected symbolic or aesthetic order ("each in its ordered
place") and an unsatisfying or, at best, imperfect achievement of a
similar order in the lives of the characters. In the case of "Oxen of
the Sun," we cannot say, of course, that *because* Mrs. Purefoy's
baby is born or *because* the rains come Bloom and Stephen will
*therefore* succeed in their meeting. We can say, however, that
Bloom moves, however hesitantly and imperfectly, toward participation in the world symbolized by birth and the life-giving rain.
His compassion, his "stark ruth of man," has brought him to the
house of birth, and his paternal feeling for Stephen emerges with
an almost startling force in the course of the chapter. The sym-

5. My argument that the disjunction between style and substance in "Oxen of the Sun"
is an instance of contraception has been anticipated (but in reverse form) by Kenner:
" 'Coition,' as Joyce is exploiting it in these pages, is the basic Aristotelian and Aquinatian
metaphor for the intercourse between mind and things" (*Dublin's Joyce*, Beacon Paperbacks [Boston: Beacon Press, 1962] p. 19).

bolic level of the chapter projects a world which Bloom, Stephen, and Molly reach out to encounter, but they have not fully encompassed it even by the end of the book. The large symbols of "Oxen of the Sun" thus represent a world which is at present beyond the characters' grasp, but which is not therefore forever unattainable.

The situation of Bloom presents perhaps the most interesting discrepancy in the chapter—the one between intention and act. Like Ulysses in the *Odyssey*, Bloom refuses to join his companions in their profanation of the Lord of Life. Ulysses is innocent of slaying the oxen of the sun and he therefore escapes the wrath of the gods. Bloom retains his own innocence outwardly by turning down offers of drink and inwardly by offering up compassion for Mrs. Purefoy. Bloom finds something primitively irreverent in the sexual jokes which pass back and forth between the young men even as they sit in earshot of the screams of Mrs. Purefoy in the agony of labor. And yet there is something paradoxical about this reverence of Bloom's, since he himself sins in another way against the Lord of Life:

> Has he not nearer home a seedfield that lies fallow for the want of a ploughshare? A habit reprehensible at puberty is second nature and an opprobrium in middle life. If he must dispense his balm of Gilead in nostrums and apothegms of dubious taste to restore to health a generation of unfledged profligates let his practice consist better with the doctrines that now engross him. (409)

This eighteenth-century diatribe—which I believe we should read as a refraction of Bloom's own thoughts—pinpoints Bloom's *vorrei e non vorrei* attitude before the process of birth and sexuality.

The disjunction within Bloom between attitude and act is perhaps rendered best in the De Quincey pastiche (414), one of the richest passages in the chapter. The passage, which recasts a reverie of Bloom's into an opium dream, closely parallels Bloom's thoughts as he returns home from the butcher's in "Calypso" (60–61). Both passages begin with the dream of an earthly paradise, alter to a scene of desolation dominated by the Dead Sea, and end with the hope of a renewal which takes form in the image of a young woman: "Quick warm sunlight came running from Berkeley Road, swiftly, in slim sandals" (61); "How serene does she now arise . . . shod in sandals of bright gold" (414). The pattern of dream-depression-recovery, so very typical of Bloom, is familiar by now; what gives the De Quincey passage its particular interest is its use of the three major women in Bloom's life to trace out this familiar curve.

The passage begins with a description of "a mare leading her fillyfoal"—a transformed picture of Molly and Milly. The immediate shift from this pleasant picture to the scene of desolation has a logic which is hidden but not difficult to follow: it is caused by the upset Bloom feels in regarding Molly under her maternal aspect. Bloom frees himself of depression by forcing his thoughts toward the two women who serve in his mind as surrogates of Molly: "It is she, Martha, thou lost one, Millicent, the young, the dear, the radiant." And now occurs the final and most interesting shift in Bloom's thought. The starry constellation representing these women transforms itself—"till after a myriad metamorphoses of symbol, it blazes, Alpha, a ruby and triangled sign upon the forehead of Taurus."

Bloom has drifted off into a reverie while gazing at a bottle of Bass's Ale, and his eyes have become fixed upon the red triangle on the Bass label. The reverie here is like the sleep of innocence Ulysses takes while his men are slaughtering the oxen of the sun. Bloom's reverie contains his own particular form of innocence. Notice how, throughout the De Quincey passage, Bloom thinks of a "she," but her identity constantly shifts. Unable to think with equanimity of Molly, he transfers his thoughts to Martha and Milly. This is the kind of psychological dodge we have become familiar with in Bloom, but here more than ever we realize it is not simply a dodge. Bloom is troubled in his relation to individual women, but he remains faithful in his reverence for woman. His fixed gaze upon the female sign of the triangle suggests his continuing attraction toward an essence common to Molly, Milly, and Martha. This is the place of Bloom in "Oxen of the Sun": the impotent priest of the Lord of Life.

If we now draw together these examples of disjunction and incommensurability within the chapter, one of the details of Joyce's schema takes on a new clarity: his description of contraception as the true sin of the chapter, the murder of the oxen of the sun. In the very disparities I have been discussing—those between style and substance, symbol and event, or intention and act—Joyce creates a version of incompleteness, of imperfect fertilization. "Oxen of the

Sun" as a whole thus offers another of those metaphors of incompleteness which fill the book (and through which the book describes itself) : the disappointed bridge, the condition of almosting it, the Pisgah sight of Palestine, the life of Stephen's Shakespeare, "untaught by the wisdom he has written or by the laws he has revealed."

If we were to look in the chapter for a metaphor of actual consummation, that metaphor would be the Incarnation, a symbol at once of completed fertilization and of the perfected expression of the Word. In the perfected Incarnation, the distinction between substance and expression or between intention and act would disappear. And, indeed, twice in the chapter the Incarnation is announced, but in both cases the event is really one of contraception or miscarriage. First, Stephen draws an analogy between the Incarnation and art :

> Mark me now. In woman's womb word is made flesh but in the spirit of the maker all flesh that passes becomes the word that shall not pass away. This is the postcreation. (391)

If in "Scylla and Charybdis" Stephen tried to argue away the embarrassing existence of his own father ("Fatherhood, in the sense of conscious begetting, is unknown to man"), in "Oxen of the Sun" he tries, like the fetus struggling to be born, to establish independence of his mother : the artist usurps the power of the woman to gestate and give birth. But Stephen is claiming a power here which he does not yet possess. He is making false claims even as he describes the act of artistic incarnation; for he has just bragged that his teacher's wages, which he proudly displays, are payment for "a song which he writ" (391). Rather like Bloom, Stephen proclaims himself the priest of a religion whose mysteries he is (as yet, at least) incapable of practicing.

Stephen's boastful claim to artistry receives a sharp rebuff later in the chapter :

> You have spoken of the past and its phantoms, Stephen said. Why think of them? If I call them into life across the waters of Lethe will not the poor ghosts troop to my call? Who supposes it? I, Bous Stephanoumenos, bullockbefriending bard, am lord and giver of their life. He encircled his gadding hair with a coronal of vineleaves, smiling at Vincent. That answer and those leaves, Vincent said to him, will adorn you more fitly

when something more, and greatly more, than a capful of light odes can call your genius father. All who wish you well hope this for you. All desire to see you bring forth the work you meditate. I heartily wish you may not fail them. O no, Vincent, Lenehan said, laying a hand on the shoulder near him, have no fear. He could not leave his mother an orphan. The young man's face grew dark. All could see how hard it was for him to be reminded of his promise and of his recent loss. (415)

Stephen now claims male power as "lord and giver of their life" to his artistic creations, but Lynch manages to rebuff both sexes of the androgynous artist: Stephen's genius, says Lynch, is a father which has as yet brought forth no child. (In a chapter in which hats, cloaks, and umbrellas symbolize condoms, "a capful of light odes" is itself an image of contraception.) But Lenehan's witticism stings Stephen even more. Lenehan tactlessly brings to Stephen's mind the memory of his dead mother, but he inadvertently blunders even further into Stephen's true desire, which *is* actually to leave his mother an orphan. Earlier in the chapter, Stephen quoted St. Bernard's appellation of the Virgin, *vergine madre figlia di tuo figlio*, the phrase by which the male Church kicks free of the mother—by claiming that she is "but creature of her creature" (391), the daughter of the autonomous son to whom she gives birth. Lenehan's *mot* is thus a perfectly precise—if unwitting—description of Stephen's attempt to deny his relation to May Dedalus.

Stephen announces the Incarnation a second time near the end of the chapter:

> But as before the lightning the serried stormclouds, heavy with preponderant excess of moisture, in swollen masses turgidly distended, compass earth and sky in one vast slumber, impending above parched field and drowsy oxen and blighted growth of shrub and verdure till in an instant a flash rives their centres and with the reverberation of the thunder the cloudburst pours its torrent, so and not otherwise was the transformation, violent and instantaneous, upon the utterance of the Word.
>
> Burke's! Outflings my lord Stephen . . . . (422-23)

Once we have noticed again the connection established between rain and birth (the two images are fused in the description of the pregnant rainclouds), there is little to say except that the passage is devastatingly anticlimactic. The chapter builds toward this crucial point—the announcement that the already-drunken revelers will retire to a nearby pub for yet more drinking. There is a weak pun here on Burke's-birth, but once again the proclamation of fertility is in reality a statement of the contrary. Not only is drunkenness a paralyzing force in Dublin life; it is also a contraceptive device, preventing the act itself.

Like Bloom, then, Stephen proclaims ideals which he does not fulfill in his own actions. In particular, he announces the artist's ability to perform an incarnation, but as yet he himself has no artistic children. A bad and unpleasant drunk, he has (in terms of the chapter's dominant imagery) regressed to an infantile state of petulance and self-will; there is little sign in this chapter of those tentative steps toward maturity he took in "Proteus," "Aeolus," and "Scylla and Charybdis."

Simply in terms of the book's two heroes, however, "Oxen of the Sun" is very much like "Aeolus." In both of these chapters the two heroes appear, but there is practically no direct communication between them, and in both chapters the failed encounter is accompanied by a ruling image of failed fruition: the Pisgah sight of Palestine and contraception. "Oxen of the Sun," in fact, would be a *mere* repetition of "Aeolus" as a functioning part of the plot were it not for the birth of a new spirit within Bloom. (In spite of the analogy between Stephen and the embryo, after all, it is Bloom who truly undergoes a new birth in the chapter.) Bloom's paternal feelings emerge with great force as he gazes upon Stephen, and those qualities of charity and compassion which have heretofore been important but unobtrusive touches in Joyce's portrayal of Bloom's character now become determinant influences upon the action, as Bloom calls at the hospital out of respect for Mrs. Purefoy and then follows Stephen from the hospital to the pub and from the pub into nighttown at the end of the chapter.

Perhaps more than any other chapter in *Ulysses,* "Oxen of the Sun" calls forth a response of "Yes, but . . . ." It is the most complex rendering within the novel of that equivocal vision of Bloom and Stephen—compounded of success and failure—which Joyce returns to again and again, each time with a new metaphor or situational analogy. The "sin" of the chapter is contraception, but the scene in the hospital closes with a joyful announcement of birth. Bloom and Stephen are profaners of their respective religions of birth and art, but they are celebrants as well. This celebration of the goal not quite reached, the consummation not quite accomplished, takes place also within the style and form of "Oxen of the Sun." The chapter marches resolutely through the history of English prose, right up to the present—and ends in confusion. It is time to discuss this modern language.

The first thing to notice about the language of the closing pages is that the style has fallen back into the chaos from which it first issued at the beginning of the chapter. This evolution from chaos through order to chaos come again is the clearest sign (the only clear sign, really) of Joyce's presentation of an historical process underlying the evolution of language and style. We can appropriately see this "style" as reflecting the modern period, cut off from traditional forms of order; such an idea is at least implicit already within the Homeric parallel itself. It is also possible to see this descent into chaos as a reflection of the historical scheme of Giambattista Vico, whose *La scienza nuova* Joyce appropriated to supply the structure of *Finnegans Wake*. But even though I am convinced that Joyce had Vico in mind as he wrote the chapter, I believe that the very context of *Ulysses* offers a more immediately satisfying analogy for describing this deterioration of language: the Apocalypse.

The Apocalypse, of course, is both the ending of an old order and the beginning of a new. It thus becomes, especially in "Circe," a symbolic accompaniment to that passage from one epoch to another in the encounter between Stephen and Bloom. The Apocalypse, though, has a more private meaning for Stephen, as is evident in his conversation with Mr. Deasy:

> —The ways of the Creator are not our ways, Mr Deasy said. All history moves towards one great goal, the manifestation of God.
> Stephen jerked his thumb towards the window, saying:
> —That is God.
> Hooray! Ay! Whrrwhee!
> —What? Mr Deasy asked.
> —A shout in the street, Stephen answered, shrugging his shoulders.

(34)

The weary, blasé attitude of Stephen's shrug conceals the terrifying implications of his atheism. Stephen identifies God with the phenomenal world (not even the *things* in the street, notice, but their *noise*). Rejecting the tyranny of Deasy's traditional Christianity, Stephen opts for a world which is even more terrifying because chaotic and senseless. The nature of his dilemma is clear in his reaction to the thunder in "Oxen of the Sun":

> A black crack of noise in the street here, alack, bawled, back. Loud on left Thor thundered: in anger awful the hammerhurler. Came now the storm that hist his heart. (394)

Stephen is caught here between the vestigial religious fears of the lapsed Catholic and the alternate terrors of living in a Godless world. He jeers at "old Nobodaddy," but his mockery—which "was only to dye his desperation"—grows out of a childish and powerful fear. Nor is he comforted by Bloom's calming words that the thunder is "all of the order of a natural phenomenon," for "the land of Phenomenon" has its own existential terrors (395). Stephen is unable to shake free from a religion which he has rejected and just as unable to accept a world to which he has given intellectual assent.

Stephen's intimations of an Apocalypse—whether in the traditional sense or as the full revelation of a world without meaning or order—are justified at the end of "Oxen of the Sun." Indeed, the Homeric parallel underlying the end of the chapter is closely akin to the Apocalypse: the wrathful Neptune raises a storm which destroys Ulysses's ship, and only Ulysses, the one just man, survives. This sense of the end of things is accompanied stylistically by the shipwreck of language. There is no longer that sense of stylistic coherence which predominates in the earlier pages of the chapter but instead a litter of slang, that linguistic ragbag which Joyce mentioned in his letter to Budgen: "it ends in a frightful jumble of pidgin English, nigger English, Cockney, Irish Bowery slang and broken doggerel."

In Joyce's list of argots and in the closing pages themselves, American slang in particular looms large—and the American language is for Joyce the appropriate vehicle for conveying chaos. The few references to America in *Ulysses* portray the new country as a land of frightening but energetic confusion. I have mentioned earlier Stephen's conception of his own linguistic Scylla and Charybdis: "Between the Saxon smile and yankee yawp. The devil and the deep sea" (187). Stephen sees himself fixed between the oppression of the English language (compare his conversation with the dean of studies in Chapter v of the *Portrait*) and the chaos of the American. But the description of America most appropriate to the ending of "Oxen of the Sun" is Mr. Kernan's recollection of his recent conversation with Mr. Crimmins in "Wandering Rocks," and in particular their discussion of "that General Slocum explosion":

> And America they say is the land of the free. I thought we were bad here.
>     I smiled at him. *America,* I said, quietly, just like that. *What is it? The sweepings of every country including our own. Isn't that true?* That's a fact. (239)

America is the land of catastrophic ship disasters (like that of Ulysses) and a country of many nationalities—and languages. In this light, it is not simply the peculiarly *American* slang but the very *variety* of languages which makes the closing pages of "Oxen of the Sun" the apocalyptic revelation of a new world, the frightening, chaotic world of America.

If the linguistic confusion at the end of "Oxen of the Sun" is a particularly American confusion, it is appropriate that the last words of the chapter are given to the major American of *Ulysses,* the Reverend Dowie:

> The Deity ain't no nickel dime bumshow. I put it to you that he's on the square and a corking fine business proposition. He's the grandest thing yet and don't you forget it. Shout salvation in king Jesus. You'll need to rise precious early, you sinner there, if you want to diddle the Almighty God. Pflaaaap! Not half. He's got a coughmixture with a punch in it for you, my friend, in his backpocket. Just you try it on. (428)

This is God as a shout in the street—raucous, vulgar, demotic, but possessed of an undeniable energy. And this is not quite chaos; at the very end of the chapter a recognizable "style" reappears. We are witnessing here what we witnessed at the very beginning of the chapter—the emergence of a new form out of chaos.[6]

In terms of Joyce's own career, the ending of "Oxen of the Sun" is indeed the language of the future, since no other part of *Ulysses* is so similar to the language of *Finnegans Wake*. The drunken atmosphere, the polyglot mixture of tongues, and the sprinkling of puns throughout these pages all anticipate the language of the later work. And in *Finnegans Wake* as well, the projected new order of things is American. On the first page of the *Wake*, the world is without form and void, and the narrative foretells those events which have not yet happened:

> . . . nor had topsawyer's rocks by the stream Oconee exaggerated themselse to Laurens County's gorgios while they went doublin their mumper all the time . . . . (*FW*, 3)

At its beginning, the *Wake* looks forward to the reestablishment of a new order in the cyclical course of things, Dublin, Ireland doubled in Dublin, Laurens County, Georgia—in America, the home of Top Sawyer and Huckleberry Finn-again.

The Reverend Dowie's "new order" is, to put it mildly, a mixed blessing. Although Dowie is a Christian, the God he proclaims is not at all the traditional Christian God. No longer enthroned in awful majesty, surrounded by thunder and lightning, Dowie's God is associated instead with the vulgarities of the here and now. He is the most garish result of that effort in *Ulysses* which begins with Mulligan's false Mass and ends with Bloom's and Stephen's communion over their cups of Epps's cocoa: the effort to accommodate the religious impulse with a completely secularized world. And yet, Bloom and Stephen must shout salvation in this king Jesus, frightening though he is. He represents that world of process which Stephen tries to force himself to accept and to which Bloom already swears partial allegiance. Both Bloom and Stephen must, in a sense, learn to speak American.

I would propose one other Biblical account of God's wrath as an analogy to these final pages of "Oxen of the Sun": the destruction of the Tower of Babel. That destruction entailed the fragmentation

6. See French, *The Book as World*, p. 174.

of one *Ur*-language into diverse languages and therefore gave rise to an awareness of language as a medium apart from and alien to the world which it attempts to register and reflect. An awareness of the diversity of language leads to an awareness of the imperfections of any language's signs and symbols. The fragmented style of the closing of "Oxen of the Sun" is therefore the inevitable conclusion to Joyce's history of English prose. The chapter is based upon the relativity of language—upon the inability of any single language to convey the whole truth—and the chapter ends with so many fragments of linguistic wreckage floating upon the ocean of the unnamable.

Yes, but . . . . *The Unnamable* is Beckett's title, not Joyce's. In spite of the somber tone I have sometimes fallen into in describing the course of language in "Oxen of the Sun," it would be false to call the tone of the chapter nihilistic or even to any great extent pessimistic. While the chapter is based upon the principle that no single language or style can fully describe and convey reality, in practice the chapter celebrates the variety and energy of the linguistic attempts themselves. What happens in the closing pages of "Oxen of the Sun" is a version of what happens when, at the very end of the novel, Joyce hands over the narrative to Molly Bloom. In so doing, Joyce acknowledges the final superiority of unformed experience to any of the shapes which the preceding chapters have attempted to impose upon it. Just so, in "Oxen of the Sun," Joyce demonstrates the various historical attempts to describe reality and ends with the babbling chaos of a thousand shouts in the street, that baby's squall which is the material out of which any new language must arise.

## "Ithaca"

Problem ye ferst, construct ann aquilittoral dryankle Probe loom! (*FW*, 286)

From beginning to end, Joyce's work is characterized by a balance of *l'esprit de géométrie* and *l'esprit de finesse*. The very experience of reading his prose frequently creates something like the dual impression which Lily Briscoe in Woolf's *To the Lighthouse* imagines as the perfect goal of her own art: the sense of a gossamer-thin butterfly's wing at rest upon strong steel girders. This double effect is especially clear in the masterful closing paragraph of "The Dead":

> A few light taps upon the pane made him turn to the window. It had begun to snow again. He watched sleepily the flakes, silver and dark, falling obliquely against the lamplight. The time had come for him to set out on his journey westward. Yes, the newspapers were right: snow was general all over Ireland. It was falling on every part of the dark central plain, on the treeless hills, falling softly upon the Bog of Allen and, farther westward, softly falling into the dark mutinous Shannon waves. It was falling, too, upon every part of the lonely churchyard on the hill where Michael Furey lay buried. It lay thickly drifted on the crooked crosses and headstones, on the spears of the little gate, on the barren thorns. His soul swooned slowly as he heard the snow falling faintly through the universe and faintly falling, like the descent of their last end, upon all the living and the dead.

At any distance at all from this passage, the critical mind seizes upon at least some of the devices which give the passage its effect. Apart from the motifs from throughout the story which are brought together here (the tapping at the window pane, the snow, the journey westward), there are noticeable, even somewhat obtrusive, rhetorical devices: alliteration ("swooned slowly," "faintly falling"), anaphora ("It was falling . . . falling softly. . . . It was falling, too . . ."), and various combinations of repetition combined with inversion ("falling softly . . . softly falling"; "falling faintly . . . faintly falling") which Joyce later resorted to in his description of the bird-girl in *Portrait*:

> Her bosom was as a bird's soft and slight, slight and soft as the breast of some darkplumaged dove. But her long fair hair was girlish: and girlish, and touched with the wonder of mortal beauty, her face. (*PA*, 171)

But—and this is the point I want to stress here—even *before* the reader has consciously stepped back from the closing of "The Dead," he is aware of this supple yet formal and balanced rhetoric. We are reminded of Frank Budgen's report that Joyce spent an entire day adjusting the word-order of "Perfume of embraces all him assailed. With hungered flesh obscurely, he mutely craved to adore" (168). As in the more formal passage from "The Dead," this highly wrought prose is in tandem with the formlessness, the dissolution, of the character's consciousness. The power of such passages arises out of the pairing of the overwhelming experience which is the subject described by the prose and the obtrusive shape of the prose itself.

The experience of reading a paragraph of Joyce's prose frequently creates a response which, in Stephen's terms from the *Portrait,* is at once lyrical and dramatic: we are impressed both by the immediacy of the action and—often with equal force—by the shape of the language which conveys that action. This description, however, is too close to being a truism, for it would apply equally well to James, Faulkner, or Woolf. What I seek here is the particularly *abstract* sense of shape which appears in Joyce's sentences themselves and again in the form of his works. We come close to this spirit in Joyce when we recall Stephen's fascination in the *Portrait* with the poetry of the expanding and contracting forms of algebraic equations. I would propose that Joyce's intense concern with form of all sorts—religious ritual, social decorum, artistic shape—is directly continuous with a fascination with abstract geometrical forms, especially the circle and the triangle.

On the first page of *Dubliners,* the narrator of "The Sisters" names three words which once had a strong power over his mind: "paralysis," "simony," and "gnomon." The first two are obviously relevant to the *Dubliners* stories themselves; the application of the third, "gnomon," is less immediately clear. A gnomon is "the part of a parallelogram which remains after a similar parallelogram is taken away from one of its corners" (*OED*). It is, in effect, an imperfect—or better, incomplete—geometrical figure. We might apply the conception "gnomon" to certain themes and motifs of *Dubliners*—the incomplete lives of the characters, for example, or the tendency of the characters (such as old Cotter in "The Sisters") to speak in incomplete sentences. But the word is more enlightening if we apply it to the form of the *Dubliners* stories: they are incomplete, open-ended, no story more so than "The Sisters" itself. Like the motif of "almosting it" in *Ulysses,* the gnomon describes the form of Joyce's fiction.

Joyce's use of geometrical form became most prominent during the composition of the *Wake*. In his manuscripts and in the *Wake* itself at several points, Joyce used abstract symbols to stand for the major characters—a sideways E for Earwicker, a delta for Anna Livia, and so forth. The "Anna Livia Plurabelle" chapter begins:

O
tell me all about
Anna Livia! I want to hear all
(*FW*, 196)

Here the very typography is symbolic. The lone-standing "O" suggests the circularity of the experience which Anna Livia embodies; and it even enacts this meaning, as it stands as the first word in the chapter but represents the end, Omega. Moreover, the arrangement of letters on the page forms a delta, which is both the delta of the Liffey and the female triangle, the true subject of the chapter. But it is in Book Two, Chapter Two of the *Wake* that Joyce's geometrical spirit reaches its height. Here Joyce includes within the text a geometrical figure, an equilateral triangle enclosed within two intersecting circles. In the course of the accompanying geometry lesson—one of the most dazzling passages in the *Wake*—not only do the twin brothers construct a triangle; in the process, they discover the secret of female sexuality. As Dolph the sexually knowledgeable son says to his brother Kev: "I'll make you to see figuratleavely the whome of your eternal geomater" (296–97). Like the gnomon in *Dubliners*, this geometrical figure stands for the form of *Finnegans Wake* itself. The two circles, representing cyclical experience, are held together by the triangle, the symbol of feminine permanence which links together generations.

Joyce's geometric spirit in *Ulysses* reaches its climax in "Ithaca"; it passes over, in fact, into self-parody. Just as a chapter such as "Nausicaa" at once affirms and mocks the pathos of transience, so does the style of "Ithaca" reveal most fully the abstract configuration of Stephen, Bloom, and Molly and simultaneously question the ability of the mathematical spirit to account for the complexities of the characters' behavior. As the last "male" chapter in the book, "Ithaca" is therefore appropriately mathematical in technique. It brings to an end point the attempts of Stephen and Bloom to impose shape upon experience; then, after the large full-stop at the end of the chapter the book plunges into the formlessness of Molly's consciousness which is, in a sense, the very material out of which the two men seek all day to create form. "Ithaca" dramatizes the triumph and the limitations of the form-making imagination.

Let us look first at some of the self-evident and purposeful inadequacies of the "Ithaca" style. As every reader of the chapter knows, the style is capable of telling us everything—except, very often, what we most want to know. Thus it can describe the passage of water from Roundwood reservoir to Bloom's faucet (671), but it perversely avoids precisely the details of attitude and motive which most interest us. ("Ithaca" does not even deign to recount one of the most significant "facts" which takes place within its temporal scope, Bloom's demand for breakfast.) On one occasion, the style pretends to remove "the enclosures of reticence" (682), but it does so only in order to tell us the names of the two men's parents. Taken as a whole, the style brings the two men together by comparing them in various ways, but it repeatedly shies away from intimately uniting Bloom and Stephen. In this way, the style operates to reflect the on-again, off-again approach and withdrawal which characterizes the interview itself.

The question "What relation existed between their ages?" and the ensuing response typify the "Ithaca" prose. The response to the question begins by drawing the two men together, as it points out the decreasing disparity between their levels of maturity as additional years are added to their ages. But then, as in an ill-programmed computer, the ensuing calculations separate the two men by tens of thousands of years, by maintaining the original ratio between their ages through successive additions of years—so that should Stephen reach "the maximun antediluvian age, that of Methusalah, 969 years," then Bloom "would have been obliged to have been alive 83,300 years . . ." (679). The effect of this passage is clear, and is especially typical of "Ithaca": the style loses sight of the human significance of the question and becomes absorbed in a purely mathematical calculation.

Now this kind of thinking is not unlike Bloom's. Repeatedly throughout the day Bloom mentally approaches some thought of major emotional import but then shies away from it—frequently by substituting some mathematical or scientific speculation. He particularly likes the kind of extended calculation which is involved in determining the relation between his and Stephen's ages in "Ithaca." For example:

> A million pounds, wait a moment. Twopence a pint, fourpence a quart, eightpence a gallon of porter, no, one and fourpence a gallon of porter. One and four into twenty: fifteen about. Yes, exactly. Fifteen millions of barrels of porter.
> What am I saying barrels? Gallons. About a million barrels all the same. (79)

This is Bloom's mind, sharp, active, calculating—and always tending toward errors of computation. This latter tendency is also apparent in the question and answer concerning the ages of Stephen and Bloom; for, as many readers have noticed, the computation of Bloom's and Stephen's ages is in error. There is, in fact, enough error in "Ithaca" to at least suggest the use of error as a motif—as if the style itself were committing Bloomisms.

The "Ithaca" style, then, partakes of certain very definite qualities of Bloom's mind. The "art" of the chapter, after all, is science, and Bloom is described in the chapter as a scientist:

> What two temperaments did they individually represent?
> The scientific. The artistic. (683)

To see this kinship between style and consciousness is to become newly aware of the strengths and weaknesses of Bloom's mentality. The style is at once truthful and evasive, honestly searching and repressive. The style, like Bloom's mind, has the virtues and the limitations of empiricism: it can deal successfully with the physical paraphernalia of Dublin life, but it is painfully inept at confronting the more complex and intangible realities of desire and trauma.

The limitations of the "Ithaca" style are clear—and I will return to them later in discussing the degree to which "Ithaca" successfully closes the action of the book. But this style does have one supreme virtue: its very qualities of abstractness and (when it can find the right subject) lucidity allow for an intense and depersonalized vision of the book's most elemental patterns. In particular, there are four uses of scientific and mathematical language which act as closing metaphors for the book's central themes: the relation between potential and kinetic energy, the quadrature of the circle, the image of the triangle, and the pervasive use of the language of astronomy.

As a part of the scientific terminology of "Ithaca," Joyce opposes the conceptions of "potential" and "kinetic." The two words denote forms of energy, but they are also closely related to Stephen's Aristotelian terminology in the early chapters: the self has a potential energy which, in the process of maturation, will reach its kinetic actualization. The language of physical science thus becomes a kind of shorthand notation for the evolution of the self. Within "Ithaca" the terms "potential" and "kinetic" are also in part self-referential, suggesting the actualization, the completion, of *Ulysses* itself.

The first occurrence of the terms describes Bloom's early poetic endeavors. There is a hidden logic in the series of questions which contain the terms:

> What lines concluded his first piece of original verse written by him, potential poet, at the age of 11 in 1877 on the occasion of the offering of three prizes at 10/-, 5/- and 2/6 respectively by the *Shamrock,* a weekly newspaper?

> > *An ambition to squint*
> > *At my verses in print*
> > *Makes me hope that for these you'll find room.*
> > *If you so condescend*
> > *Then please place at the end*
> > *The name of yours truly, L. Bloom.*

> Did he find four separating forces between his temporary guest and him?

> > Name, age, race, creed.

> What anagrams had he made on his name in youth?

> > Leopold Bloom
> > Ellpodbomool
> > Molldopeloob.
> > Bollopedoom
> > Old Ollebo, M.P.

What acrostic upon the abbreviation of his first name had he (kinetic poet) sent to Miss Marion Tweedy on the 14 February 1888?

> Poets oft have sung in rhyme
> Of music sweet their praise divine.
> Let them hymn it nine times nine.
> Dearer far than song or wine,
> You are mine. The world is mine. (677–78)

This portrait of the artist is witty and charming and it contains a useful lesson about the passage from potential poet to kinetic poet. Bloom's first poem, his anagrams, and his acrostic poem all refer to himself, but in interestingly—and humorously—different ways. The first poem states nothing except that it *is* a poem by one L. Bloom. The anagrams are even more obviously self-enclosed. In the second poem, it is ridiculous but true to say that the poet's personality has diffused itself into its subject. The artistic passage from potential poet to kinetic poet is the human passage from self-enclosure to love. The seemingly irrelevant insertion—"Did he find four separating forces between his temporary guest and him?"—is actually a well-placed indication of the distance between Stephen's potentiality and Bloom's actuality.

The passage from potential to kinetic is one small contribution to the strong sense within "Ithaca" of things coming to fulfillment. Another occurrence of the words, however, has something like the opposite effect:

Why did he not elaborate these calculations to a more precise result?

Because some years previously in 1886 when occupied with the problem of the quadrature of the circle he had learned of the existence of a number computed to a relative degree of accuracy to be of such magnitude and of so many places, e.g., the 9th power of the 9th power of 9, that, the result having been obtained, 33 closely printed volumes of 1000 pages each of innumerable quires and reams of India paper would have to be requisitioned in order to contain the complete tale of its printed integers of units, tens, hundreds, thousands, tens of thousands, hundreds of thousands, millions, tens of millions, hundreds of millions, billions, the nucleus of the nebula of every digit of every series containing succinctly the potentiality of being raised to the utmost kinetic elaboration of any power of any of its powers. (699)

Here there is a sense, not of potentiality issuing finally in some one sharply realized moment, but of potentiality containing within itself virtually infinite possibilities. There are, then, two senses of potential energy in "Ithaca." We may look upon the potentiality of a given subject as realizing itself in one ineluctable conclusion *or,* in the present's ignorance of the future, we may see the subject as holding within itself infinite possibilities, any one of which may be realized. Stephen, indeed, considered this very distinction earlier in the day, in "Nestor":

> Had Pyrrhus not fallen by a beldam's hand in Argos or Julius Caesar not been knifed to death? They are not to be thought away. Time has branded them and fettered they are lodged in the room of the infinite possibilities they have ousted. But can those have been possible seeing that they never were? Or was that only possible which came to pass? Weave, weaver of the wind. (25)

By suggesting final resolution and simultaneously opening up a large number of possibilities, the language of potentiality and actualization serves as an index to the double direction of "Ithaca." For repeatedly the chapter gives us the sense of two contrary possibilities at once—the one closed, the other open-ended, the one centripetal, the other centrifugal. By the end of the chapter, all action has come to a complete rest, but we are aware that it is a rest not of resolution but of incipience.

A second scientific motif within the chapter occurs in a passage I have already quoted: the quadrature of the circle. In "Circe" Lipoti Virag mocks Bloom for having "intended to devote . . . the summer months of 1882 to square the circle and win that million" (514–15). The problem apparently fascinated Bloom for some long time, since he was still considering it in 1886 (699). Even today, in 1904, one of the get-rich-quick schemes in the back of Bloom's mind involves "A solution of the secular problem of the quadrature of the circle, government premium £1,000,000 sterling" (718). The squaring of the circle is another of those mathematical or scientific motifs within "Ithaca" which act as references to the form of *Ulysses* itself. The attempt to square the circle is an attempt to reduce a figure of infinite tangents to a figure of four sides. It is an attempt to reduce the infinite to the finite, the irrational to the rational; and in this respect it is an epitome of "Ithaca," which attempts to know the unknown, the void itself, through purely mathematical means. And here once more we run up against the double impression created by "Ithaca." No chapter tells us more about Bloom, and no chapter is more incapable of illuminating the true mysteries of his identity. The chapter attempts to know, but finally its apparatus for knowing is incommensurate with the subject it so relentlessly assaults. The circle cannot be squared.

The problem of the squaring of the circle epitomizes the artistic effort of all of *Ulysses* up through "Ithaca"; for the book at once celebrates the ability of the imagination to give shape and coherence to its world and finally acknowledges that the irrational and infinite nature of the world is superior to any order placed upon it. This dilemma of consciousness confronting the unknown (because unknowable) receives one final expression as Bloom drifts off to sleep at the end of the chapter:

When?
Going to a dark bed there was a square round Sinbad the Sailor roc's auk's egg in the night of the bed of all the auks of the rocs of Darkinbad the Brightdayler. (737)

The curious picture of the egg within the square is one final version of the squaring of the circle. The circle has here become the very image of feminine fertility, the cyclical reality which Bloom and Stephen confront and avoid throughout the day. And with Sinbad-Bloom's approach to the egg, the "Ithaca" chapter—and the book's efforts to achieve mathematical form—come to an end.

The third motif within "Ithaca" is the figure of the triangle. In "Scylla and Charybdis" Eglinton complains to Stephen: "You have brought us all this way to show us a French triangle" (213). Like many other remarks about Stephen's Shakespeare theory, this one applies aptly to *Ulysses,* which brings us through over 700 pages of difficult reading to present us with the triangular relationship of Stephen, Bloom, and Molly. As Joyce uses the abstract figure of the triangle in *Ulysses*, it may signify a pattern of relationships among characters (as in "French triangle") or it may be a female symbol (as it is in the De Quincey pastiche in "Oxen of the Sun"). Both of these senses come together in "Ithaca," since it is the woman, Molly, who completes the ideal relationship between Stephen and Bloom.

Early in "Ithaca" Joyce describes Bloom's and Stephen's divergent explanations of Stephen's collapse in "Circe." Bloom cites empirical evidence such as "gastric inanition." Stephen, however, attributes the collapse "to the reapparition of a matutinal cloud (perceived by both from two different points of observation, Sandycove and Dublin) at first no bigger than a woman's hand" (667). This is one of those passages which draw together an astonishing number of disparate motifs. The description recalls the moment, rendered in "Telemachus" (9) and "Calypso" (61), when Bloom and Stephen observe the sun slowly covered by a cloud. To both men, the darkened light evokes a deathly woman: Stephen remembers his mother, and Bloom, reflecting on the "bent hag" he sees crossing the street, imagines "the grey sunken cunt of the world." The cloud itself is the first sign of the breaking of the drought in Dublin, and the symbolic suggestions of water are reinforced by a Biblical allusion. In I Kings 18:44, Elijah's servant reports to him, "Behold there ariseth a little cloud out of the sea, like a man's hand." This Elijah recognizes as the cloud which will break the drought he himself has caused. By altering the phrase from "man's hand" to "woman's hand," Joyce establishes a complex and powerful symbol: Bloom and Stephen are united in their consciousness of woman, through a symbol which suggests the life-giving force of rain. The deathly nature of the woman evoked by the cloud only reinforces our awareness of the need the two men have of one another. Each of the men needs what the other has in excess, if either of them is ever to approach a woman without the obsessive and traumatic consciousness of death. A pictorial representation of the two men observing the cloud yields a triangle, with the cloud at its apex (a configuration which calls to mind the parallactic observation of a star). The geometrical figure of the triangle stresses in the simplest way the most essential theme of *Ulysses:* the complementarity of Bloom and Stephen and their shared need of a woman's love.

A second triangular relationship makes much the same point:

> Were they indefinitely inactive?
> At Stephen's suggestion, at Bloom's instigation both, first Stephen, then Bloom, in penumbra urinated, their sides contiguous, their organs of micturition reciprocally rendered invisible by manual circumposition, their gazes, first Bloom's, then Stephen's, elevated to the projected luminous and semiluminous shadow. (702)

The geometrical arrangement here recalls the sighting of the cloud, but now it is Molly's window which is the apex of the triangle. This second triangular image is less complex but more explicit. The two men's "organs of micturition" are also the organs of generation; and there is something at once pathetic and childishly funny about this substitution of urination for copulation—"Shy but willing, like an ass pissing," in Bloom's words (553).

This image of a triangle formed by two men and a woman is so precisely repeated in *Finnegans Wake* as to be worth a digression. The fable of Burrus and Caseous (*FW*, 160–68) is an especially clear example of Joyce's habit of abstracting and reworking in the *Wake* a pattern already present in his earlier work. In the higgledy-piggledy mixture of the sublime and the ridiculous which is *Finnegans Wake*, the names of Burrus and Caseous suggest two son-figures guilty of parricide (Brutus and Cassius) and two forms of milk, butter and cheese (French *beurre* and Latin *caseus*). Already implicit in these etymologies is much of the sexual mythology of *Finnegans Wake*. The two men are incomplete, as if in their murder of the father the father's primal identity had split in two; and the two men are joined by their relation to the mother, whose milk forms their basic natures. The two men are fragmentary and complementary.

The fable, narrated by one Jones, focuses upon the quarrel between Burrus and Caseous over the meltingly beautiful maiden Margareena:

> Positing, as above, two males pooles, the one the pictor of the other and
> the omber the *Skotia* of the one, and looking wantingly around our un-
> distributed middle between males we feel we must waistfully woent a
> female to focus and on this stage there pleasantly appears the cowry-
> maid M . . . . (*FW*, 164)

Notice first how the two males here are both opposite and similar.
They are warring rivals (Pict and Scot), but one is the picture of
the other and the second the shadow ("omber") of the first. Jones,
who makes the fable into something of a geometry lesson, first
establishes the two males as polar opposites ("two males pooles")
and then transforms the bipolar straight line into a triangle by intro-
ducing the girl. And yet a triangle is not quite the right term for
describing the relation of Burrus, Caseous, and Margareena. Instead, in Jones's words, Burrus and Caseous form an "isoscelating
biangle" (*FW*, 165). This bizarre geometrical form is apparently
a truncated triangle without its apex, so that the two men stand
looking up at the unattainable woman (like Bloom and Stephen
looking up at Molly's window).

The fable reaches its conclusion when Margareena, grown weary
of the dispute between Burrus and Caseous, turns to a third hero:

> A cleopatrician in her own right she at once complicates the position
> while Burrus and Caseous are contending for her misstery by implicat-
> ing herself with an elusive Antonius, a wop who would appear to hug a
> personal interest in refined chees of all chades at the same time as he wags
> an antomine art of being rude like the boor. (*FW*, 166–67)

That Cleopatra chose Antony rather than Brutus or Cassius is
history; what is not recorded is that Antony relished both cheese
and butter. Margareena chooses a man who combines the natures of
the conflicting rivals. The result is a triangle ABC, "an Antonius-
Burrus-Caseous grouptriad" (*FW*, 167).

*Finnegans Wake* only makes more explicit (if, paradoxically,
more obscure) what was already implicit in *Ulysses*. The Stephen-
Bloom-Molly triangles of "Ithaca," like the fable of Burrus and
Caseous, emphasize the necessity of a union of the two men's natures
if they are ever to approach the woman in any liberated way.
Stephen's self-awareness and Bloom's sheer skill at living are not

finally hostile but, ideally, compatible. "Ideally" is the operative word here. For once we have brought the fantastical triangle back within the bounds of *Ulysses,* we have to remember that it remains an abstract image; it does not at all *predict* the fates of Bloom, Stephen, and Molly. The severe abstractions of "Ithaca" bring into sharp focus the patterns implicit in the characters' lives, but it is the nature of these abstractions only to show us patterns, not to resolve the novel's human dilemmas.

There is one other important use of scientific phraseology in "Ithaca," although it is much more general than the figures and terminology I have discussed above: the pervasive language of astronomy. Joyce listed the comet as the presiding symbol of "Ithaca," and if one science predominates in the chapter it is certainly astronomy. Perhaps the most uncanny and memorable effect of the chapter is its placement of the characters—and especially Bloom—beneath the infinitude of the heavens. "The cold of interstellar space" (704) and "the apathy of the stars" (734) rule over the chapter and at times render Bloom and his problems completely insignificant.

On one occasion, the heavens are not simply an indifferent backdrop; they seem, instead, to be in sympathy with the characters:

> What celestial sign was by both simultaneously observed?
> A star precipitated with great apparent velocity across the firmament from Vega in the Lyre above the zenith beyond the stargroup of the Tress of Berenice towards the zodiacal sign of Leo. (703)

Here the very heavens seem to declare the union of Stephen, Bloom, and Molly by uniting the stars which symbolize the three characters. Like the triangular images, this falling meteor freezes for a moment the image of an ideal.

But this image of the meteor is an exception to the general use of astronomy in the chapter. Here, for example, is a more complex statement of the relation between human beings and the heavens:

> Which various features of the constellations were in turn considered?
> . . . the appearance of a star (1st magnitude) of exceeding brilliancy dominating by night and day (a new luminous sun generated by the collision and amalgamation in incandescence of two nonluminous exsuns)

about the period of the birth of William Shakespeare over delta in the re-
cumbent neversetting constellation of Cassiopeia and of a star (2nd magnitude) of similar origin but lesser brilliancy which had appeared in and
disappeared from the constellation of the Corona Septentrionalis about
the period of the birth of Leopold Bloom and of other stars of (presumably) similar origin which had (effectively or presumably) appeared
in and disappeared from the constellation of Andromeda about the period
of the birth of Stephen Dedalus, and in and from the constellation of
Auriga some years after the birth and death of Rudolph Bloom, junior,
and in and from other constellations some years before or after the birth
or death of other persons . . . . (700–701)

There is a marked transition within the passage. It begins by implying a significant correlation between astral and human events but
gradually undercuts that significance, as it robs Shakespeare's and
Bloom's natal stars of their uniqueness and goes on to imply that
the correlation of stars with human births and deaths is completely haphazard.

The effect of the style is teasing here (as it often is throughout
the chapter). The style frequently seems to offer us glimpses of
some ideal truth applicable—or at least relevant—to Stephen,
Bloom, and Molly, but those glimpses are quickly lost, overwhelmed
by the spectacle of infinitude. This is one major justification for the
digressions and catalogues of "Ithaca" (the account of the water's
flow from reservoir to tap, the list of Molly's putative lovers, etc.) :
they stress the insignificance of the individual unit when it is considered among the infinite set of which it is an integer. The astro-
nomical language of "Ithaca" is only the most pronounced version
of this sort of reduction.

The language of astronomy, then, epitomizes all the scientific and
mathematical language of the chapter. "Ithaca" repeatedly draws
the characters together into patterns which seem, by usual novelistic
standards, full of significance. But then the style—which is not particularly concerned with "significance," the human applicability of
raw data—by a sudden shift reminds us of the arbitrariness of
choosing one fact or pattern rather than another.

Now this tendency to establish some small node of "meaning"
surrounded by the larger consciousness of the inherent meaninglessness of any human activity in the infinite context of the universe

shows one final continuity (and the most important one) between the procedure of "Ithaca" and the movements of Bloom's consciousness. Nothing is more typical of Bloom than the establishment of a small ordered world which is dissipated by his consciousness of infinity. Within "Ithaca" itself, for example, it is Bloom who has the most sanguine hopes for an acquaintance with Stephen, but it is also Bloom who, in his weary wisdom, foresees the probable failure of such an acquaintance because of "the irreparability of the past" and "the imprevidibility of the future" (696). Thus does the sense of future possibility alternately glimmer and fade in the course of "Ithaca."

The continuity between the "Ithaca" style and Bloom's mind is clearest once Stephen has left Bloom alone, for it is now that Bloom attempts to hold his world intact even as the consciousness of his own insignificance floods over him. One such attempt occurs as he sits alone and brings the day into a satisfying focus for himself before he goes to bed. Here Bloom's reasonable nature (in the Homeric parallel Bloom's reason is Ulysses's bow) creates an orderly microcosm set in juxtaposition to the frightening incertitude of the void. The mental creation of the suburban home of his dreams, Flowerville, is a jocoserious triumph of the empirical mind beset by the knowledge of its own futility (712–13). Like the flight from Boylan at the end of "Lestrygonians," this exercise of the imagination creates order by simply fixing intently upon a large number of objects which are held together only by the workings of Bloom's consciousness.

Bloom's vision of Flowerville, it should be noted, does not involve any significant change in his mode of life: it is the projection of his current state, once he has gained more years and his money has gained more interest. The ultimate goal of "ameliorating the soil, multiplying wisdom, achieving longevity" (715) is the logical and reasonable extension of the present Bloom of 7 Eccles Street. It is essential to the spirit of "Ithaca" that, unlike Stephen and Molly, Bloom does not foresee any real possibility of significant change in his future life: he can foresee only the possibility of incremental change along a straight line. It is thus Bloom's mind which lends to "Ithaca" the strong sense of an ending: Bloom assesses the status quo and seeks to be content with that assessment.

Before he goes to bed, Bloom's thoughts reach a point of rest:

> What were habitually his final meditations?
> Of some one sole unique advertisement to cause passers to stop in wonder, a poster novelty, with all extraneous accretions excluded, reduced to its simplest and most efficient terms not exceeding the span of casual vision and congruous with the velocity of modern life. (720)

Notice first the implications of "habitually." This is the description of a mind which reaches peace through a programmed and predictable series of steps (not entirely unlike the spiritual exercises of Stephen's St. Ignatius). Or we might say that Bloom's mind comes to rest here upon what amounts to a commercial epiphany. (Bloom's concern for the economical and strategic placement of detail marks perhaps his closest approach to his creator.) This final meditation brings to its sharpest point Bloom's ability to achieve a static contentment through the pure exercise of mind.

Exactly the same process is at work as Bloom lies in Molly's bed. As Bloom stretches out and senses "the imprint of a human form, male, not his" (731), the cold and brilliant prose of "Ithaca" describes the mental exercise by which Bloom finally slays the suitors. The precise, logical movement from envy to equanimity is, like Bloom's final meditation before retiring, a triumph of reason—although of a reason which has as its starting point the status quo and which will not deeply consider the possibility of altering the basic premises of Molly's adultery and Bloom's own sexual abstinence (732–33).

Thus does Bloom drift off to sleep, his mind having categorized and (at least for today) rendered neutral the unhappiness of his own existence. And this is a triumph, the epitome of a theme which runs throughout *Ulysses*, the wonder of having reached any goal at all, of having "proceeded energetically from the unknown to the known through the incertitude of the void" (697). Hence Bloom's contentment earlier in the chapter:

> His mood?
> He had not risked, he did not expect, he had not been disappointed, he was satisfied.

What satisfied him?

To have sustained no positive loss. To have brought a positive gain to others. Light to the gentiles. (676)

This is the logical and conservative statement of a man satisfied only to have survived.

And yet, one wonders, is not this sort of victory too modest? If "Ithaca" displays the triumph of an orderly and rational mind, it also calls into question the adequacy of order and rationality. The chapter pretends to square the circle and thereby ignores the unaccountable, irrational margin which the square cannot encompass. Once, as if by inadvertence, the chapter makes an excursion into pure lyricism—"The heaventree of stars hung with humid nightblue fruit" (698)—but a few pages later this momentary slip is corrected: "it was not a heaventree" (701). More generally, the chapter leaves unasked (not to say unanswered) the questions which the rest of the book so pressingly puts forward—questions involving the future lives of all three major characters. By ignoring those questions the chapter reaches a sense of closure, signaled by the large period at the end. But the chapter also dramatizes the futility of its own methods, and brings into existence that necessary opposing voice which will go on speaking after reason has gone to sleep.

# A Short Conclusion,
## Placed before the Postscript

So much for Bloom's day. Had we miraculously been within the book itself, actual witnesses to Mr. Bloom's journey, we might have found cause for some modest celebration in his safe return home. But, of course, we are readers, not the "objective observers" of the physics textbooks, and the true celebration must be for the fact that Bloom has survived, not only the sometimes trying events of this day, but also the machinations of Joyce himself. To that "objective observer," the day has been a continuum, punctuated no doubt by climaxes of different sorts, but relatively even in tone and texture. To the reader, however, the day has been a decathlon—or, rather, whatever the word is for a competition with fourteen events—testing Bloom's ability to remain faithful to the promptings of his own soul. The book assaults, flays, claws at Bloom in an attempt to know him, to pin him wriggling to the wall—or, if it cannot do that, at least to humiliate him.

Bloom's victory over the trials placed in his way—the trials which he actually encounters and those which Joyce the stylist imposes—is to a considerable extent an ethical one; it is no accident that the very best of the book's critics—Goldberg, Ellmann, French—have stressed the charity and compassion which are fundamental to Bloom's very nature. In this study I have been less concerned with ethics per se than with the structures of personality which make

ethics possible and operative in the world. And perhaps the most
important discovery we make when we attempt to define such structures is that they are founded upon an unfathomable mystery. We
can chart the sine curve of feeling which Bloom undergoes dozens
of times throughout the day, but the generative core, the soul out of
which that pattern of response grows, is noumenous, beyond the
powers of analysis—Joyce's or our own. The closest we can come
to a final formulation of character in *Ulysses* is the character's
"rhythm," which is itself only a phenomenon of a deeper-lying impulse. In Bloom, this rhythm consists of the alternate powers of
self-dispersal and reassimilation. He is far more willing than
Stephen to let go, to become a passive receptor to the information
fed to him by his senses, and he is far more capable than Molly of
codifying those sensory events.

The crisis for all of Joyce's great heroes occurs when they must
reach beyond the bounds of themselves and see themselves as parts
of the given, the things that are. Such is the nature of Gabriel Conroy's crisis, and such, set in an adolescent mode, is the nature of
Stephen's moment at the climax of the *Portrait,* as he awakes after
his rapturous vision of the bird-like girl and finds himself beneath
"the vast indifferent dome and the calm processes of the heavenly
bodies" (*PA,* 172). Such moments are respites from the most mor-
bid form of the romantic disease, the disease of seeing the world as
subservient to one's own imperial self. Of all Joyce's heroes, Bloom
is the most capable of this depersonalized form of consciousness.
The source of both his compassion and his intimacy with the physical
world is this ability to go forth and encounter experience, to place
himself within the person or object seen.

The trouble is that Bloom returns from each of these mental ex-
cursions with his awareness of his own insignificance newly ratified.
The ability to accept one's position beneath the apathy of the stars
may increase one's humility, but it does not increase one's determi-
nation to act. It is interesting in this light to notice what frequently
goes on in Bloom's mind after one of his acts of charity: he is quick
to modify or criticize in his own thoughts the good act he has just
performed. Having gone forth to identify with the world as it is—
to place himself as much as possible within the skin of the blind
stripling or even inside the feathers of the gulls—he is unable to

generate any self-esteem when he returns within himself. This capacity to project himself outward freely, spontaneously—coupled with his inability to return to himself in any approving way—is characteristic of Bloom and is the very hallmark of what René Girard has brilliantly described as the all-too-common modern type of the masochist.[1]

In the last pages in which we see Bloom awake, Stephen turns down the offer of a place to spend the night, and Bloom characteristically withdraws back into himself, willing once more to denigrate his own minimal plans for self-assertion. This is Bloom's final retreat back into himself before he goes to sleep. Given all the conditions of his life, Bloom's acquiescence, his acceptance of his wife's adultery, is praiseworthy. *But* Bloom's acquiescence is, after all, the line of least resistance; if he accepts, he does not have to act. And, lest we overpraise Bloom for his selflessness in sanctioning the adultery, we should note that Molly is actually the victim of Bloom's passivity and not simply the beneficiary of his good will.

For all of Bloom's great power to loosen the hold on his own ego and to go forth and encounter the present world, he resists those changes which would relegislate the laws of his ego. As long as Stephen the young man is present to remind him of his own youth and of the possibility of having a son, Bloom can furtively imagine such a change; when Stephen leaves, Bloom's ideas of change leave with him. Bloom in the end chooses to rest content with Mount Pisgah, rather than enter into the promised land; he almosts it but stops short of the goal.

By leaving us with a Bloom who shows no tangible sign of change in his attitude toward his marriage, Joyce does more than thumb his nose at the sanguine reader who might have expected a happy end-

---

1. René Girard, *Deceit, Desire, and the Novel: Self and Other in Literary Structure,* trans. Yvonne Freccero (Baltimore: Johns Hopkins University Press, 1965), pp. 176–92. Girard's treatment of masochism and his entire exposition of "triangular desire" shed much light on Bloom's psychology. The Other—Mulvey, Menton, Boylan, or whoever—is constantly on Bloom's mind as a possible or actual sexual rival. Moreover, even though Bloom resolves to take Stephen home to help oust Boylan, his showing of Molly's photograph to Stephen strongly suggests that he considers even his ally his potential rival. (As is well known, Joyce too tended—even desired—to look upon his closest friends as possible sexual rivals.) Even as Bloom moves tentatively toward renewing his and Molly's sexual life, he retains his habitual triangular model of jealously and rivalry. As an exact mirror image of this equivocal vision of Stephen in Bloom's mind, Molly thinks of Stephen both as a son-surrogate and as a lover.

ing. If we back off and complain that Joyce is teasing us by leaving so many questions unanswered, or if we insist that the questions themselves are irrelevant (these are, after all, only characters in a book), we miss the exciting sense of bristling possibilities with which the book closes. *Ulysses* does reach a point of stasis at the end of "Ithaca," but it is a stasis of incipience and potentiality, not simply a stasis of completion and closure. Bloom has entertained and then repressed the thought of change within his marriage; the stasis he achieves is that of a man who is holding compressed a coiled spring. Stephen earlier in the day mused upon the number of possible futures which might be contained within one moment's potentiality. The large period at the end of "Ithaca" is a sign of closure but also an auk's egg containing the infinite possibilities which the present moment holds within itself. It is left to Molly to imagine what those possibilities are.

## Chapter VIII

# Molly Bloom

What song the Syrens sang, or what name Achilles assumed when he
hid himself among women, though puzzling questions, are not beyond all
conjecture.—Sir Thomas Browne

## "Penelope"

All first-time readers of *Ulysses* enter "Penelope" in a state of confusion. The ideal first-time reader—if that hypothetical creature
exists—enters the last chapter in a very particular state of confusion. The three chapters leading up to "Penelope"—"Circe,"
"Eumaeus," and "Ithaca"—have established two contradictory
moods in Bloom: a very tentative resolve for future action and a
resignation to the state of affairs in the present. At the end of
"Circe," Bloom's painfully repressed desire for a son has become
clear—even, apparently, to himself. In "Eumaeus," Bloom foresees
the practical advantages of Stephen's coming to live at 7 Eccles
Street: not only might he teach Italian to Molly, his very presence
might interrupt the affair with Boylan. This hopeful mood continues
into "Ithaca," until Stephen turns down Bloom's offer of a place to
spend the night. After that point, Bloom, alone once more, directs
his mind back into the channel of resignation and acceptance.
Bloom's sense of future possibilities has opened up during his encounter with Stephen but has then closed again at Stephen's de-

parture. All we can say is that the basic equation of Bloom's mind has altered slightly with the addition of this new term—but it is impossible to tell just how much.

All male intellectual conceptualization ends with the large period at the end of "Ithaca." It is as if the only sound left, Molly's voice, has been a low murmur—like the sound of the sea accompanying Stephen's abstrusiosities in "Proteus"—which we hear clearly for the first time now that the men have left the scene. Molly's voice does, indeed, have about it the sea's formlessness, out of which the men seek to wrest some meaning: "Listen: a fourworded wave-speech: seesoo, hrss, rsseeiss, ooos" (49). Her soliloquy seems formless most of all in its very indiscriminateness: she wants Bloom back; she wants him to stay in his place so that she can continue her affair with Boylan; she dislikes Boylan for his crudeness, especially when she imagines, poor woman, the poetic refinement of Stephen the young "professor"; none of these men can measure up to the memory of Mulvey; etc. There is something here that seems frighteningly messy, indifferent, indiscriminate. But there is also a powerful motive force here, desiring and willing something better than her barren married life. Whatever Molly wants, she does not want simply to maintain the status quo which Bloom opts for at the end of "Ithaca."

In comparing Molly to the sea, I have touched upon one of the central critical problems surrounding her character: she is both the dissatisfied housewife of 7 Eccles Street and a representative of Nature. While a host of historical, literary, and mythological figures stand behind Bloom and help to define his character, the major force standing or lying behind Molly is prehuman. Containing the sea—"O patience above its pouring out of me like the sea" (769)—she is the earth delighting in seasonal cycles: "Im always like that in the spring Id like a new fellow every year" (760). To her mind, her most effective and final put-down of Bloom is the assertion that his grotesqueries are not "natural" (745, 771), and there is almost something of self-praise in her words as she moves toward her final lyrical outburst: "Id love to have the whole place swimming in roses God of heaven theres nothing like nature" (781).

Implicit in the "naturalness" of Molly Bloom is an assumption that grows more and more explicit from book to book in Joyce's career: the woman represents a principle prior to man, roughly analogous to the earth preexisting the cities men build or unformed feeling preexisting consciousness. Joyce's women have a private life which antedates the arrival of the husbands and which the jealous husbands can never triumph over—hence Gretta Conroy and Michael Furey, Molly and Mulvey, Anna Livia and Michael Arklow. For Joyce and his characters, the visible sign of the woman's priority is her menstrual blood. Her "monthlies" are the woman's tie to the natural order of things: the menstrual cycle enforces the woman's awareness of her own body and grounds her identity within her body to a far greater extent than is ever possible for the male characters. Such are some of the limitations within which Joyce creates his female characters. He chooses to portray women of a certain limited character type, and he passes back and forth between the "mythic" and the "realistic" with more facility in his creation of women than in his creation of men.

But Molly's mythic status never completely subsumes her particularized personality. The view of Molly as mythic, in fact, has the danger of blinding us to the underlying rhythm of her character. Again and again we confront in Molly psychological patterns as well-defined and sometimes as intricate as Bloom's and Stephen's—psychological patterns, moreover, which hold a deep interest since they show Molly's different approach to problems which Bloom and Stephen both face.[1]

Marilyn French has illuminated the most basic pattern within Molly's thought: her enormous power of self-contradiction.[2] Throughout *Ulysses* Joyce is interested in portraying personality as founded upon self-contradiction and in testing the personality's ability not only to steer between but actually to include both Scylla and Charybdis. Mulligan is so elusive because he seems to us nothing but a collection of contradictory poses; Stephen is caught between the poles of will and emotion; Bloom is so supple and yet

---

1. For an intelligent reading of Molly's character, see David Hayman, "The Empirical Molly," *Approaches to "Ulysses,"* ed. Thomas F. Staley and Bernard Benstock (Pittsburgh: University of Pittsburgh Press, 1970), pp. 103–35.

2. *The Book as World* (Cambridge, Mass.: Harvard University Press, 1976) pp. 244–50.

so paralyzed (already a contradiction) because he is usually willing
to acknowledge both a truth and a countertruth, so that he is batted
back and forth between the contradictory tendencies of his own
mind. Molly is superficially like Bloom (in this respect and in
many others) in that she practically never makes a statement without at some point reversing her position. But Molly is not made
uncomfortable by her self-contradictions; indeed, she is seldom
aware of them. The psychological pattern of her contradictions is
something like the reverse of Bloom's typical cycle of euphoria-
depression-normalcy. Molly usually criticizes first and then feels
free to celebrate. This is a repeated pattern within her monologue
and the pattern of her monologue as a whole.

Molly's self-contradictions are especially important in shaping
her attitudes toward other people, including, in the most complex
ways, Bloom himself. She is quick to criticize because her first
mental impulse is to establish her dominance over the other person;
but once she has gained that dominance, she is often willing to
grant sympathy and sometimes admiration. (Her thoughts of Boylan reverse this process: she begins by admiring him, but in the
course of her monologue she gradually turns on him and puts him
in his place.) This succession of dominance and sympathy is most
obvious in Molly's thoughts about the old—who represent that
dread wasteland lying beyond the age of thirty-five. She is at first
harsh and only then forgiving toward Mrs. Riordan (738), Mrs.
Fleming (768), and Rudolph Virag: "his father must have been a
bit queer to go and poison himself after her still poor old man I
suppose he felt lost" (767). To be sure, Molly's evaluations do
not always end in sympathy and generosity: she is not the goddess
of charity. Even so, she has the ability to affirm what she at first
looks upon as negative—and this ability is tremendously important
in her evaluation of Bloom.

Molly's power to wrest a positive meaning out of negative
evidence, to state the worst and then to remember the best, makes
of her the muse of two of the most important (and interrelated)
arts of *Ulysses,* sentiment and memory. One could do worse than
read *Ulysses* as an examination of true and false sentiment. The
picture of false sentiment is so prevalent in the book as to rank as
the most dominant Dublin drug. One definition of false sentiment is

contained in Stephen's telegram to Mulligan, cribbed from *The Ordeal of Richard Feverel: "The sentimentalist is he who would enjoy without incurring the immense debtorship for a thing done"* (199). Stephen's borrowed phrase attacks Mulligan's habit of sponging off Stephen and, more generally, Mulligan's insincerity. But the unpaying sentimentalist is present in many other forms in the book: in Simon Dedalus's self-pitying tears at the cemetery (in combination with his ill-treatment of his children), in the self-indulgent praise of the past notable in "Aeolus" and "Sirens," in the conveniently one-eyed vision of the Citizen, and in the more forgivable insipidities of Gerty MacDowell. Of all the major characters, Stephen is the most distrustful of sentiment, even though he is capable of it in his thoughts: outwardly, he is too acutely self-aware and too obsessively guarded to allow a sentimental impulse to escape him. Bloom, as always, seems halfway between Stephen and Molly. Sentiment is not at all foreign to his character, but he will never let it go uncriticized for long.

Molly is the most prominent character of sentiment in the novel, the focus for Joyce's examination of the power and the failings of pure feeling. Her sentiment is based in part upon a naïve and uncomplex vision of the world and a rejection of those unpleasantnesses which she does not even try to understand: "I hate the mention of politics after the war" (748); "as for them saying theres no God I wouldnt give a snap of my two fingers . . . who was the first person in the universe before there was anybody that made it all who ah that they dont know neither do I so there you are" (782). When Bloom tries to speak out against war in "Cyclops," he soon gets balled up in his own vague philosophy of futility. Molly deals with war and atheism as the usual result of men's meddling—and she simply rejects them. Another basis of Molly's sentiment is a rapturous appreciation of the plenitude of the world—not only in her evocations of Gibraltar (the most lyrical sections of "Penelope") but in such a detail as her appreciation of shopping in the morning: "I might go over to the markets to see all the vegetables and cabbages and tomatoes and carrots and all kinds of splendid fruits all coming in lovely and fresh" (780).

But, undoubtedly, Molly is most unabashedly sentimental in her thoughts of sex. In one of her more amusing efforts to be one up on

Milly, Molly equates the power to feel with the capacity to experience orgasm: "of course she cant feel anything deep yet I never
came properly till I was what 22 or so" (767). So desirous is she of
"feeling" that she is willing to disregard any misgivings she may
have about the specific content of the emotion. There is, for example, her recollection of this afternoon with Boylan:

> O thanks be to the great God I got somebody to give me what I badly
> wanted to put some heart up into me youve no chances at all in this place
> like you used long ago I wish somebody would write me a loveletter his
> wasnt much and I told him he could write what he liked yours ever
> Hugh Boylan in Old Madrid silly women believe love is sighing I am
> dying still if he wrote it I suppose thered be some truth in it true or no
> it fills up your whole day and life always something to think about every
> moment and see it all around you like a new world (758)

Again, there is much here that is rather like Bloom, but the total
effect, of course, is quite unlike Bloom's thought process. Bloom
always balances what he wishes against what he knows to be true;
opposed to his tendency to dream is a deep-running pessimism about
the nature of things. Bloom's fantasies about Martha are so
furtive and guilty—and so exciting to him as well—because he
knows they are stolen moments which could not withstand the touch
of reality. Molly, in this passage about Boylan, also takes negative
information into account, but only in order to outstrip it and to
ratify the truth of the moment. She indirectly registers some feeling
of guilt that she has gone beyond Poldy ("youve no chance at all
in this place like you used long ago"), she reiterates her dissatisfaction with Boylan's style ("his wasnt much"), and she even provides a parody of sentiment ("in Old Madrid silly women believe
love is sighing I am dying"). But then wham! there is the sudden
break beyond these reservations and the creation of a "new world."
Bloom's doubts are always there, hovering about his fantasies, de-
limiting them and threatening to bring them crashing down. Molly
nods to all her doubts on the way up to the peak and then enjoys
the view from there undoubtingly, serenely.

"True or no it fills up your whole day": here is the strength as
well as the considerable weakness of Molly's emotive power.
Whereas Bloom's more sanguine thoughts collapse as soon as he

reminds himself that the relevant facts will not support them, for Molly the test of "truth" is the emotion itself, not the specific facts: "of course a woman wants to be embraced 20 times a day almost to make her look young no matter by who so long as to be in love or loved by somebody if the fellow you want isnt there" (777). Molly's insistence upon defining love as an intense moment of ecstasy is at many points continuous with Gerty's adolescent fantasies, and it sometimes serves the same purpose Gerty's fantasies serve: to relieve and redeem a drab and disappointing existence. But in this very willingness to believe in the validity of her own feelings Molly has a power the two men lack—and I think it is clear that if the Blooms ever break the logjam of their marriage, the initiative must come from Molly, acting on the strength of her feelings.

Molly's greatest sentimental moments—like Gretta Conroy's and Anna Livia's—are directed toward the past: she is the muse of memory. The workings of memory, that force which binds together the self, have troubled the two heroes throughout the day. Stephen, forever analyzing his own experience, ceaselessly asks who he is in relation to his past selves. Even Bloom, whose conscious moments of self-conception are rare, can think, "I was happier then. Or was that I? Or am I now I?" (168). Molly does not have these problems of self-conception, mainly because she has such a complete, unmediated identification with her own past. Like Bloom, she prefers to return in thought to the early days before the marital troubles began, but she has no problem recalling episodes from more recent years. In fact, we probably learn more details about the Blooms' married life—including those wonderful comic scenes which Bloom has quite understandably suppressed, such as the episode of the soup and the train or the episode showing Bloom-Ulysses unable to manage a rowboat—from Molly's monologue than from all of Bloom's thoughts in the book.

In this respect it is interesting to notice some of the few things Molly has trouble remembering. In one droll passage, she seems blessed with virtually total recall, as she apparently remembers verbatim a letter she received from Hester Stanhope many years before; the one detail she has trouble remembering is the name of this close "friend" Hester. She is uncertain, too, about another name, a name involved in her most radiant memory: "what was his name Jack Joe Harry Mulvey was it yes" (761). These two failures of memory are instances of that gigantic egoism which has appalled so many readers; Molly can recall what Hester and Mulvey did for her, but she has trouble recalling them as distinct personalities. Notice, incidentally, how important to Molly are the memories of receiving letters from Hester and Mulvey. How she loves to receive letters! She judges Boylan on his letter writing, she remembers Bloom's letters, and she looks forward to receiving poetry from Stephen. Letters are for her—what Martha's letters are for Bloom—more easily assimilable experience than direct encounters are. The touch of solipsism in Molly's liking for letters —and in her difficulties in remembering the names of the writers— is most evident in one of her memories of Gibraltar: "not a letter from a living soul except the odd few I posted to myself with bits of paper in them so bored sometimes" (757).

But the lapses of memory are relatively few. Molly's ability to remember things that have happened *to her* is an index of her egoism but by the same token also an index of her powerful, robust selfhood. She has in overplus what the two heroes lack: an undisturbed, unreflective sense of her own being. She has self-doubts only, as it were, on the periphery of her character. She is the power of self-affirmation. She wanders back and forth between her different selves with delight and with no feeling that one of her serial personalities is really separate from another. In no other way is she more significantly different from the two men.

Her freedom of memory sometimes adds to her status as a mythic force. In spite of her detailed recall of Gibraltar, her phrasing often makes that period in her life seem eons away. Especially in her recollection of the Stanhopes, the life in Gibraltar takes on an antique quality, as if like the earth she really were age-old: "Lord how long ago it seems centuries" (756); "old Sprague the consul that was there from before the flood" (757); "ages ago the days like years" (757). And yet again, when she thinks of Mulvey, the pastness of the past falls away, and the dear dead days surge up into the immediate present: "Lord its just like yesterday to me" (761); "I declare to God I dont feel a day older than then" (779). "Ages ago" and "just like yesterday" remain clichés, but they reinforce one's sense of the relativity of Molly's past; her past is fluid, not frozen into the rigid shape of Stephen's or Bloom's. Molly is therefore not nearly so wistful or regretful in her memories as Bloom is. Carrying her own past inside her with virtually no barriers between her and it, Molly has the extraordinary power actually to reduplicate and relive it. One recalls Beckett's remark that Proust had a poor memory; had Proust's memory been better, his recapturing of the past would not have been so shocking and earthshaking an experience. Molly differs from Marcel, that other bedridden narrator, in that her affective memories are so constantly available to her. Like "The Halcyon Days" which appear to Bloom in "Circe," Molly's early days shout to her, "Live us again"—and she does just that (548).

A true sentimentalist, Molly considers the present less important than either the past or the future. She both remembers from the past and projects into the future a world different from and more radiant than her current life. The two songs most in her head have this same Janus-like quality: "Love's Old Sweet Song" with its phrase "the dear dead days beyond recall" looks toward the past, while "Waiting," a song suitable for Penelope, anticipates the future. Her whole day, in fact, has been spent anticipating and then remembering the meeting with Boylan—and then anticipating again: "Thursday Friday one Saturday two Sunday three O Lord I cant wait till Monday" (754). Joyce, of course, has heightened this past- and future-directedness by placing Molly in a darkened room, in which sensory awareness of the present is at a minimum. Yet, it is clear that this placement of Molly is symbolically appropriate. She is mentally vague about her location in the present: "the 4 years more I have of life up to 35 no Im what am I at all Ill be 33 in September" (751). Molly's wish to think of herself as young enters into her confusion here, but that wish itself is an instance of her vague awareness of the present. At one point she blames this vagueness on a gift she received from Bloom: "I never know the time even that watch he gave me never seems to go properly" (747). Bloom's own watch, like his mind, was for a while stopped, traumatized, at four-thirty; Molly's watch (an example of poor Bloom's attempt to impose some order upon Molly's chaos) does not acknowledge the present.

Molly's ambivalent attitudes toward time and the past are
perhaps clearest in her reactions to Milly's maturing. First, like
her memories of Gibraltar, Molly's thoughts about Milly create in
her a memory and replication of her own youth. Some of the most
charming passages in "Penelope" are those in which Molly begins
as the harsh mother and ends by identifying with the daughter:
"wouldnt even teem the potatoes for you of course shes right not
to ruin her hands" (766); "I had to tell her not to cock her legs
up like that on show on the windowsill before all the people passing
they all look at her like me when I was her age" (767). It is psychologically necessary for Molly to criticize before she offers sympathy,
but the sympathetic identification with Milly is almost always there:
"of course shes restless knowing shes pretty with her lips so red a
pity they wont stay that way I was too" (767); "well if he doesnt
correct her faith I will that was the last time she turned on the
teartrap I was just like that myself" (768).

Molly's identification with Milly, though, is not complete:
Milly's sexual coming of age is a threat, reminding Molly of her
age—and Molly's only real fear is of growing old. Her voice thus
becomes harsh and resentful when she perceives Milly as a rival.
There is resentment (and another mention of letters) in her first
mention of Milly: "only his letter and the card from Milly this
morning see she wrote a letter to him" (758). There is a quickness
to take offense here which springs from Molly's awareness that
Milly, no longer simply a daughter but now a sexual rival as well,
has begun to usurp Bloom's attention. There is even more of this
resentment in one of Molly's most defensive thought-sequences in
the chapter:

> but if there was anything wrong with her its me shed tell not him he
> cant say I pretend things can he Im too honest as a matter of fact I sup-
> pose he thinks Im finished out and laid on the shelf well Im not no nor
> anything like it well see well see (766)

Molly is seldom so plainly insecure as she is here. Her jealous
reaction to Milly's preference for Bloom, her guilt at having committed adultery (which shows itself in her protesting too much),
and her sense of growing old briefly come together in a critical
moment which she tries to shake off with a determined "well see

well see." Milly is for Molly, as well as for Bloom, the focus of
their marital problems: at once a reminder of the passing of time
and an abrogation of time, a reincarnation of Molly's own youth.
Molly's resentment of this younger version of herself is one of
the clearest signs in the chapter of her resistance to the idea of
losing Bloom.

Molly's reaction to Milly raises the question of what Molly
thinks of Bloom—and that question is very complex. We can best
approach it by considering what she thinks of men as a class. In
general, Molly has a wry, condescending attitude toward men. She
thinks of them as ailing, infantile, dependent upon women: "theyre
so weak and puling when theyre sick they want a woman to get
well" (738). The undifferentiated "they" and the confused refer-
ents of "he" in Molly's memories of men have the effect of reducing
them to an easily known and handleable reality. (Even in this regard, however, she can be self-contradictory; she acknowledges the
quirky uniqueness of Bloom and she at least admits that Boylan
has his particular fetishes: "theyre all so different Boylan talking
about the shape of my foot" [744].)

Her view of men as children, of course, seems at times a psychological strategy designed to establish her dominance. She begins one
of her paragraphs with the memory of Boylan at her breasts this
afternoon: "yes I think he made them a bit firmer sucking them like
that" (753); from here she moves to the almost inevitable comparison: "an hour he was at them Im sure by the clock like some
kind of big infant I had at me" (754); and finally, in her next
paragraph, she universalizes this man-infant: "theyre all mad to
get in there where they come out of" (760). Thus does Molly
succeed in transforming dominant, cocky Boylan into an infant.

But Molly's association of men and infants is more than a
psychological ploy which assures her of dominance; it is also sometimes a sublimated expression of her desire for a son.[3] This is

---

3. There is considerable critical dispute about the source of the Blooms' marital troubles.
There has not been full sexual intercourse between Bloom and Molly for over ten years
(736). Given Molly's resentment and Bloom's silent remark "Could never like it again
after Rudy" (168), it seems clear to me that Bloom's trauma at the death of Rudy is
the continuing cause of their abstinence. Other readers find the fault to be Molly's.
Darcy O'Brien, for example, says (somewhat cryptically): "Bloom, of course, is prevented
by Molly from having any more children" (*The Conscience of James Joyce* [Princeton:

clearest in her thoughts about Stephen. In what is perhaps the most interesting warp in Molly's thinking, her mental approaches to Stephen twice begin in the attitude of mother and end in the attitude of lover. Like her thoughts about Milly, her thoughts about Stephen bring up in her mind the most serious conflict in her conception of herself: unable to think calmly of her maternal role, since therein lies the source of the tragedy of her marriage, she makes herself young again and thinks of Milly as a sexual rival and of Stephen as sexual prey.

Here is her first major approach to the thought of Stephen:

> I saw him driving down to the Kingsbridge station with his father and mother I was in mourning thats 11 years ago now yes hed be 11 though what was the good in going into mourning for what was neither one thing nor the other of course he insisted hed go into mourning for the cat I suppose hes a man now by this time he was an innocent boy then and a darling little fellow in his lord Fauntleroy suit and curly hair like a prince on the stage when I saw him at Mat Dillons he liked me too I remember they all do wait by God yes wait yes hold on he was on the cards this morning when I laid out the deck union with a young stranger neither dark nor fair you met before (774)

Molly is unaware of the "Ithaca"-like coincidence contained in "thats 11 years ago now yes hed be 11" (Rudy would be eleven today, Stephen would be eleven eleven years ago), but the subliminal linkage between Stephen and Rudy is there. Molly's desire for sexual pleasure and her desire for a son both find temporary satisfaction in her fantasy of having a surrogate son for a sex partner. Only very gradually does the image of Stephen bring her back to Bloom and to the possibility of renewed sex with him.

Molly's second mental approach to Stephen also begins with maternal thoughts:

---

Princeton University Press, 1968], p. 166n.); David Hayman says: "The death of the Blooms' only son, Rudy, at eleven days in 1894 has soured Molly on the whole process of childbearing and turned her marriage awry" ("The Empirical Molly," p. 104). Hayman, however, also finds in Molly an "unrecognized son-fixation" (p. 129). I am in agreement with Hayman, at least to the extent that he sees Molly as a woman who has convinced herself to get along without a son but who strongly desires one unconsciously. In this, she is like Bloom.

well its a poor case that those that have a fine son like that theyre not
satisfied and I none was he not able to make one it wasnt my fault we
came together when I was watching the two dogs up in her behind in the
middle of the naked street that disheartened me altogether I suppose I
oughtnt to have buried him in that little woolly jacket I knitted crying
as I was but give it to some poor child but I knew well Id never have
another our 1st death too it was we were never the same since O Im
not going to think myself into the glooms about that any more I wonder
why he wouldnt stay the night (778)

The clearest difference between Molly's thoughts here and her
thoughts in the passage I quoted just previously is that she has now
dropped that earlier defensive callousness ("what was the use of
going into mourning for what was neither one thing nor the
other") and is more willing to remember her real grief again.
Again she catches herself up ("O Im not going to think myself into
the glooms about that any more"), but by now the suppressed
image of Rudy has begun to act powerfully beneath the level of
thought.

By the end of Molly's seventh paragraph and the beginning
of her eighth, Stephen's image has defeated Boylan's:

and I can teach him the other part Ill make him feel all over him till he
half faints under me then hell write about me lover and mistress publicly
too with our 2 photographs in all the papers when he becomes famous
O but then what am I going to do about him though
    no thats no way for him has he no manners nor no refinement nor no
nothing in his nature slapping us behind like that on my bottom because
I didn't [sic] call him Hugh the ignoramus (776)

Thus does Stephen-Telemachus finally assist in defeating the
suitors—at least to the extent that Molly now clearly expresses her
dissatisfaction with Boylan. And Stephen's image does even more
than this in Molly's mind. For both Bloom and Molly he is a
mediating figure whose image brings each of them back toward the
other. Molly's final thought of Stephen (which I will discuss presently) is the catalyst which sets in motion the reacceptance of
Bloom.

In thinking of Boylan, Milly, or Stephen, Molly is also thinking indirectly of Bloom. He is the true center of her thoughts, and she is quite frankly perplexed by him. Disarmingly submissive to her, Poldy nevertheless possesses a mysterious, quirky integrity which she cannot touch and which she both resents and respects: "I had the devils own job to get [a proposal] out of him though I liked him for that it showed he could hold in and wasnt to be got for the asking" (743). The very source of his attractiveness in the old days was a combination of submissiveness which repeatedly toppled over into the perverse and an erotic power which grew in part out of his strangeness, his otherness. Notice, for example, the character-istic ambivalence in her memory of the time he threatened to kneel in the rain and "beseeched of" her to lift her petticoat: *"O Maria Santissima* he did look a big fool dreeping in the rain splendid set of teeth he had made me hungry to look at them" (746).

Her description of Bloom is nowhere closer to our own impres-sion of him than when she says: "he annoyed me so much I couldnt put him into a temper" (743). This remark—delightful because it reminds us of both characters' most typical behavior, Molly's attempt to elicit a response from her lover and Bloom's elusive, Ulyssean refusal to be cornered—is suggestive of Molly's always active but never satisfied desire to touch upon Bloom's secret self and secret life. She is repelled—but not simply repelled; Molly often has a secret attraction to Bloom's perversities—by his probing of her secret life:

> who is in your mind now tell me who are you thinking of who is it tell me his name who tell me who the German Emperor is it yes imagine Im him think of him can you feel him trying to make a whore of me what he never will (740)

Yet, as is often the case (as in her thoughts about exhibitionism), Molly shares the very qualities which she singles out to criticize in men. She uses means more devious than direct questioning—she looks for women's hairs on Bloom's clothes and searches his wallet —but she is just as curious as Bloom is to know the other's secrets. And, unable to know fully what Bloom is like, she uses various arguments to convince herself to remain content in her ignorance.

No other woman, she reflects, could know him as well as she does: "if they only knew him as well as I do" (739). She adopts an ill-feigned indifference: "not that I care two straws who he does it with or knew before that way though Id like to find out" (739). And she stands back and looks upon this sport of nature with mingled amusement and perplexity:

> then he wanted to milk me into the tea well hes beyond everything I declare somebody ought to put him in the budget if I only could remember the one half of the things and write a book out of it the works of Master Poldy (754)

Molly's relation to Bloom inevitably raises the most hotly debated question in recent Joyce criticism: how sexually experienced is Molly? There is, of course, something inherently comic in learned discussions of the matter, but the question is nevertheless very pertinent. First of all, it seems logical and even necessary to follow Stanley Sultan and others in reading Bloom's list of Molly's suitors (731) as a projection of Bloom's own suspicions and fears, not as an objective list of the men who have had sexual dealings with Molly.[4] So far can we reduce this list, in fact, that we cannot find any definite evidence to show that before this afternoon Molly has ever committed adultery, or even had sexual intercourse with anyone other then Bloom. And yet there does seem to be one possible candidate for this honor other than Bloom and Boylan: Lieutenant Gardner, with whom Molly had some kind of affair after her marriage and who does not appear on Bloom's list. I am afraid the truth is that Joyce did not intend us to know for certain all the details of Molly's sexual history—although the burden of the evidence strongly suggests that Molly has not committed adultery before June 16, 1904. Joyce does for Molly with Gardner what he does for Bloom with freemasonry: he establishes a zone of mystery which we will never succeed in understanding fully.

Despite the scarcity of evidence about Molly's specific adventures, many readers still agree with Robert M. Adams, who recoils

---

4. Sultan, *The Argument of "Ulysses"* (Columbus: Ohio State University Press, 1964) pp. 431–33.

from the character he describes as "a slut, a sloven, and a vora-cious sexual animal."[5] It is true that Molly has a supercharged sexual imagination, inspired in part by the renewal this afternoon of her long-frustrated sexual life. But what is the nature of this sexual imagination? The men she chooses in her fantasies are men she does not know or knows only by sight, and sometimes they are completely anonymous: "pick up a sailor off the sea . . . or one of those wildlooking gipsies in Rathfarnham" (777). Stephen him-self is a young man she has not seen since he was a boy. Like many people, including her husband, Molly can create and enjoy her sexual fantasies only when the object of the fantasies is at a safe distance. At such a distance, virtually *anyone* is prey: Bloom's list of the suitors is in this respect perfectly correct. One of her thoughts which I have already quoted is very apropos: "of course a woman wants to be embraced 20 times a day almost to make her look young no matter by who so long as to be in love or loved by somebody if the fellow you want isnt there" (777). The combina-tion of sexual indiscriminateness with the phrase "if the fellow you want isnt there" brings Molly's eroticism into clear focus. Molly has a roving eye because she is unwilling to set her sights exclusively on one man beyond Bloom, the fellow she wants who isn't there. She can remain infatuated with Boylan only as long as she can sus-tain an orgasmic imaginative intensity about him; she passes from him to the conveniently unknown quantity, Stephen; and Stephen eventually leads her back to Bloom. Molly's "sluttishness" is not simply a characteristic that Joyce has assigned to whorish Woman; it exists in a dynamic relation to her feelings about Bloom. She is a highly sexed woman, and her sexuality finds an outlet in imagined promiscuity as a direct result of her unfulfilled life with Bloom.

Molly's notorious obscene moments also need to be examined in

5. Robert M. Adams, *James Joyce: Common Sense and Beyond* (New York: Random House, 1966), p. 166. For those who find Molly a negative character, there exists a full arsenal of epithets. Darcy O'Brien has been the most inventive of the indignant critics; he calls Molly "at heart a thirty-shilling whore" (*The Conscience of James Joyce,* p. 211) and—best of all—a "great lust-lump" ("Some Determinants of Molly Bloom," *Approaches to "Ulysses,"* p. 148). Readers of a more classical temper may prefer the simplicity of J. Mitchell Morse's description of Molly as "a swine" (*The Sympathetic Alien: James Joyce and Catholicism* [New York: New York University Press, 1959], p. 86). Phillip Herring offers a good survey of the critical attitudes toward Molly in "The Bedsteadfast-ness of Molly Bloom," *Modern Fiction Studies,* xv (1969), 49–61.

the light of her varied psychology. Like her roving eye, her obscene tongue helps her to expel her resentment and dissatisfaction. And, interestingly, Molly's obscenities very often reveal a woman who is actually tentative and conservative about sexual acts themselves even as she is curious about variations from the sexual norm. Like her imaginative promiscuity, Molly's sexual frankness is very often a kind of *faute de mieux*. A good example of her sexual attitude appears when she remembers how heavy Boylan was, lying on her this afternoon: "better for him put it into me from behind the way Mrs Mastiansky told me her husband made her like the dogs do it and stick out her tongue as far as ever she could" (749). The idea has an erotic appeal for Molly, but it is typical of her that she very quickly retreats from it with the remark: "can you ever be up to men the way it takes them" (749). There is the same combination of erotic curiosity and reticence in her consideration of the small statue of Narcissus:

> I wanted to kiss him all over also his lovely young cock there so simply I wouldnt mind taking him in my mouth if nobody was looking as if it was asking you to suck it so clean and white he looked with his boyish face I would too in ½ a minute even if some of it went down what its only like gruel or the dew theres no danger besides hed be so clean compared with those pigs of men I suppose never dream of washing it from 1 years end to the other the most of them only thats what gives the women the moustaches (776)

This is Molly's version of Bloom's attraction to cool, white goddesses. Although she at one point says of men, "they want everything in their mouths," she herself once again possesses those same "unnatural" traits. Even here, though, she is able to feel her superiority to those "pigs of men." The entire passage has a bluff bravado about it—"I would too in a minute"—which is only one step removed from a young girl's giggles. And there is the final safety valve: perhaps, after all, she should rest content with conventional sex since cock-sucking might lead to a sprouting moustache. Similarly, Molly's account of what she wanted to shout out while having sex with Boylan is an account of a freedom she did not take:

I was coming for about 5 minutes with my legs round him I had to hug
him after O Lord I wanted to shout out all sorts of things fuck or shit
or anything at all only not to look ugly or those lines from the strain
who knows the way hed take it (754)

She likes to imagine herself as sexually daring and adventurous,
but she is adept at finding excuses for refraining from anything very
far from the very ordinary. Molly is the mirror image of Gerty
who, beneath her innocence, possesses already a considerable sexual
awareness; beneath Molly's image of herself as a sexual dynamo,
there is reticence and a girlish curiosity.

Molly's combination of bravado and reticence makes her in some
ways the ideal partner in Bloom's sexual fantasies. With the knowledge gained from both "Circe" and "Penelope" we can in fact see
how Bloom's and Molly's sexual proclivities have come to mesh in
some ways. She feels resentment toward Bloom because of his
sexual failures, and her resentment sometimes goes forth to meet
what she hazily knows to be his guilty need of punishment. One
such instance occurs as she remembers Bartell d'Arcy's kiss:

Bartell dArcy too that he used to make fun of when he commenced kiss-
ing me on the choir stairs after I sang Gounods *Ave Maria* . . . Ill
tell him about that some day not now and surprise him ay and I'll [*sic*]
take him there and show him the very place too we did it so now there
you are like it or lump it he thinks nothing can happen without him
knowing (745)

Resentful of the ill-treatment she receives from Bloom and further
exasperated by the thought that she cannot even commit adultery
without Bloom's knowledge ("he thinks nothing can happen without him knowing"), Molly treasures the memory of a flirtatious
moment of which Bloom is unaware and goes on to imagine what
she thinks of as a daring (and clearly unlikely) scene. Even here,
though, there is again the safety valve: "Ill tell him about that
some day not now."

Such passages as these give us the chance to see how both Molly
and Bloom have gradually created for themselves the psychological
ploys and dodges which make life livable within the bounds established by Bloom's trauma. In response to Bloom's own sexual

dilemma, Molly has developed certain fantasies and psychological defenses which in their most extreme form make her resemble some of the sadistic women in "Circe." Only in this sense is she the creation of obsessive male sexual anxieties: she has readjusted her life in response to Bloom's failures in an effort to accommodate herself to an impossible situation.

And now, on June 16, that complex psychological interplay between husband and wife has reached a crisis, as Molly has finally acted out her fantasies. Bloom's response to that crisis—Molly's adultery—has been twofold: self-torment which in itself leads him nowhere and, through Stephen, a very painful and also very tentative desire for a new son. Molly's response is clear only when we take into account the slow, unconscious psychological process of her monologue as a whole. As she does with virtually everyone else she thinks of, she compiles the negative evidence against Bloom before she begins her movement toward the final decision to give him one last chance.

Underlying all her resentment of Bloom is a desire not to lose him and an unwillingness to leave him. Indeed, she criticizes her own desire to run away by attributing it to an inbred part of her character rather than to the particular circumstances of her married life: in Gibraltar, "I was almost planning to run away mad out of it somewhere were never easy where we are father or aunt or marriage waiting always waiting to guiiiide him toooo me" (757). There is something very moving in the thought-sequence here. Not only does Molly dismiss as girlish the idea of running away; she ends by singing to herself of that resented and exasperating condition of waiting for the errant husband which is her real, sad lot. Similarly, when she thinks of another kind of escape, the idea of having Boylan's child, she refuses and again comes back to Bloom, in the process paying him a physiological compliment: "supposing I risked having another not off him though still if he was married Im sure hed have a fine strong child but I dont know Poldy has more spunk in him yes" (742).

Molly's ambivalence toward Bloom centers in his "womanly" qualities. Twice she gives him credit for intuiting the way a woman feels (747, 782), and many times she pays tribute to those qualities of kindness and gentleness which are missing in his more "mas-

culine" fellow citizens: "still I like that in him polite to old women
like that and waiters and beggars too" (738). (And this kindness is
not foreign to Molly's own nature: it was she, not Father Conmee,
who threw a coin to the one-legged sailor in "Wandering Rocks.")
She has a good understanding of Bloom's weak and vulnerable position in Dublin, and she is quick to jump to his defense: "well
theyre not going to get my husband again into their clutches if I
can help it making fun of him then behind his back" (773).

But Molly is well aware of what the reader also knows by now,
that Bloom's delicacy leads not only to thoughtfulness and kindness
but also to the deep insecurity which has led to their present unhappiness. Molly circles around this problem on one of those occasions
when she praises Bloom's ability to understand a woman:

> I liked the way he made love then he knew the way to take a woman
> when he sent me the 8 big poppies because mine was the 8th then I wrote
> the night he kissed my heart at Dolphins barn I couldnt describe it
> simply it makes you feel like nothing on earth but he never knew how to
> embrace well like Gardner I hope hell come on Monday as he said at the
> same time four (747)

At first it seems that Molly is describing Bloom's (former) physical
prowess as a lover when she speaks of his knowing "the way to take
a woman," but actually she is lingering over his thoughtfulness in
sending those eight poppies for her birthday. When she thinks of
the more possessive and "masculine" act of an embrace, she prefers
Gardner to Bloom, and then the further transition to brawny,
cocky Boylan is swift and inevitable. What she finds most lacking in
Bloom is that masculine assertiveness which is Boylan's trump card
and which Molly remembers in her father. Her desire for this
strong maleness is clear in her two wistful comparisons of Bloom to
Major Tweedy: "he looked more like a man with his beard a bit
grown in the bed father was the same" (738); "I wish hed even
smoke a pipe like father to get the smell of a man" (752).

What, then, do we make of Bloom's one tentative step toward
self-assertion, his request for breakfast in bed the next morning? In
the published criticism on Joyce, perhaps only Stephen's and
Bloom's communion over "Epps's massproduct, the creature cocoa"

ranks with this request for breakfast as a crux of interpretation.
Richard Ellmann, for one, has worked to tone down the claims of
earlier criticism that the request for breakfast heralds an imminent
change in the Blooms' marriage: "His request for breakfast may
be just what it appears to be, an expression of fatigue after a late
night which is most unusual for him."[6] But this revisionism goes too
far. The fact is that Molly herself is very impressed by the request.
She is not at all sure of its meaning, but (like other critics of Bloom)
she is sensitive to its possible import. The request for breakfast
does not signal the arrival of male dominance at 7 Eccles Street:
we can make a pretty good guess that the Bloom household will
never be male-dominated. It is significant, though, that Molly—in
a statement which combines sardonic irony with covert wish-fulfill-
ment—sees the request as precisely that: "then he starts giving us
his orders for eggs and tea Findon haddy and hot buttered toast
I suppose well have him sitting up like the king of the country"
(764).

What the request more obviously conveys to Molly is a change
in those mental habits which have been built up over the last eleven
years: "Yes because he never did a thing like that before as ask to
get his breakfast in bed with a couple of eggs since the *City Arms*
hotel" (738)—that is, around the time of Rudy's birth and death.
I do not think that Molly overemphasizes the importance of the
request; for clearly any transformation of the long-established
mental patterns of the Blooms must begin in such small changes.

Molly thinks about breakfast again in the most highly charged
passage of her chapter (779–81). She has returned to her thoughts
about Stephen, and it is not surprising that these thoughts now
bring her to her most hopeful and most hating thoughts of Bloom
in her entire reverie; for in Molly's fantasy, Stephen is both the
sexual partner and the sexual result, the son, and therefore the
crystallization of the problems of the Bloom marriage. She is here
as close to the nub of things as she comes anywhere in her monologue. What follows is a rapid alternation between angry resentment of the past and possible prospects for the future. The alternation is clearest in her consideration of breakfast the next morning

6. Ellmann, *Ulysses on the Liffey* (New York: Oxford University Press, 1972) p. 161.

and breakfasts in general: "I could have brought [Stephen] in his breakfast in bed with a bit of toast" (779); "if [Stephen] wants to read in bed in the morning like me as [Bloom is] making the breakfast for 1 he can make it for 2" (779); "Ill just give [Bloom] one more chance Ill get up early in the morning" (780). This last remark, Molly's most explicit acknowledgment that breakfast is to be a crucial event, gives Bloom the same chance she offers him in the two musical phrases she plans to sing to entice him in the morning: *"mi fa pietà Masetto . . . presto non son piu forte"* (780). Unknown to Molly, these phrases reverse the novel's pattern of allusions to *Don Giovanni*. Whereas earlier Boylan is Don Giovanni attempting to seduce Zerlina and Bloom is at best the stone Commendatore returning to seek revenge, Molly's musical phrases transform Bloom into the seducer while Molly remains the yielding Zerlina.[7]

There is also resentment aplenty in Molly's thoughts in these pages: "Ill let him know if thats what he wanted that his wife is fucked yes and damn well fucked too . . . serve him right its all his own fault if I am an adulteress" (780). And yet even these plans of Molly's, which can rival anything in "Circe," have the ultimate goal of seduction:

> Ill tighten my bottom well and let out a few smutty words smellrump or lick my shit or the first mad thing comes into my head *then Ill suggest about yes O wait now sonny my turn is coming Ill be quite gay and friendly over it* . . . [then, remembering that she has her period,] Ill wipe him off me just like a business his omission then Ill go out *Ill have him eyeing up at the ceiling where is she gone now make him want me thats the only way* (781, italics mine)

And with this vision of Bloom lying in bed desirously awaiting her return (an interesting reversal of their roles on June 16), Molly's fantasy breaks off. The words I have italicized are of extreme importance: Molly has evidently decided to give Bloom all his perverse fancy may desire before she goes out in the morning and seduce him the way *she* wishes on her return: "thats the only way."

---

7. Sultan offers a good analysis of the phrases from *Don Giovanni* in *The Argument of* "*Ulysses*" p. 449.

In Molly's mind, Bloom is to be the goal of her odyssey, just as she is the goal of his. We will never know what happened on June 17, 1904, but the powerful motive force in Molly's words makes it clear that, for better or worse, June 17 will not be a simple repetition of June 16.

Immediately after Molly's vision of tomorrow morning, there is a full stop in her monologue: "let me see if I can doze off 1 2 3 4 5" (781). What follows is a coda to her chapter, just as her chapter is a coda to the book. When she resumes her thoughts she reverts to Stephen: "Ill go to Lambes there beside Findlaters and get them to send us some flowers to put about the place in case he brings him home tomorrow today I mean" (781). But again the thought of Stephen carries Molly back to Bloom, just as the thought of Stephen carries Bloom back to Molly: the plan to deck out the house with flowers leads directly to Molly's recreation of the bank of rhododendrons on Howth Head and to the ecstatic closing of the book.

Molly's plan, formed just previously, to give Bloom one more chance is a repetition of the initial capture sixteen years ago on Howth—in leapyear (1888 and 1904) when the woman has the right to propose—and that moment itself is a recollection of the first moment with Mulvey. Molly's repetition of the past in these last moments of waking consciousness is not a simple escape from the present; it is the recollection of the Edenic memory which she has just resolved upon reenacting tomorrow. The phrase of indifference which crops up just before sleep comes—"well as well him as another"—indicates the true dominance she once had and which she has willed to have again: the dominant power of assuming indifference and of saying "yes" to the man she has seduced.

In all the powerful scenes of sentiment he created, Joyce always provided some down-to-earth ballast. If we cast a cold eye on these scenes, it is apparent that Michael Furey did not die because of Gretta but because of consumption, that Stephen's vision of the dove-like girl takes place in the context of his physical revulsion from the very element she wades in, and that Molly's evocation of the Moorish wall and the rhododendrons on Howth takes place as she lies in bed with arse-kissing Poldy. In every case, Joyce provides enough of an ironic distance for us to see the subjectivity of

the experiences, but the very power of the experiences is great
enough to call into question the sufficiency of irony and detachment.
Joyce, whose work is open to the charge of overintellectualization,
gestures beyond intellectualism in his insistence that epiphanic moments of sentiment, based, certainly, in the subjectivity of the character's consciousness, are nevertheless capable of changing the
character's life. *Ulysses,* an extensive critique of false sentiment,
ends on a moment of true sentiment: Molly is reviving those dear
dead days not yet beyond recall precisely in order to reenact them
tomorrow.

Despite the book's skepticism at the idea of radical change in the
lives of the middle aged, then, Joyce is far from ruling out the idea
of such change. The possibilities of renewal which I have suggested
are ratified by two symbolic details within "Penelope." The first
is a phrase of Molly's: "that thunder woke me up as if the world
was coming to an end" (741). That Apocalyptic thunder was the
occasion for Bloom's move to comfort Stephen in "Oxen of the
Sun." In Molly's phrase, the book's complex Apocalyptic imagery
comes to a climax. The possible change in the lives of the major
characters is like that change prophesied in the very last words of
the Old Testament, the book whose title recalls Mulligan, the
priest of the old order:

> Behold, I will send you Elijah the prophet before the coming of the
> great and dreadful day of the Lord: And he shall turn the heart of the
> fathers to the children, and the heart of the children to the fathers, lest I
> come and smite the earth with a curse. (Malachi 4:5–6)[8]

The two moments of great Biblical change—the First Coming and
the Second—are conflated here: Molly awakes thinking of the
Apocalypse just as Bloom's paternal heart turns toward Stephen.[9]

---

8. Foster Damon in his excellent, unjustly neglected article first noted the importance
of this Biblical passage ("The Odyssey in Dublin," *James Joyce: Two Decades of
Criticism,* ed. Seon Givens [New York: Vanguard Press, 1963] pp. 240–41).

9. The passage from one Biblical age to another is also faintly suggested near the end
of Molly's soliloquy: "Ill go to Lambes there beside Findlaters and get them to send us
some flowers to put about the place in case he brings him home tomorrow today I mean"
(781). The pairing of Lambe and Adam (Findlater) comes just before Molly swings into
the lyrical closing words.

The second detail is Homeric. Like Penelope, Molly spends the night unweaving a web. In its most specific sense, the web she unweaves is the woolly jacket she wove for her dead son. By returning to Bloom through the mediating filial image of Stephen, Molly begins to unweave the death shroud surrounding her marriage. But more generally, Molly unweaves the intricate tapestry of rationality which the two men have woven during the day. In her subversive opposition to the carefully structured and defensive thought-patterns which the two men and the seventeen previous chapters have evolved, Molly is the voice of the unexpected, the unforeseen; she is the voice of potentiality.

Bloom, after some signs of rejuvenation, opts for the way things are at the end of "Ithaca"; Molly opts for change. The battle will be decided in the morning.

# Index